Attorney's Guide to
Effective
Discovery Techniques

Attorney's Guide to Effective Discovery Techniques

WALTER BARTHOLD

Prentice-Hall, Inc.   Englewood Cliffs, N.J.

PRENTICE-HALL INTERNATIONAL, INC., *London*
PRENTICE-HALL OF AUSTRALIA, PTY. LTD., *Sydney*
PRENTICE-HALL OF CANADA, LTD., *Toronto*
PRENTICE-HALL OF INDIA PRIVATE LTD., *New Delhi*
PRENTICE-HALL OF JAPAN, INC., *Tokyo*

Library of Congress Cataloging in Publication Data

Barthold, Walter.
    Attorney's guide to effective discovery techniques.

    Includes bibliographical references.
    1. Discovery (Law)—United States. I. Title.
KF8900.B3   347'.73'72   74-20666
ISBN 0-13-050484-X

This publication is designed to provide accurate and
authoritative information in regard to the subject
matter covered. It is sold with the understanding that
the publisher is not engaged in rendering legal, accounting, or other professional service. If legal advice
or other expert assistance is required, the services
of a competent professional person should be sought.

*—From a Declaration of Principles jointly
adopted by a Committee of American Bar
Association and a Committee of Publishers
and Associations.*

PRINTED IN THE UNITED STATES OF AMERICA

PREFACE

On the premise that today's lawyer can rarely if ever prepare a case for trial without resort to some form of discovery, the author offers this book to the practicing bar. He has in mind both trial specialists and general practitioners. All, no matter in what jurisdiction they practice, should find something of value in each of the chapters that follow.

The full-time litigator will read of the kinds of problems and opportunities he has been dealing with for years. He will find new approaches to these known situations. He will wish to compare these new approaches with the techniques that he himself has developed. Some of the author's ideas may strike him as worthy to replace his own established methods. He may wish to keep the volume handy to remind him that recurring situations call not for stereotyped approaches, but for constant rethinking. The illustrative examples found in every section of the book should adapt it to such use.

The general practitioner, too, will encounter discovery situations already known to him. He will realize that even sophisticated talent can begin to decay once self-satisfaction extinguishes the eagerness to learn without which none of us can do his best. This book, coupled with that realization, should put the occasional litigator on equal terms in discovery with almost any trial specialist he finds himself opposing.

The attorney who handles litigation as one part of a general practice should derive additional benefits. He will encounter in these pages situations unprecedented in his own practice. These he will approach, if he is wise, as if he were newly admitted to the bar. He will deceive no one but himself if he thinks that years of experience endow him with refined skill in every new task that confronts him.

The non-specialist has an obvious need for the kind of help this book extends. He can look up applicable statutes, rules and court decisions as he approaches each new discovery problem. But how can he avoid the awkwardness and the blunders that will brand him a novice? How can he make effective, astute use of discovery tools that he is handling for the first time? The author hopes to solve that problem by sharing the lessons that he and many others have learned in decades of actual practice. This sharing should bolster the competence and the confidence of the lawyer approaching a new discovery situation.

Consider some examples. At the commencement of an action, counsel must decide what he is going to do about discovery. The inexperienced lawyer studies the rules pertaining to depositions. He finds a form to adapt for a notice of deposition and serves it. He thinks that he is ready to proceed. Is he really? Doubts trouble him as the day for the hearing approaches. He wonders what he can do in preparing for the deposition to help get the truth from a shrewd witness of whose scruples he has serious doubts. How can he make the best use of some helpful documentary evidence he has found, but of which he thinks the other side is unaware? What is he to say when his own client asks for permission to attend the deposition? An offer by his adversary to let his secretary transcribe the testimony, thereby saving a court reporter's fee, bewilders him. He worries whether paying strict attention to technical rules of evidence will render him ridiculous in the eyes of his experienced opponent. What will he do about the stipulations that he notices in varying form at the beginning of several deposition transcripts he has read? The author wishes this book to remove such worries. He hopes that it will also pose and answer questions that would not otherwise occur to the non-specialist practitioner.

Problems of the sort just discussed do not trouble the case-hardened veteran who has taken scores or hundreds of depositions. He nevertheless has some thinking to do before he pushes ahead. Having fought, for example, many battles over priority of depositions, should he hasten to take the deposition of the opposing party before he must let the testimony of his own client be taken, or is this the one case where letting the other side move first would be wiser? Should he, for that matter, take the deposition of a key witness before taking that of the opposing party? Our experienced trial specialist takes pride in the many successes achieved in depositions by a severe demeanor calculated to frighten the witness out of any temptation to lie or distort. Is the present situation, however, one where a friendly demeanor will work better? Should he follow his usual practice of serving written interrogatories before the deposition, or might they better be foregone here? Is this, in fact, a case where the time and expense of a deposition could advantageously be eliminated altogether? This book contains no formulae answering all such questions for all cases that arise. It does set forth ideas that should help every lawyer, trial specialist or not, find his own way to the answers that are right for his case. It raises questions intended to make the experienced practitioner reconsider his established approaches to discovery, examine the premises on which they are based and, where necessary, adopt new techniques.

Every section of the book contains examples illustrating the ideas advanced. Many of the examples come from reported cases. Citations appear in those instances. Other examples come from the author's own experience or from the experience of the many colleagues with whom he has compared notes on common problems encountered in litigation. Such examples, for obvious reasons, are disguised by the use of fictitious names and the alteration of factual details not essential to the points made. As a third category, some examples are purely hypothetical. They nevertheless represent kinds of situations that lawyers will recognize as real.

The reader presumably brings with him some acquaintance with the rules of evidence and with the code and decisions governing discovery in his jurisdiction. The book, therefore, makes no effort to present a compendium of such provisions. It cites and quotes from statutes, rules and decisions of almost all U. S. jurisdictions. The Federal Rules and cases decided under them appear more frequently than corresponding material from state sources for two reasons. First, most trial lawyers in every American jurisdiction participate in federal practice. Secondly, many states have adopted practice codes substantially or totally identical to the Federal Rules. We have not developed a nationwide federal and state common law of discovery, but reliance by courts on decisions from other jurisdictions is surely on the increase.

Wherever we practice, all of us know that pre-trial discovery has been assuming a steadily greater role in litigation for at least three decades. Less and less evidence comes to light in the courtroom and more and more in the office or conference room before trial. This is the essence of pre-trial discovery.

Courtroom skill, then, no longer suffices to insure success in litigation. Trial lawyers have always known that exhaustive, thoughtful preparation pays tangible dividends. Courtroom developments like the devastating cross-examination or the eloquent summation may strike the spectator as flashes of spontaneous brilliance. Today, as always, they more likely represent the product of hours of painstaking effort. Now, however, discovery, too, must play a part in trial preparation. This book, therefore, will help equip the practicing lawyer with the refined and tested techniques that he needs to apply in today's litigation.

WALTER BARTHOLD

CONTENTS

Chapter I

LAUNCHING A DISCOVERY PROGRAM

A. WILL DISCOVERY PAY IN YOUR CASE?

1. An Early Question to Ask

Before we take up our review of individual discovery techniques, let us consider some questions common to the entire field of discovery. First comes the basic question whether to engage in discovery at all.

When we speak in these pages of "discovery," we use that term in its generic sense, that is, as comprehending the whole field of depositions, interrogatories, etc.[1] Care must be taken not to confuse this broad term with "discovery and inspection," a specific technique dealt with in Chapter V.

In later chapters we shall consider the relative strengths and weaknesses of different forms of discovery. Let us concentrate for the moment on the pros and cons of discovery as a whole.

2. Advantages of Discovery

a. Getting the Whole Story

Discovery's advantages come easily to mind. One thinks first of the tremendous asset of access to evidence in his opponent's sole

---

[1] That is the definition used in the Federal Rules. See, e.g., Rule 26(a), "Discovery Methods." In some states, New York and to some extent Connecticut, for example, the term "disclosure" designates the broad range of procedures of the kind with which we are concerned. N. Y. Civil Practice Law and Rules §3101; Conn. Gen. Stats. Ann. §§52–197 and 52–198.

possession. As the Supreme Court of the United States said in
Hickman v. *Taylor,* 329 U.S. 495, 507, 67 S.Ct. 385, 392, 91 L.Ed.
451, 460 (1947):

> We agree, of course, that the deposition-discovery rules are
> to be accorded a broad and liberal treatment. No longer can the
> time-honored cry of "fishing expedition" serve to preclude a party
> from inquiring into the facts underlying his opponent's case. . . .
> The deposition-discovery procedure simply advances the stage at
> which the disclosure can be compelled from the time of trial to
> the period preceding it, thus reducing the possibility of surprise.

Knowing all the facts, not just those available from friendly sources,
can spell the difference between defeat and victory. Take this actual
case as an example:

> Plaintiff in a malpractice suit was unconscious during a sup-
> posedly routine operation by defendant surgeons. He knows only
> that upon coming to, he was partly paralyzed. By taking the
> surgeons' deposition, he will be able to find out just what hap-
> pened while he was under anesthesia.[2]

Any lawyer can continue with examples from his own experience.
Discovery, it is plain, gives counsel factual resources that would
have been difficult to conceive of just a few decades ago.

b. The Other Side's Theories

Discovery can usually give us much more than the facts in an
adversary's possession. Discovery devices, notably interrogatories,
have come to perform the function of the common-law bill of particulars. You may, in other words, use discovery devices to learn
what an opponent is contending.[3] For example, as amended in 1970,
Federal Rule 33(b) provides in part:

> An interrogatory otherwise proper is not necessarily objec-
> tionable merely because an answer to the interrogatory involves
> an opinion or contention that relates to fact or the application
> of law to fact, but the court may order that such an interrogatory
> need not be answered until after designated discovery has been
> completed or until a pre-trial conference or other later time.

---

[2] *Rodriguez* v. *Hrinda,* 16 F.R. Serv.2d 592 (W.D. Pa. 1972).
[3] *Fernandes* v. *United Fruit Co.,* 50 F.R.D. 82, 84 (D. Md. 1970).

Using discovery to ascertain a party's contentions does more than tell you what those contentions are. It tends to commit the other party to the theory or version of that fact which he discloses. This can help you materially. The court, to be sure, may have discretion to let a party change his theory by amending his answers to your interrogatories. However, that does not mean that it will exercise that discretion in his favor.[4]

c. Evaluating the Case

Knowing all the facts plus the other side's theories makes it easier to size up a case for settlement and other purposes. As one court has expressed it:

> . . . by "educating the parties in advance of trial as to the real value of their claims and defenses" . . . the ascertainment of the truth and ultimate disposition of the lawsuit in accordance therewith is expedited.[5]

We owe it to our clients and to our overburdened courts to settle before trial as many cases as we fairly can. Thorough discovery helps us meet this obligation. It thereby enables many lawyers to increase their case loads substantially.

d. Improving Productivity

Discovery makes the process of gathering evidence more efficient. Counsel for a personal-injury plaintiff might spend weeks tracking down eye-witnesses to an accident that left his client unconscious. A deposition or set of interrogatories, on the other hand, might enable him to get from defendant a complete list of persons who saw the occurrence.[6]

Again, the short-cuts that modern discovery makes possible enable every trial lawyer to take on more work. They also enable him to do that work better.

---

[4] *Matlack, Inc.* v. *Hupp Corp.*, 16 F.R. Serv.2d 1429 (E.D. Pa. 1973).

[5] *Monier* v. *Chamberlain*, 35 Ill.2d 351, 361, 221 N.E.2d 410, 417 (1966). A similar statement of policy appears in *Surf Drugs, Inc.* v. *Vermette*, 236 So.2d 108, 111 (Fla. 1970).

[6] See Fed. Rules Civ. Proc., Rule 26(b)(1); *Edgar* v. *Finley*, 312 F.2d 533 (8 Cir. 1963); *Ballard* v. *Terrak*, 58 F.R.D. 184 (E.D. Wisc. 1972); *Smith* v. *Superior Court*, 189 Cal. App.2d 6, 11 Cal. Rptr. 165, (1961); *Grant* v. *Huff*, 122 Ga App. 783, 178 S.E.2d 734 (1970); *Road Commission* v. *Petty*, 17 Utah 2d 382, 412 P.2d 914 (1966); *Hodge* v. *Myers*, 255 S.C. 542, 180 S.E.2d 203 (1971).

e. Preserving the Evidence

Discovery procedures make it possible to preserve evidence until the trial. Today's elongated dockets make this advantage all the more important. The death or disappearance of a key witness can destroy a case. Taking the witness's deposition will avoid that disaster.

f. Safety in Questioning

Discovery eliminates one of the greatest risks of the trial. One can, in discovery, safely ask a question of an opposing party or hostile witness without any idea what the answer will be. You may, for example, suspect another party or one of his witnesses of having a criminal record. On cross-examination at the trial, you have the right to ask if he has ever been convicted of a crime. You hesitate to do so. A negative answer, likely to be delivered with emphasis, will only improve the witness's standing. In discovery, on the other hand, you may ask the question without hesitation.[7] If the answer is what you want, you may use it at the trial. If it is not, you can forget about it with no harm done.

Resourceful counsel can use various discovery devices in a variety of ways to reduce the risks of cross-examination. In a medical malpractice case [8] a Florida court upheld interrogatories calling for a list of textbooks considered reliable by the defendant physician. Such a list would make plaintiff's cross-examination easier and more secure. Without it, counsel would have to make his own selection of treatises without knowing which, if any, the defendant doctor would acknowledge as authoritative.

3. Discovery's Drawbacks

a. Expense

We have reviewed some of discovery's advantages. We shall deal with all of them again, as we consider individual discovery devices. Let us turn for a moment to some features that may give one pause before embarking on discovery.

The lawyer of limited experience may wonder what negative factors could outweigh discovery's advantages. To be sure, it pays

---

[7] *Mellon* v. *Cooper-Jarrett, Inc.,* 424 F.2d 499 (6 Cir. 1970).
[8] *Buga* v. *Wiener,* 277 So.2d 296, 297 (Fla. App. 1973).

to engage in some form of discovery in at least nine cases out of ten. However, that should not keep you from taking a fresh look at each case to determine if discovery will be worthwhile there.

Discovery can cost plenty. You may have to pay in time, in money or in both. In a small case, this element may tip the scales against any discovery at all. If you represent a salesman suing a former employer for $500 in commissions, spending $250 in reporter's charges plus hours of your own time taking the depositions of defendant's sales manager and accountant will hardly be worthwhile, no matter how much evidence you elicit. In all but the largest cases, the cost of discovery must be taken into account.

You can mitigate the cost of discovery, we shall see, by selecting the least expensive technique adequate to fulfilling your needs. If, for example, your only purpose in discovery is the authentication of documentary evidence, the availability of interrogatories and the request to admit may obviate depositions altogether.

If you prevail in an action, you may tax the costs of discovery against your adversary.[9] Your award, however, will not cover everything. What you pay for extra copies of a deposition may not, for example, be included.[10]

b. Delay

Discovery consumes time in another way. If extensive, it will delay bringing a matter to trial. If your case requires prompt disposition, you owe it to your client to consider either doing without discovery or curtailing it materially.

c. Retaliation

Discovery invites repayment in kind. In theory, your discovery program or lack thereof has no effect on how much or how little discovery your opponent engages in. In fact, what you do often determines in large measure what the other side does. If you decide against taking the deposition of your adversary, you have no guarantee that his lawyer will likewise forego taking your client's testimony, but if you do serve a notice of deposition, you can count on getting one back. The same goes for interrogatories and other proceedings.

---

[9] See, e.g., for purposes of federal practice, 28 U.S.C. §1920; 4 MOORE'S FEDERAL PRACTICE (2d Ed. 1970) ¶26.82; Peck, *Taxation of Costs in United States District Courts,* 37 F.R.D. 481, 487–488 (1965).

[10] *Mercon Corp.* v. *Goodyear Tire & Rubber Co.,* 16 F.R. Serv.2d 1210 (D. Minn. 1972).

If, therefore, you represent the party holding the bulk of the discoverable evidence, it may work to your advantage if both sides do without discovery. You may in such a situation decide to wait and see if your adversary, in the absence of initiative on your part, fails to embark on discovery or does only to a limited extent. Your patience and forbearance may avoid an exchange from which your client stands to lose more than he gains.

d. Disclosing Your Own Case

Another possibly disadvantageous exchange comes to mind. One's own discovery can sometimes convey more to the opposition than it garners for oneself. One has difficulty asking questions, orally or in writing, or seeking physical evidence, without showing what the inquirer considers the important parts of his case.

Consider this example:

> In a breach-of-warranty action, defense counsel failed to realize that the statute of limitations ran from the date of the sale, not from the date on which the breach manifested itself.[11] He did not plead the statute. Plaintiff's attorney served interrogatories. Several of them attempted to fix the exact date of the sale. (The parties had dealt by mail, so several documents of different dates made up the sales transaction.) These questions alerted defense counsel to an affirmative defense that enabled him, after an amendment to his answer, to win the dismissal of a major cause of action.

Plaintiff's attorney would plainly have been better off not to have served interrogatories. Other examples of how discovery can do more harm than good abound in almost everyone's experience.

e. Forcing Preparation

Discovery may have another disadvantage. By making your opponent answer exhaustive questioning or do extensive research, you are forcing him to prepare his case. He might otherwise be inclined to devote less effort to preparation. Therefore, whatever you stand to gain from your discovery has its price tag. Only you can decide if you are apt to be paying too much.

Our review of some of the advantages and disadvantages of dis-

---

[11] Uniform Commercial Code §2–725(2).

covery does not give us a means of computing discovery's value in any given case. It does teach us that the lawyer should neither undertake nor reject discovery automatically. He must evaluate discovery in the circumstances of each case that comes to him.

B. PLEADINGS: KEY TO DISCOVERY

1. Problems for Plaintiff

Today we hear many voices proclaim the art of pleading dead.[12] An action, to be sure, will survive casual, even slipshod pleading. It does not follow that such slovenly practice makes sense. A look at how pleadings affect discovery will show why the astute lawyer does not pride himself in how little time he takes to dash off a complaint, answer or counterclaim. He devotes serious, unhurried thought to the ramifications of each paragraph of his pleading.

Courts now divide on whether pleadings limit the scope of discovery. The trend is to avoid such a limitation.[13] A leading authority [14] has expressed the principle in federal practice thus:

> The cases make it quite clear that relevance is not to be measured by the precise issues framed by the pleadings, but by the general relevance to the subject matter. [Footnote, citing cases, omitted.]

A prevalent attitude on the subject was expressed thus in *Montgomery Ward & Co.* v. *Fotopoulos,* 32 F.R.D. 333, 334–35 (D. Minn. 1963):

> In many cases, it is difficult to fully determine from the pleadings what the issues at trial will be. . . . A liberal grant of discovery is preferred to a denial when the answers sought might prove to be relevant at the time of trial. [Footnote, citing case, omitted.]

Judges nevertheless look to pleadings for help in determining what discovery they will and will not allow. The most liberal jurisdictions

---

[12] See, e.g., McCaskill *Modern Philosophy of Pleading: A Dialogue Outside the Shades,* 38 A.B.A. Journal 123 (1952), commenting on, *inter alia, Dioguardi* v. *Durning,* 139 F.2d 774 (2d Cir. 1944), further proceedings, 151 F.2d 501 (1945).

[13] See, e.g., *Allen* v. *Crowell-Collier Publishing Co.,* 21 N.Y.2d 403, 408, 235 N.E.2d 430, 433 (1968); *Charles Sales Corp.* v. *Rovenger,* 88 So.2d 551 (Fla. 1956).

[14] 4 MOORE'S FEDERAL PRACTICE ¶26.56[1].

impose some standard of relevance or materiality on discovery proceedings. True, most judges today will not let the pleadings have the last word on how far discovery may go.[15] Yet the pleadings may be the first source to which they turn for guidance on where to draw the line.[16]

Consider, as an illustration, *Pacific Tel. & Tel. Co.* v. *Superior Court*, 2 Cal.3d 161, 84 Cal. Rptr. 718, 465 P.2d 854 (1970). There the Supreme Court of California, in a right-of-privacy case, introduced its consideration of the propriety of deposition questions with this typical pronouncement: (2 Cal.3d at 172–173; 84 Cal. Rptr. at 762; 465 P.2d at 862):

> In addition, because all issues and arguments that will come to light at trial often cannot be ascertained at a time when discovery is sought, courts may appropriately give the applicant substantial leeway, especially when the precise issues of the litigation of [*sic*] the governing legal standards are not clearly established. . . .

Throughout the balance of its opinion, however, the court repeatedly referred to the parties' pleadings as justification for the allowance of broad discovery. This, for example, appears at page 178 of 2 Cal.3d, page 730 of 84 Cal. Rptr., and page 866 of 465 P.2d:

> In addition, evidence of defendants' past practice of widespread monitoring, which may be revealed by the questions challenged here, may quite possibly be admissible at trial on the issue of "malice," an issue expressly in dispute under the present pleadings.

In New York, whose highest court has held discovery not limited by the scope of the pleadings,[17] an appellate court, ruling on interrogatories, has nonetheless said:

> The test of materiality should be relevancy of the material to the issues pleaded. . . .[18]

---

[15] The federal authorities are collected at 4 MOORE'S FEDERAL PRACTICE ¶26.56[1], note 17.

[16] See, e.g., *Hesselbine* v. von *Wedel*, 44 F.R.D. 431, 434 (W.D. Okl. 1968); *Sandee Mfg. Co.* v. *Rohm & Haas Co.*, 24 F.R.D. 53 (N.D. Ill. 1959); *Nagel* v. *Prescott & Co.*, 36 F.R.D. 445 (N.D. Ohio 1964); *Myers* v. *St. Francis Hospital*, 91 N.J. Super. 377, 387, 220 A.2d 693, 698 (1966).

[17] *Allen* v. *Crowell-Collier Publishing Co.*, footnote 13.

[18] *Avco Security Corp.* v. *Post*, 42 A.D.2d 395, 397, 348 N.Y.S.2d 409, 412 (4th Dept. 1973).

It follows that the attorney drafting a pleading is, whether he realizes it or not, determining in advance the scope of discovery. Let us consider an example:

> The attorney for a national distributor plans to sue a manufacturer for defects in a new line of upholstery fabric. Plaintiff's attorney is first inclined to allege merely breach of warranty. This, he reasons, will simplify his case, since to recover he need only prove the defects. Upon considering the effect that the complaint will have on his discovery program, he changes his mind. He realizes that adding a cause of action for negligent manufacture and inspection will increase his chances of being allowed discovery of defendant's factory procedures. This, he concludes, may help him strengthen his proof of defects.

Our hypothetical plaintiff's counsel might well go further. He might decide to plead a third cause of action, fraudulent misrepresentation. This might entitle him to still broader discovery. He could ask, for example, about complaints received by the manufacturer before the sale to his client. This, he might argue, would have relevance to the question of scienter, not an element in his first two claims. On the same theory, plaintiffs in some product-failure actions allege a design defect in the hope of obtaining discovery of the details of other failures of the same product.[19]

Plaintiff's attorney in the hypothetical example above might nevertheless stick to his original single cause of action. With solid proof of breach of warranty, he might reason that broadening his allegations would only give defendant the chance to drag the case out by raising defenses and engaging in discovery that would be irrelevant to the warranty claim. Whatever his decision, this attorney has shown good sense. He has not blindly thrown everything into his complaint for good measure. Nor has he, with equal blindness, stuck to his original plan just to keep the case simple. He has evaluated all possible allegations in terms of his own and his adversary's contemplated discovery programs.

Take another, quite different example:

> Plaintiff's counsel in a contemplated personal-injury action is all set to incorporate into his complaint a routine clause alleging loss of earnings. Thinking it over, he realizes that such

---

[19] See, e.g., *Self* v. *American Home Assurance Co.*, 51 F.R.D. 222 (N.D. Miss. 1970).

an allegation may give the defense access to his client's income tax
returns.[20] As a federal judge in California has said:

> Plaintiff placed the issue of earnings in question in this
> action and, therefore, any interrogatory dealing with past
> earnings is clearly relevant and material or reasonably cal-
> culated to lead to the discovery of admissible evidence.[21]

After a confidential talk with the client, plaintiff's attorney
decides that the allegations in question may damage his case far
beyond the amount of lost earnings plaintiff has sustained.

Before making his final decision, however, counsel takes into account
the likelihood that omitting loss of earnings may provide his adversary,
in closing argument or in settlement negotiations, with ammunition
to minimize the seriousness of the injuries. Again, the crucial fact
is that the attorney has thought the matter through.

We have looked at two elements of a complaint, the cause or
causes of action selected, and the nature of the relief demanded. We
have seen how each element can have a material effect on discovery
at later stages of the action. Our brief review will suggest other ways
in which the possibilities of discovery can play a part in the decisions
made in drafting an initial pleading.

2. Decisions for Defendant

Not just plaintiff's counsel should consider what effect his pleading
will have on discovery. A defendant has much the same problem.

Defense counsel, as one possibility, may have one or more marginal
defenses, that is, items that might be helpful but then again might
turn out to be more bother than they are worth. Before he decides
to use or discard each such defense, he should think about what its
inclusion or deletion will do to discovery.

Illustrations proving this point come readily to mind. Here is one:

> In the suit by a distributor against an upholstery manufacturer
> mentioned above, defense counsel wonders whether to plead as

---

[20] See, e.g., *Freehill* v. *DeWitt County Service Co.*, 125 Ill.App.2d 306, 261 N.E.2d
52 (1970). On the other hand, the absence of a claim for lost earnings may make
income information irrelevant for discovery purposes. *Nichols* v. *Philadelphia Tribune
Co.*, 22 F.R.D. 89, 92 (E.D. Pa. 1958).

[21] Sweigert, D. J., in *Reichert* v. *United States*, 51 F.R.D. 500, 503 (N.D. Calif.
1970).

an affirmative defense plaintiff's waiver of the alleged breach of warranty by its renewal of the distributorship contract after discovery of the alleged defects. He may reason that including it will make it easier to persuade a judge that he, defense counsel, should have access to plaintiff's correspondence with its customers. On the other hand, he may prefer to take his chances and hope to prove the waiver under his denials, thereby keeping plaintiff's counsel in the dark, for the time being, as to the theory of his defense.

By adding an affirmative defense, an attorney may materially help his discovery program. Take this Florida case:

> Defendant was accused of having defamed plaintiff by calling him, among other things, "sick" and "psychotic." Defense counsel sought a psychological examination of plaintiff. In unanimously holding the examination to have been properly allowed, an appellate court relied on defendant's plea of truth as a defense.[22]

Including or omitting a worthwhile affirmative defense calls for consultation of applicable substantive law and rules of pleading. In addition, as we have seen, it calls for consideration of what effect the presence or absence of the defense will have on one's own and one's opponent's discovery program.[23]

From defense counsel's standpoint, this conclusion applies not just to affirmative defenses. By admitting an allegation, defendant's attorney will often remove that issue from the area of permissible discovery.[24] By denying it, he will make the topic accessible to plaintiff's discovery proceedings.[25] As an example:

> A personal-injury action involves allegedly negligent maintenance of real property leased to defendant. The latter's attorney decides to admit possession and control of the premises. He sees that denial would facilitate plaintiff's attorney's gaining discovery

---

[22] *Gordon* v. *Davis*, 267 So.2d 874 (Fla. App. 1972).

[23] See *General Industries Co.* v. *Birmingham Sound Reproducers, Ltd.*, 194 F. Supp. 693 (E.D. N.Y. 1961); *Avco Security Corp.* v. *Post*, footnote 18, 42 A.D.2d at page 399, 348 N.Y.S.2d at page 413.

[24] *Swartz* v. *Darling Co.*, 14 F.R. Serv. 33.323, Case 1 (N.D. Ohio 1950); *Fletcher* v. *Foremost Dairies, Inc.*, 29 F. Supp. 744 (E.D. N.Y. 1939); *Norton* v. *Cooper, Jarrett, Inc.*, 1 F.R.D. 92 (N.D. N.Y. 1938); *Avco Security Corp.* v. *Post*, footnote 18, 42 A.D.2d at page 397, 348 N.Y.S.2d at page 412. To the contrary is *Pacific Tel. & Tel. Co.* v. *Superior Court*, 2 Cal.3d 161, 174, 84 Cal. Rptr. 718, 465 P.2d 854, 863–864 (1970).

[25] *Wills* v. *Towns Cadillac-Oldsmobile, Inc.*, 490 S.W.2d 257, 260 (Mo. 1973).

of the lease and thereby learning the amount for which defendant has agreed to keep the property insured.

Take again as an example:

A personal-injury action involves a claim for lost earnings. His investigation has convinced defense counsel that the lost earnings part of the claim is not exaggerated and probably will be established. He denies it anyway. He hopes that by placing plaintiff's loss of earnings in issue, he will get a look at the latter's income tax returns. He thinks that they may help him in some legitimate way.

When it comes to a counterclaim, of course, defendant must weigh the same considerations as occupy a plaintiff's attorney in drafting a complaint. Plaintiff's counsel likewise finds himself momentarily in defendant's shoes when he considers his reply to the counterclaim.

3. Ideas for Both Sides

Including or omitting allegations, defenses and denials are not the only matters relating to discovery that will concern counsel at the pleadings stage. Sometimes the degree of detail into which a pleading goes will have its effect on discovery. Today's trend favors brevity and simplicity in pleading.[26] Every lawyer should do his best to further that trend. Some latitude is nevertheless permissible and may be desirable for reasons of discovery.

Here is an example:

In an automobile negligence case, it would suffice, under the rules in some courts, to allege that "Defendant negligently drove a motor vehicle against plaintiff." [27] Adding a few words to describe what defendant did negligently, *e.g.*, that he drove too fast, did not keep a proper lookout, or was under the influence of liquor, could help plaintiff demonstrate the relevance of evidence that might otherwise appear remote to the issues of the case. Specifying that defendant was negligent in driving without his glasses might enable plaintiff to have an ophthalmo-

---

[26] Federal Rule 8(a), for example, calls for "a short and plain statement of the claim showing that the pleader is entitled to relief." Rule 8(b) requires a party to "state in short and plain terms his defenses to each claim asserted. . . ."

[27] Official Form 9, as amended, Federal Rules of Civil Procedure (1972).

logical examination of his adversary. To get such relief otherwise, he might have to make a special showing, perhaps even reveal some of his proof.

The helpfulness of detail in pleading manifests itself more often in complex litigation, such as commercial and antitrust suits. Consider as an example:

A salesman sues his ex-employer for unpaid commissions. He needs discovery of the company's records to find out exactly what it owes him. Although it is not strictly necessary, his complaint sets forth a list of the transactions on which he is relying. This gives him a good start toward defeating any charge by defense counsel that plaintiff is engaged in a "fishing expedition."

Finally, both parties have the right under proper circumstances to amend their pleadings. Amendment may open new avenues of discovery.[28]

We have seen some ways in which pleadings can have an effect, helpful or otherwise, on discovery. Let us turn to motion practice, the next phase of most actions, and consider its relationship to discovery.

C. MOTION PRACTICE AND DISCOVERY

1. Judgment on the Pleadings

Most motions before trial justify themselves in terms of the immediate relief that they seek. Many also have important effects on your discovery program.

All jurisdictions provide for a motion for judgment on the pleadings or its equivalent, usually replacing the common-law demurrer.[29] Such a motion enables a litigant to dismiss one or more causes of action on the ground of legal insufficiency. Experienced counsel sometimes avoid such motions even when grounds appear to exist. They argue that they can gain the same relief at trial at the cost of

---

[28]*Keely* v. *Price*, 27 Cal. App3d 209, 103 Cal. Rptr. 531 (1972).

[29] See, e.g., Federal Rules 7(c) and 12(c); Pennsylvania Rules of Civil Procedure, Rule 1034. At least one state has combined the motion for judgment on the pleadings with the motion for summary judgment. 6 Callaghan's Michigan Pleading and Practice §42.07.

far less preparation and with less risk of the court's nullifying the result by allowing amendment. Such reasoning often has validity. It should never, however, become an automatic thought pattern. The motion for judgment on the pleadings or its equivalent, among its other benefits, can solve some of the problems that discovery by one's adversary creates.

Take this case:

> A small manufacturer sues a large supplier of component parts for violations of the antitrust laws. Among other things, plaintiff has tried to plead a cause of action for price discrimination in violation of the Robinson-Patman Act. Defendant's attorney sees that this part of the pleading has a flaw. It alleges only the quotation rather than the actual charging of a discriminatory price.[30] Counsel ponders whether to move to dismiss the deficient cause of action in view of his certainty that the trial judge will eventually dismiss the claim anyway. He decides to make the motion. He realizes that letting the price-discrimination cause of action stand will invite extensive discovery into his client's complex pricing practices. Revealing such confidential data will cost the client far more in customer-aggravation and perhaps future litigation than will the counsel fees that the motion to dismiss generates.

The same dilemma can confront plaintiff's attorney when he must decide whether moving to strike a deficient defense is worth his while. Two federal decisions illustrate the problem from his point of view.

> In *Bourget* v. *Government Employees Ins. Co.,* 313 F. Supp. 367 (D. Conn. 1970), *further proceedings,* 456 F.2d 282 (2 Cir. 1972), an injured truck driver sued a tort-feasor's insurance carrier to recover the difference between the amount of his judgment and the amount of the policy. Defendant asserted various affirmative defenses, one based on an alleged lack of diversity of citizenship and another based on an agreement made in the prior action. Plaintiff moved to strike these defenses. Chief Judge Timbers granted his motion. He simultaneously denied defendant's motion for production under Rule 34 on the ground that it was based on two of the stricken defenses.

---

[30] *Shaw's, Inc.* v. *Wilson-Jones Co.,* 105 F.2d 331, 333 (3d Cir. 1939); *Rutledge* v. *Electric Hose & Rubber Co.,* 327 F. Supp. 1267, 1275 (C.D. Calif. 1971); *Becker* v. *Safelite Glass Corp.,* 244 F. Supp. 625, 635 (D. Kan. 1965).

Had plaintiff in *Bourget* not bothered to move against the invalid defenses, defendant might well have obtained the discovery that he sought. Thus:

> In *Paramount Film Distributing Corp.* v. *Ram.* 15 F.R.D. 404 (E.D. S.C. 1954), plaintiffs objected to certain interrogatories on the ground that they related to an invalid defense. Judge Wyche overruled the objections. He pointed out that "no motion has been made by the plaintiffs to strike this defense."

A motion to strike a defense or to dismiss a cause of action often does not seem worth the effort. Considering the motion's impact on discovery can sometimes change that appraisal.

2. Corrective Motions

The motion disposing of an entire cause of action or defense is not the only kind that can affect discovery. Practice codes provide for motions to strike superfluous, scandalous, redundant and other undesirable material from pleadings.[31] A motion in this category may seek to eliminate no more than a sentence or a few words from a pleading. It may be worthwhile or not in and of itself, but counsel should not reject it without considering its impact on discovery.

As an example:

> A department store in a small community brought suit against a labor union and its officers for conspiracy to induce plaintiff's employees to commit breaches of their employment contracts. Among other things, the complaint alleged that one individual defendant was "a person known to have a long criminal record and extensive underworld connections." Defendants' attorney did not wish that subject gone into via discovery or in any other way. He had no difficulty deciding to move to strike the allegations as "scandalous" and "impertinent."

A corrective device known as the motion to make more definite and certain or motion for more definite statement [32] may serve a purpose with respect to discovery. A complaint, for example, pleading a claim for breach of contract, may refer simply to defendant's "nu-

---

[31] See, e.g., Federal Rule 12(f); N.Y. CPLR, Rule 3024.
[32] Federal Rule 12(e).

merous orders of merchandise" from plaintiff. If plaintiff and defendant engage in thousands of transactions involving scores of different products every year, defendant has difficulty determining both what he is charged with and where he should begin discovery. A motion to make more definite and certain will solve his problems. We might note, however, that interrogatories can often achieve the same purpose with considerably less effort. Courts sometimes deny motions to make more definite and certain on this very ground.[33]

The modern lawyer tends to write off corrective motions as pointless exercises in procedural refinements. Reflection will show that in some cases these devices can pay practical dividends.

3. Summary Judgment

a. As a Quasi-Discovery Device

The motion for summary judgment has a unique relationship to discovery. Depositions, interrogatories and other discovery procedures can provide substantial help to both the moving party and his opponent.

Because of the motion's dispositive character, courts often allow discovery for the purpose of gathering evidence to oppose a motion for summary judgment.[34] That does not mean that a request to engage in discovery can be counted on to thwart the motion for summary judgment in every instance. If it appears to the court that discovery will not generate material facts sufficient to defeat the motion, (*e.g.,* where questions of law predominate), it may deny discovery.[35]

In some jurisdictions, the making of a motion for summary judgment or some other dispositive motion automatically suspends discovery unless the court orders otherwise.[36] In other jurisdictions a court may take it upon itself to suspend discovery pending resolution of a dispositive motion.[37]

---

[33] See, e.g., *Doug Sanders Golf Intercontinental* v. *American Manhattan Industries, Inc.,* 359 F. Supp. 918, 921 (E.D. Wisc. 1973).

[34] Federal Rule 56(f); *NAACP, Western Region* v. *Hodgson,* 57 F.R.D. 81, 83 (D.C. D.C. 1972). A litigant's right to discovery for the purpose of opposing a motion for summary judgment is not unlimited. *First National Bank of Arizona* v. *Cities Service Co.,* 391 U.S. 253, 88 S. Ct. 1575, 20 L. Ed.2d 1575 (1968).

[35] See *Rosin* v. *N. Y. Stock Exchange, Inc.,* 484 F.2d 179, 185 (7th Cir. 1973).

[36] N.Y. CPLR §3214(b); *Schneider* v. *Rockefeller,* 31 N.Y.2d 420, 435, 293 N.E.2d 67, 75 (1972).

[37] *Webster* v. *Midland Electric Coal Corp.,* 43 Ill. App.2d 359, 372, 193 N.E.2d 212, 218 (1963), *cert. denied,* 377 U.S. 964, 84 S.Ct. 1645, 12 L.E.2d 735 (1964).

The foregoing make up some of the ways in which summary judgment and discovery relate, directly and immediately. Let us now consider how the motion for summary judgment can itself serve as a form of discovery.

Disposal of the case on its merits is, of course, the goal of every motion for summary judgment. Factual affidavits of admissible evidence by competent witnesses must support the motion.[38] The opponent of such a motion may not rest on formal denials. He must come forward with concrete evidence showing at least that a question of fact worthy of a trial exists.[39]

The motion, therefore, presents an obvious way to flush out your adversary's evidence. If you wish to find out how and by what witnesses he intends to refute your allegations, move for summary judgment.

Consider an example such as this:

> In an action for breach of a sales contract, plaintiff buyer pleaded issuance and acceptance of an order, defendant seller's failure to deliver the goods and plaintiff's resulting damages. Defendants simply denied the material allegations. Plaintiff's attorney moved for summary judgment. He established the necessary elements of his case by means of affidavits by his client's employees. Defendant opposed the motion by affidavits showing that the sales manager alleged to have accepted plaintiff's order had in fact left defendant's employ a week earlier. Defendant's affidavits showed also that it had notified plaintiff of the severance. Plaintiff's attorney lost his motion but gained insight into the case that might otherwise have required weeks, even months of discovery.

No ethical lawyer moves for summary judgment without what he considers adequate grounds. A court might well not require a response to a sham motion. Employed in good faith, however, the motion for summary judgment, even if denied, may provide comprehensive discovery as a by-product.

b. Discovery as Support for the Motion

We have seen how the motion for summary judgment can function as a form of discovery. The techniques of discovery, on the other hand, can do much to improve a litigant's chances of winning or defeating a motion.

---

[38] Federal Rules of Civil Procedure, Rule 56(e); Calif. Code of Civil Procedure §437c.

[39] *Ibid.*

Factual affidavits usually provide the main support for a motion for summary judgment. Most procedural codes also permit the use of depositions and other discovery material. Federal Rule 56(c), for example, provides in part:

> The judgment sought shall be rendered forthwith if the pleadings, depositions, answers to interrogatories, and admissions on file, together with the affidavits, if any, show that there is no genuine issue as to any material fact and that the moving party is entitled to a judgment as a matter of law.[40]

Certain restrictions, as we shall see, govern the use of a deposition at trial. They do not apply to the use of the deposition in a motion for summary judgment.[41] The trial concerns itself with the resolution of questions of fact, the motion for summary judgment with whether such a question exists. As one federal appellate court has explained:

> The trial court may not make a factual finding by reference to deposition or affidavit wherein the disputed issue of fact appears but may explore whether or not such disputed issue does exist by reference to deposition and affidavits.[42]

Where relevant, discovery material supporting a motion for summary judgment can have a decisive advantage over the traditional affidavit. The affidavits that a moving party relies on will necessarily be those of his own witnesses. If his adversary has any case at all, he will then usually have no difficulty getting from his own side affidavits sufficiently contradictory to establish a question of fact. That will require the court to deny the motion.

The opponent of the motion has a harder job when discovery material supports the motion. If you, as attorney for the moving party, have taken the deposition of the opposing party or one of his key witnesses or employees, and if you submit all or part of the deposition transcript in support of your motion, the lawyer on the other side may be in trouble. He can hardly contradict his own client or one of his witnesses without crippling his case or at least

---

[40] See *Ransburg Electro-Coating Corp. v. Landsdale Finishers, Inc.*, 484 F.2d 1037, 1039 (3d Cir. 1973).
[41] 6 MOORE'S FEDERAL PRACTICE ¶56.11[4].
[42] *Bolack v. Underwood*, 340 F.2d 816, 819 (10th Cir. 1965).

putting it in a bad light in the judge's eyes. As one leading scholar has said, speaking of support for motions for summary judgment:

> As a general proposition a deposition is better than an affidavit. For while an affidavit must contain evidentiary materials and be under oath, the affiant is not subject to cross-examination. The deposition, on the other hand, not only contains evidentiary materials that are under oath, but the deponent is subject to cross-examination.[43]

As you plan and carry out your discovery program, you should keep summary judgment in mind. Thus if a deposition goes particularly well, or if your adversary's answers to your interrogatories reveal a basic weakness in his case, you may perceive a short-cut to final judgment.[44] Summary judgment that disposes of only part of a case, *e.g.*, one or more causes of action, will still probably save you time and anxiety and your client money.

Here is an example of how efficacious discovery can prove as support for a motion for summary judgment:

> In a federal case in Pennsylvania, a longshoreman sued a ship-owner for injuries sustained on the job. Defendant's attorney took the longshoreman's deposition. He elicited testimony that plaintiff had not worked during the period in which the alleged injury occurred. District Judge E. Mac Troutman granted defendant's motion for summary judgment.[45]

The possibility of rapid disposition of the action via summary judgment adds to the importance, which we shall discuss in greater detail, of thoughtful, exhaustive preparation for depositions and other discovery proceedings. Evidence supporting or opposing summary judgment must be of a kind which, if presented in court through a witness, would be admissible in evidence.[46] You must, therefore, take special pains to insure the propriety of your deposition questions. Similarly, since documents produced on discovery and inspection

---

[43] 6 MOORE'S FEDERAL PRACTICE ¶56.11[4]. Professor Moore adds, "The deposition, like the affidavit, is subject to the weakness that the court is unable to observe the demeanor of the deponent."

[44] See, e.g., *Johnson* v. *Nationwide Ins. Co.*, 276 F.2d 574 (4th Cir. 1960); and *Cabales* v. *United States*, 51 F.R.D. 498 (S.D. N.Y. 1970), affd., 447 F.2d 1358 (2 Cir. 1971).

[45] *James* v. *Port Lyttleton Port Line Ltd.*, 51 F.R.D. 216 (E.D. Pa. 1971).

[46] Illinois Supreme Court Rule 191(a); Pennsylvania Rules of Civil Procedure, Rule 1035(d).

may also come in handy on a motion for summary judgment, you would be well advised to authenticate such papers as meticulously as you would if you expected to use them all in court. You may do this by deposition, by interrogatories, by notice to admit or by stipulation.

Its potential use as support for a motion for summary judgment justifies the bother involved in the technical detail of filing your deposition transcript in court. That may be a prerequisite to its use in such a motion. Even if it is not, the presence of the transcript in the court's files will enable you to submit with your motion those passages essential to the point you are making and yet not be charged with unfairly presenting only part of the testimony.

We have dealt principally with depositions as aids to motions for summary judgment. Other discovery material, e.g., answers to interrogatories and admissions, may be used to support such motions.[47]

Discovery material may also provide the means of successfully opposing a motion for summary judgment. Here again, if it emanates from the moving party himself or a witness crucial to his side of the case, it can provide a decisive weapon. But just as a party may not offer in evidence his own answers to interrogatories or his own responses to another party's request for admissions, at least some courts will not let him use that material to oppose a motion for summary judgment by, for example, seeking to prove the existence of a question of fact.[48]

4. Other Motions

Any motion whose determination turns on factual material invites the use of discovery techniques in much the same way as does summary judgment. In most instances discovery may be used either to support the motion or oppose it, sometimes for both purposes.

In a Pennsylvania case, for example, a trial court overruled defendants' jurisdictional objections to plaintiff's complaint. An appellate court held this to have been error. Factual determinations had been involved, and "the lower court should have ordered the taking of depositions or the filing of interrogatories or both." [49]

---

[47] *Williams* v. *Howard Johnson's Inc. of Washington,* 323 F.2d 102, 105 (4th Cir. 1963).

[48] See, e.g., *Sympson* v. *Mor-Win Products, Inc.,* 501 S.W.2d 362, 364 (Tex. Civ. App. 1973).

[49] *Luria* v. *Luria,* 220 Pa. Super. 168, 286 A.2d 922 (1971).

Considerations of discovery may also motivate certain motions. A motion for change of venue, for example, might have as a motive shifting the case to a county or district where the climate is deemed more (or less) favorable to discovery. A plaintiff whose action has been removed to a federal district court might, for reasons related to discovery, make a motion to remand the case to the state tribunal. The experience of most lawyers will call to mind other instances of motions that were or should have been made with considerations of discovery in mind.

Nothing illustrates more vividly the importance that discovery has come to assume in litigation than the way in which it relates to every phase of the action. Motion practice is no exception to this phenomenon.

D. OTHER EARLY DECISIONS AFFECTING DISCOVERY

1. Your Choice of Forum

a. Selecting the Tribunal

We have seen how pleading and motion practice can both influence and be influenced by discovery factors. Let us turn to some other preliminary considerations.

The choice of forum will affect discovery in more ways than many lawyers realize. A fundamental decision here may be whether to select a state or federal court for your action.

b. Right to a Federal Forum

Generally speaking, plaintiff may sue in a federal district court if he is claiming a right under a federal statute such as the patent or the antitrust laws or if his case involves both diversity of citizenship and an amount in controversy exceeding $10,000.[50] For practical purposes, diversity of citizenship means that no plaintiff, whether corporation or natural person, may be a citizen of the same state as any defendant.[51] The law, for this purpose, considers a corporation a citizen both of the state of its incorporation and of the state where it has its principal office.[52]

---

[50] 28 U.S.C. §§1331, 1332.
[51] 1 MOORE'S FEDERAL PRACTICE ¶0.60[8.–4].
[52] 28 U.S.C. §1332(c).

c. Removal to a Federal Forum

A defendant, too, may have a choice between a federal and a state forum. If federal jurisdiction exists but if plaintiff nevertheless sues in a state court, his adversary has the right to remove the action to the appropriate U. S. District Court.[53] He may do so by filing a simple petition and a modest bond with the clerk of the district court and carrying out a few other formalities.[54]

The passages above do not purport to deal exhaustively with the subject of federal jurisdiction. They will suffice to introduce the considerations that counsel must weigh in deciding what impact his choice of forum will have on his own and on his adversary's discovery program.

d. Breadth of Discovery

We may safely generalize that in federal courts discovery is broader than in many state tribunals. We need not analyze here the historical and other reasons for this phenomenon. We should recognize that more and more states have liberalized their practice, making our generalization of greater federal liberality no longer the absolute it once was. Many states, moreover, have adopted the Federal Rules verbatim, or almost so, as their own practice codes. In a great many jurisdictions, however, a party to whom extensive discovery is vital will give serious thought to bringing his action in a federal court.

Remember, however, whether you are plaintiff or defendant, that if you invoke federal jurisdiction on a dubious basis, the federal court may refuse to allow discovery, at least pending resolution of the jurisdictional question.[55] It may, on the other hand, allow you to conduct discovery for the purpose of resolving jurisdictional issues, provided you act promptly.[56]

e. "Relevance"

While dealing with the impact that one's choice of forum will have on his own and his adversary's discovery, we might mention

---

[53] 28 U.S.C. §1441.

[54] 28 U.S.C. §1446.

[55] See *Cannon* v. *United Ins. Co.*, 352 F. Supp. 1212, 1214–15 (D. S.C. 1973); *Lantz International Corp.* v. *Industria Termotecnica Campana*, 358 F. Supp. 510, 516 (E.D. Pa. 1973).

[56] *Whittaker Corp.* v. *United Aircraft Corp.*, 482 F.2d 1079, 1086 (1st Cir. 1973), and cases cited.

some of the ways in which federal discovery differs from that practiced in some state courts, as well as some of the features that distinguish state procedures from one another. Our purpose will be
more to list these elements, as an inducement to thought and research
in individual cases, than to analyze them.

To begin with, we find differences in the standard of relevance.
Federal Rule 26, which governs the scope of discovery, establishes
the standard as "any matter, not privileged, which is relevant to the
subject matter involved in the pending action." [57]

"Relevant" as used in this context means something different from
the same word as used by the trial judge in determining admissibility
in evidence.[58] Even inadmissible matter may be obtained, if it "appears
reasonably calculated to lead to the discovery of admissible evidence." [59] Chief Judge Edelstein of the U. S. District Court for
the Southern District of New York has cited with approval and
applied a commentator's view that by the federal standard:

> . . . discovery should be relevant where there is *any possibility*
> that the information sought may be relevant to the subject matter
> of the action.[60]

Not all state courts go so far.[61] The federal standard of relevance
might thus make a federal forum attractive to the attorney whose case
will depend on obtaining extensive evidence from his adversary or
from outside sources. Conversely, the lawyer who wishes to limit his
opponent's discovery may do better by picking a state forum.

f. Types of Action

Some states have statutes, rules or case law limiting or denying
some kinds of discovery in particular kinds of cases such as stockholders' suits, matrimonial matters, etc. A New York litigant, for

---

[57] Federal Rule 26(b)(1). "Privileged," for purposes of this passage, refers to
evidentiary privilege. *United States* v. *Reynolds,* 345 U.S. 1, 73 S. Ct. 528, 97 L.Ed.
727, 32 ALR2d 382 (1953).

[58] See, e.g., *Burns* v. *Thiokol Chemical Corp.,* 483 F.2d 300, 304, note 8 (5th
Cir. 1973).

[59] Federal Rule 26(b)(1). Thus a ruling allowing discovery does not mean that
the discovered material will be admissible in evidence. *Uitts* v. *General Motors Corp.,*
58 F.R.D. 450, 452–453 (E.D. Pa. 1972).

[60] C. Wright, LAW OF FEDERAL COURTS §81, at page 359, note 47 (2d Ed. 1970),
cited in *Mallinckrodt Chemical Works* v. *Goldman, Sachs & Co.,* 58 F.R.D. 348, 353
(S.D. N.Y. 1973). (Emphasis added by the court.)

[61] Connecticut, for example, provides for disclosure on motion of matter "material to the mover's cause of action or defense, and within the knowledge, possession
or power of the adverse party." Conn. Gen. Stats. Ann. §52-197.

example, considering whether to bring a personal-injury action in state or federal court, would take into account that state's prohibition against interrogatories in actions for "personal injury, resulting from negligence." [62] The Federal Rules contain no such limitation.

Some states relegate certain forms of discovery to a particular stage of some types of actions. In a suit for an accounting, for example, plaintiff may have to establish his right to an accounting before he is entitled to discovery and inspection of books and records establishing the amount owing him.[63]

In federal practice, too, discovery may be barred or limited in certain types of actions. Habeas corpus and class actions provide two examples [64], although a federal court may allow discovery on the maintainability of a class suit.[65] Discovery under the Federal Rules is, to a limited extent, available in administrative proceedings.[66] Whether it is to be had in judicial review of such proceedings depends on the proper scope of such review by applicable statutory standard.[67]

Some types of actions, on the other hand, enjoy a favored status for purposes of discovery. Civil rights cases form one such category in federal practice.[68]

Rules such as the few mentioned here may work for you or against you in a given situation. Make sure you know about them before you decide where to sue or whether and where you wish to remove or transfer a case.

g. Depositions of Non-Parties

Another advantage to federal practice is the right to take the deposition of a non-party witness.[69] Like the right to take a party's deposition, this right is subject to any protective order necessary to prevent harrassment or other abuse.[70] Nevertheless, in contrast to

---

[62] N.Y. CPLR 3130.

[63] *Wood* v. *Brackett*, 266 So.2d 398 (Fla. App. 1972).

[64] See, as to habeas corpus, *Harris* v. *Nelson*, 394 U.S. 286, 89 S.Ct. 1082, 22 L.Ed.2d 281 (1969). As to class actions, see *Gardner* v. *Awards Marketing Corp.*, 55 F.R.D. 460 (D. Utah 1972).

[65] *Huff* v. *N. D. Cass Co. of Ala.*, 485 F.2d 710, 713 (5th Cir. 1973).

[66] See *Federal Trade Commission* v. *Bramman*, 54 F.R.D. 364, 367 (W.D. Mo. 1972), and cases cited.

[67] See, e.g., *Gables by the Sea, Inc.* v. *Lee*, 365 F. Supp. 826, 829 (S.D. Fla. 1973).

[68] *Burns* v. *Thiokol Chemical Corp.*, 483 F.2d 300, 305 (5th Cir. 1973).

[69] Federal Rule 30(a) permits the taking of "the testimony of any person, including a party, by deposition upon oral examination."

[70] Federal Rule 26(c).

the rule that obtains in some states,[71] no special showing need be made to take a non-party's deposition in a federal court.

h. Attorney's Work-Product

The litigant in a federal court may be less likely than his counterpart in a state proceeding to have his discovery thwarted by the "work product" rule. This doctrine protects from discovery material collected or created by counsel in preparation for trial. Federal Rule 26(c)(3) accords limited protection to most such material. Some states restrict the discovery of work product severely [72] or deny it absolutely.[73]

A basic split of authority exists on whether reports obtained by a liability insurance carrier are protected as work product or otherwise. In any accident case, if you have a choice of forum, you will surely wish to look into the relevant holdings.[74]

i. Discovery Concerning Expert Witnesses

A litigant who wishes to learn what any expert witness retained by the other side has found or is apt to testify to, may fare better in a federal court. As recently amended, the Federal Rules require a party, in answer to interrogatories, to identify any experts it intends to call and to summarize their testimony.[75] Under "exceptional circumstances," a party may further be required to divulge the findings of an expert retained but not expected to testify.[76] The rules of some states limit discovery of the opinions of an opponent's expert.[77]

---

[71] In New York, for example, unless the potential witness is a party to the action, is about to leave the state or meets other specified qualifications, his deposition may be taken only "where the court on motion determines that there are adequate special circumstances." N.Y. CPLR, Sec. 3101(a)(4). See *Romeo* v. *Russo*, 31 A.D.2d 935, 299 N.Y.S.2d 7 (1969).

[72] In Florida, work product is obtainable under "rare and exceptional circumstances." *Surf Drugs, Inc.* v. *Vermette*, 236 So.2d 108, 112 (Fla. 1970).

[73] See, e.g., N.Y. CPLR, Sec. 3101(c).

[74] *Brakhage* v. *Graff*, 190 Neb. 53, 206 N.W.2d 45 (1973), including the dissenting opinion of Spencer, J. at page   of 190 Neb., page 49 of 206 N.W.2d, cites decisions both ways from a number of jurisdictions.

[75] Federal Rule 26(b)(4)(A)(i).

[76] Federal Rule 26(b)(4)(B). Even federal practice, however, does not give one total access to the work product of his adversary's experts. See, e.g., *Breedlove* v. *Beech Aircraft Corp.*, 57 F.R.D. 202 (N.D. Miss. 1972); *Bailey* v. *Meister Brau, Inc.*, 57 F.R.D. 11, 14 (N.D. Ill. 1972).

[77] See, e.g., N.Y. CPLR §3101(d)(1); *LeMieux* v. *Bishop*, 209 N.W.2d 379, 385 (Minn. 1973); *State* ex rel. *New Mexico State Highway Commission* v. *Taira*, 78 N.M. 276, 430 P.2d 773 (1967).

j. Notice Procedure

The party seeking discovery in most forms under the Federal Rules has the advantage of being able to proceed by simple notice, rather than having to go before the court with a motion.[78] The party who opposes discovery must object.[79] This relieves the discovering party of a substantial burden. The practice of some states still makes discovery of some kinds available only by motion.[80]

k. Discovery of Liability Insurance

In personal-injury and other actions, plaintiff often wishes to discover defendant's liability-insurance policy. A 1970 amendment to the Federal Rules makes such material available.[81] The discovery practice of many states still denies it or grants it only in special situations.[82]

l. Supplemental Disclosure

Litigants often clash over the question whether one party, upon gaining new or corrected information, must bring up to date his response to his adversary's discovery. Federal practice, although it imposes no such duty absolutely, applies it to a considerable extent.[83]

m. Appealability

Some states let the disappointed litigant have appellate review of a discovery order, either by extraordinary writ or by interlocutory appeal.[84] Some do not.[85] In federal practice, where the final judgment rule obtains,[86] appellate review is almost always impossible.[87]

---

[78] Federal Rule 34(a).

[79] Federal Rule 34(b).

[80] See, e.g., Calif. Code of Civil Procedure §2031(a); 12 Okl. Stats. Ann. §548; Rule 88 of the Rules of Practice for the Circuit Courts of South Carolina; Section 25–1267.39 of the Revised Statutes of Nebraska. All of the above provisions deal with discovery and inspection. See also Conn. Gen. Stats. Ann. §52–197.

[81] Federal Rule 26(b)(2). This does not mean, of course, that such material will be received in evidence. *Grise* v. *Crownover*, 57 F.R.D. 210 (E.D. Tenn. 1971).

[82] See, e.g., *Fort* v. *Neal*, 79 N.M. 479, 444 P.2d 990 (1968); *Hastings* v. *Thurston*, 100 Ariz. 302, 306, 413 P.2d 767, 770 (1966); *Kenney* v. *Angerer*, 42 A.D.2d 963, 347 N.Y.S.2d 743 (2d Dept. 1973). Cf. *Carroll Cable Co.* v. *Miller*, 501 S.W.2d 299 (1973).

[83] Federal Rule 26(e). See discussion at page 231.

[84] For an example of an appeal from a discovery order, see *Baser* v. *Uniroyal, Inc.*, 39 A.D.2d 632, 331 N.Y.S.2d 74 (4th Dept. 1972). An example of the successful use of an extraordinary writ will be found in *Louisville General Hospital* v. *Hellman*, 500 S.W.2d 790 (Ky. 1973).

[85] *State* ex rel. *Daggett* v. *Cressaman*, 34 Ohio St.2d 55, 295 N.E.2d 659 (1973).

[86] 28 U.S.C. §1291.

[87] 4 MOORE'S FEDERAL PRACTICE ¶26.83[3]; *Donnelly* v. *Parker*, — App. D.C. —, 486 F.2d 402, 408 (1973); *Childs* v. *Kaplan*, 467 F.2d 628 (8th Cir. 1972); *Honig* v. *E. I. du Pont de Nemours & Co.*, 404 F.2d 410 (5th Cir. 1968).

Even in federal practice, of course, discovery orders may be reviewed in an appeal from the final judgment.[88] By that time, however, most discovery issues have become academic.

Many experienced lawyers agree that the freedom from appellate review on discovery matters tends to incline the federal judge to a pragmatic rather than a technical approach to the subject. This often leads to broader discovery.

n. Federal or State Discovery

We have listed a number of ways in which discovery practice in federal courts differs from that which prevails in many states. We can safely say that in general federal discovery is at least as broad and often broader than its state counterpart. The plaintiff or defendant whose case qualifies for federal jurisdiction will wish to weigh each of these elements carefully before he decides in what court he wants his case to be tried.

o. Different State or Federal Forums

The problem of choosing a forum will not always pose itself in state vs. federal terms. Your action may be such that you can bring it in (or transfer it to) any one of several counties within your state. You may have the right to sue or be sued in any one of several states or federal districts. Perhaps you have the right to select a state court of one or another jurisdictional level. In any of these choices, discovery should enter into your decision.

2. Choosing the Right Parties

a. As Counsel for Plaintiff

Choosing the forum is not the only early decision likely to affect the discovery phase of your action. Selecting the parties to the action will have an impact, too.

We have mentioned that in some jurisdictions a litigant has an easier time getting discovery from a party than from a non-party witness. This may induce you to include as a party someone not essential to the relief you are seeking but important for purposes of discovery.

---

[88] 4 MOORE'S FEDERAL PRACTICE ¶26.83[10].

Let us consider an example:

> A personal-injury claimant proposes to sue the taxi company
> whose vehicle knocked him down. His attorney wonders whether
> to name the driver a defendant, too. He knows that the rule of
> *respondeat superior* makes the company liable for the driver's
> negligence. The company's insurance carrier will pay any judg-
> ment. He nevertheless names the driver a defendant. Why?

If plaintiff's counsel in the above hypothetical situation practices
in a state which makes it relatively difficult to take the deposition
of a non-party,[89] his principal reason for naming the driver a defendant is obvious. To prove negligence, he must have the driver's
testimony. Naming him a defendant establishes his right to a
deposition.

Suppose, however, that our hypothetical plaintiff's counsel had
sued in a federal court or in the courts of a state that grants full
rights to take a non-party's deposition. Do the needs of his discovery
program still provide reasons for naming his essential witness a party?

Several grounds come to mind at once. First, even in the federal
courts and in the more liberal state jurisdictions, the deposition of a
party is easier to use at trial than that of a non-party witness. Generally
speaking, one has an absolute right to offer an adverse party's deposition in evidence.[90] He must, on the other hand, show the non-party
witness's unavailability or perhaps other special circumstances, sometimes a difficult job, before reading his deposition into the record as
evidence.[91]

Take a case where you have obtained helpful testimony from a
witness. You fear that if you put him on the stand at trial, he will
qualify or modify what he has said. You can in such a case use his
deposition testimony to impeach him, but then he may explain the
discrepancy. Had you named him a party, you could have read his
deposition into evidence without putting him on the stand.

Moreover, in a jurisdiction with more liberal discovery rules, a
party's deposition may be much easier to arrange than that of a witness.
You may take the party's deposition by merely sending a notice to
his attorney. To compel a non-party witness to appear and testify,

---

[89] New York, for example. See footnote 71.
[90] See, e.g., Federal Rule 32(a)(2). As one of many examples, Kans. Stats. Ann.
1972 Supp. 60–232(a)(2) is substantially identical to the federal provision.
[91] Federal Rule 32(a)(3).

you must find him and personally serve him with a subpoena.[92] True, to make him a party, you must likewise effect personal service, but once that is done you need not worry about his moving away, etc. If you fail to name him a defendant, you never know if your process-server will be able to find him with a subpoena when you need him.

If the need arises to enforce your discovery rights, your job may be simpler against one whom you have named a party. You may have trouble, for example, punishing an employer for failing to produce its employee at a deposition.[93] If you have named the employee himself a party, however, you may succeed in having meaningful sanctions imposed against him.

We have been talking just about depositions. Even the Federal Rules and the more liberal of the state codes limit other forms of discovery to parties. Federal Rule 33, for example, provides for the service of interrogatories "upon any other party." Rule 34, governing production of documents, etc., is similarly limited to parties, its sub-section (c) appearing to require "an independent action" to obtain such production from "a person not a party." Federal Rule 36 ("Requests for Admission") likewise applies to parties alone. So, in essence, does Rule 35, pertaining to physical and mental examinations.

Consider, therefore, this example:

> An appliance store sues a distributor over a design defect in a new line of electric toasters. Plaintiff's attorney deems it unnecessary to join the manufacturer as a defendant. He can claim breach of warranty against the distributor and keep his action a simple one. He reasons, however, that adding the manufacturer will give him access, via Federal Rule 34 or its state counterpart, to factory records likely to strengthen his proof of a defect.

Assume that in the personal-injury case outlined at page 44, plaintiff contended that the taxi driver's defective vision or other physical handicap caused the accident. His attorney may wish to have a physical examination of the driver. If he has sued in a federal court, Rule 35 entitles him to have examined "a party, or . . . a person in the custody or under the legal control of a party." This alone might justify naming the driver a party. Plaintiff's attorney may argue, to be sure, that the driver, even if not a party, as the taxi company's employee is under its "legal control." But what if by the time of the proposed examination the driver has changed jobs?

---

[92] 4A MOORE'S FEDERAL PRACTICE ¶30.55[1].
[93] *Serpe* v. *Yellow Cab Co.*, 10 Ill. App. 3d 1, 293 N.E.2d 742 (1973).

Again, the conclusion to draw is plain. Obtaining discovery will be easier against one you have named a party. It does not follow that your wisest course necessarily lies in naming everyone in sight a party. On the contrary, other things being equal, the fewer adversaries you have the better off your client will be as a litigant.

For one thing, every additional adverse party that you name means one more lawyer in the case seeking discovery against you and using his talents to thwart your case. If, as plaintiff's counsel, you sue one defendant, you know that your witnesses will be cross-examined once at the trial. Every added party means one more brain to pick flaws in your proof and catch points that an earlier cross-examiner missed. Adding a party not strictly necessary must promise to confer a demonstrable substantive benefit to offset such a drawback.

Other considerations emphasize the foolishness of automatically resolving all doubts in favor of making everyone you can a party. Take the case, hypothesized above, of the appliance dealer suing the distributor and adding the manufacturer as a defendant. Counsel for the dealer takes into account the likelihood that suing the manufacturer will introduce a large law firm with manpower and other resources enough to complicate and prolong the case by a series of motions and similar proceedings that might not ensue were he to limit his action to the distributor. He adds the manufacturer as a defendant, cognizant of this negative factor, because he concludes that the need for ready access to the manufacturer's records makes its presence in the case worthwhile.

Another example will show that it is not wise to automatically name all eligible witnesses defendants:

> A window designer sues a chain of jewelry stores. He alleges breach of an agreement to purchase some made-to-order display material. His attorney knows that the defendant will contend that its former area manager, named Brandon, lacked authority to make the deal. Plaintiff's attorney fears that Brandon may move out of the jurisdiction. He considers the latter's testimony of conversations with plaintiff crucial to plaintiff's case. Plaintiff's attorney is thus first inclined to name Mr. Brandon a defendant. It dawns on him, however, that by doing so he will be giving him an interest in the outcome of the litigation and tempting him to "shade" his testimony in favor of his former employer. With Brandon a mere witness, plaintiff's attorney realizes that his discharge by the corporation will insure his objectivity. That, counsel

concludes, justifies the risk of having difficulty taking or using Brandon's deposition.

The sound rule, then, is not so simple. Before adding a party for discovery's sake, one should weigh the disadvantages as well as the advantages of his presence. Elements other than discovery will figure in this consideration. One may, for example, decide to name a particular defendant for the sake of insuring a collectible judgment. Resolving the question of whom to sue without taking into account considerations of discovery, however, can impair the litigant's chances of achieving the result he desires.

b. As Counsel for Defendant

The discussion to this point has suggested that plaintiff is the only party who must decide, for reasons of discovery or otherwise, whom to bring into the case and whom to leave out. Defendant may have the same questions to ask and answer.

A defendant may bring in new parties by impleader, sometimes called third-party practice.[94] If he counterclaims or cross-claims, he may name others in addition to the plaintiff who sued him.[95] Even if he does not counterclaim, he may force others into the action as "involuntary plaintiffs." [96]

Let us take another look at the above case of the window designer suing the jewelry chain:

Defendant's attorney realizes that his having been fired may tempt the ex-manager Brandon to get even with defendant by distorting his testimony in plaintiff's favor. He might, that is, admit authority that he actually knew he lacked. Counsel decides, therefore, before any party proceeds to take Brandon's deposition, to draw up a third-party complaint against him, alleging that if defendant is held liable to plaintiff it will have been the result of Brandon's *ultra vires* acts. By bringing Brandon into the case, defense counsel reasons, he will not only guarantee his own right both to take and use Brandon's deposition, but will also give the ex-manager a potent incentive to tell the truth.

For all counsel, choosing parties can have important consequences

---

[94] See, e.g., Federal Rule 14(a).
[95] Federal Rule 13(h).
[96] Federal Rule 19(a).

in terms of discovery. The selection demands careful thought. The mechanical application of a rule-of-thumb will not do.

3. Collecting Facts: Work-Product and Litigation-Preparation

On either side of a lawsuit, you will often begin collecting and evaluating evidence before an action is commenced. You may usually not use discovery processes for this pre-action assemblage of facts, but considerations of discovery will play a part in your activity.

Your jurisdiction may give more or less protection to the attorney's work-product and to material prepared in contemplation of litigation.[97] You know that the more of your preliminary preparation you can legitimately bring under one or the other of these rubrics, the less the chances you will have to share it with your adversary. You will consider, therefore, strategems such as:

1. Interviewing witnesses yourself rather than through a hired investigator or adjustor;

2. Seeing that the reports of such investigators as you must engage are directed to you rather than, say, to your client's claims department;

3. Combining with your own factual reports (memoranda of interviews with witnesses, for example) comments and evaluations that manifest application of your professional talent.

4. Making clear that all pre-action investigatory effort, whether by you or by a hired investigator or photographer, etc., shows that it is prompted by and directed toward the possibility of litigation.

Conversely, you will not waste time collecting facts that you know you can get by discovery anyway. For example:

You represent a third-party defendant brought into a personal-injury action two years after the accident and a year and a half after the commencement of suit. The defendant who impleaded you is a large insurance company. You know that it investigated the accident immediately after it happened. If your practice gives you under these circumstances the right to obtain from that defendant such things as the names of witnesses and copies of photo-

---

[97] See the brief discussion at page 41.

graphs taken immediately after the accident, you will temper your own investigatory work accordingly.

This brief discussion does not purport to treat, for purposes of any jurisdiction, the vastly complicated subjects of work-product and litigation-preparation. It does provide suggestions how the attorney's procedure in his collection of facts for litigation can have repercussions in his and his adversary's later discovery efforts.

4. Other Things to Remember

We have mentioned the drafting of pleadings, the choice of forum and the selection of parties as early decisions in which discovery should play a part. Every experienced practitioner can think of others.

You may have the chance to decide between arbitration and a conventional lawsuit. You must ask what effect your choice will have on your ability (and that of other participants) to obtain the evidence needed to prosecute or defend the claims. Discovery may or may not be available in arbitration proceedings.[98]

The same goes for particular types of suits that may be launched in certain circumstances. A special proceeding is one such category. Some jurisdictions have devised simplified proceedings to dispense in some situations with the delays and complications of regular litigation.[99]

A litigant may have the choice of bringing an action himself or allowing a public official to sue on his behalf. Sometimes he may sue (or defend) alone or as a member of a class. As his attorney, you should never let him make such a decision without first weighing its effect on discovery and in turn the effect that discovery will have on the outcome of the proceeding.

Remember, as a last word, that you may be able to use the fruits of discovery (deposition testimony, for example) obtained in an earlier action. If the issues in prior litigation were substantially the same as in your present case, look into the possibility of using discovery material obtained there. Identity of parties is not always necessary.[100]

---

[98] See, e.g., *Cavanaugh* v. *McDonnell & Co.*, 357 Mass. 452, 258 N.E.2d 561 (1970).

[99] See, for example, the Simplified Procedure for Court Determination of Disputes provided for by N.Y. CPLR §3031 *et seq.*

[100] See, for example, *George R. Whitten, Jr., Inc.* v. *State Univ. Construction Fund*, 359 F. Supp. 1037 (D. Mass. 1973), and cases cited; *Levy* v. *Kimball*, 51 Haw. 540, 465 P.2d 580 (1970).

E. TIMING DISCOVERY

1. Priority of Discovery

a. Depositions

You have decided to engage in discovery. You must determine when to make your moves. Should you take your adversary's deposition before he takes your client's? Should your motion or notice for discovery and inspection come before or after you take depositions and serve interrogatories? These and other questions demand prompt answers.

Your statute or rules probably allow you to proceed largely as you will, once the action is commenced. Federal Rule 30(a), for example, governing depositions, provides for such proceedings "After commencement of the action," with a court order required under certain circumstances if plaintiff wishes to proceed within 30 days after service of the summons and complaint. This provision has the effect of giving defendant a head start on depositions if he wishes to take advantage of it. Whether he should do so will be discussed below.

As for written interrogatories, Federal Rule 33 allows them to be served:

> without leave of court . . . upon the plaintiff after commencement
> of the action and upon any other party with or after service of
> the summons and complaint upon that party.

Federal Rule 34 makes an identical provision for the service of a notice for discovery and inspection. Rule 36, applying to requests for admissions, does likewise. Federal Rule 35 (*Physical and Mental Examination of Persons*) does not limit the time during which a party may move for an examination.

All this does not tell you how it is best to arrange the sequence of your discovery proceedings. Neither does it say how you should time those proceedings with respect to the discovery conducted by other parties to the case.

Let us begin with the question of priority of deposition. Should you try to take the other side's deposition before your adversary takes your client's testimony? The question has many ramifications.

Most lawyers act instinctively. They want to beat their opponents to the draw in taking depositions. Their desire arises in part from wishing to show clients their alertness and aggressiveness. Some states have built up substantial case law as a result of this desire to be first.[101] Some thought may yield the conclusion that in a given case it will pay to concede priority.

Before you rush instinctively to take your adversary's deposition, ask yourself whether you are really ready to take that testimony. Would you do a more effective job of questioning at a later stage of the case? Might, for example, taking the deposition of a non-party witness provide indispensable background for examining the party opposing you? Might your adversary's line of questioning in taking your client's deposition help you question his client more effectively?

Weigh your answers to these questions against the obvious advantages of taking the first deposition. The principal such advantage, as we all know, is the desirability of committing the other side to a particular version of the facts before knowing what your client has to say.

In the personal-injury or other tort case devoid of voluminous documentary evidence, abstruse technicalities and factual complexities, trying for priority of discovery may make sense. Say, for example:

> You represent plaintiff in a case stemming from an automobile collision at an intersection. Your client and an independent eyewitness have assured you that plaintiff was proceeding through a green light when defendant's vehicle struck him. You suspect defendant of having been under the influence of liquor at the time. You reason that if defendant gets your client's version of the accident first, he will be tempted to concoct an explanation for having gone through a red light. If, on the other hand, defendant testifies first, without the benefit of your client's version and without knowing about the eye-witness, the vagueness of his recollection may lead him simply to say that he had the green light, a contention that you know you can refute.

This is not to say that you should necessarily seek priority of deposition in every simple personal-injury case. Your accumulation of evi-

---

[101] See, e.g., 3A Weinstein-Korn-Miller, New York Civil Practice ¶¶3106.01 *et seq.*

dence with the passage of time may suggest that you will be in a stronger position to elicit helpful testimony if you wait for a while. Think about this example:

> You represent defendant in a personal-injury case. You suspect plaintiff of exaggerating his inquiries. His complaint alleges that a loss of mobility in his shoulder has kept him from earning a living in his usual trade. His ex-wife, however, has told you that he has been seen playing tennis at an out-of-town court. You have just hired an investigator to corroborate the report, preferably by taking movies of plaintiff in the act. You reason that if you take plaintiff's deposition immediately, you can simply ask him if he has engaged in any sports since his accident. He may deny it and call an immediate halt to his tennis games. If, however, you wait until you have movies or other objective proof to back you up, you can ask him whether he did not play tennis at a specific place on a named date. Then you think that he will have to admit it or risk provable perjury.

Particularly if you think that your case on the facts of the accident is all but hopeless and that your only chance of emerging with a reasonable settlement or verdict is to prove plaintiff a malingerer, you may well decide in this situation to defer your deposition and let plaintiff's attorney examine your client first.

To show the variety of possibilities, let us vary the facts slightly and assume that:

> Again as defense counsel in the same case, you have, at the outset of the case or shortly thereafter, movies of the allegedly disabled plaintiff engaged in athletic activity. You desire to take plaintiff's deposition as early as possible. You would like him to testify before his lawyer, through his discovery program or otherwise, finds out about the movies. You hope not merely to force an admission from plaintiff. You want to catch him in an outright, demonstrable lie.

Some lawyers maintain that, as the suggestion has been made above, one should invariably yield priority of deposition. They contend that the questions asked by opposing counsel help one prepare one's own questioning for the deposition of the other side. This principle may not qualify as a hard-and-fast rule. It does deserve consideration in every case.

Take another example:

> A small manufacturing corporation sued a design consultant for
> conspiracy to divert the corporation's principal source of business
> to another firm and to pirate plaintiff's trade secrets. The com-
> plaint spoke in broad terms. Defense counsel had no idea which
> of the dozens of projects and transactions that had taken place
> would constitute the true subject-matter of the action.
> He first satisfied himself that his client's conduct throughout the
> parties' dealings had been lawful and fair. He then decided to let
> plaintiff's counsel take defendant's deposition first. This, he
> thought, would save him time in preparing for and taking plain-
> tiff's deposition. It would show him which of his client's actual
> or alleged deeds were under attack.

Racing to take the first deposition, some may argue, can never be
a fatal mistake. If your opponent's later deposition of your client
brings out aspects of the case that you failed to perceive when it was
your turn, you can take a second deposition of his client. Such a
procedure, however, will cost much in time and money. It may
require seeking court permission or facing a motion for a protective
order on the ground of harassment. In any such proceedings you
will have to "telegraph your punch" by telling the court, and thereby
your opponent, exactly what you propose to question the latter's
client about. Remember, too, that just as you can get many ideas
from your adversary's questioning of your client, he can learn much
from the deposition that you take. We have pointed out how your
discovery can induce opposing counsel to prepare his case more
thoroughly than he might do otherwise. Part of this extra preparation
may consist of questions to your client that would otherwise have
gone unasked. For your adversary, as for you, a second deposition
may prove impossible or seem not worthwhile.

One's own discovery and the other side's questioning on deposition
are not the only sources of information that may persuade you to take
your deposition later rather than sooner. Other preliminary proceedings may have the same effect.

The motion for summary judgment, we saw, often serves as a
form of discovery device.[102] In an action where you contemplate
such a motion, you may conclude that you will save time and effort
by deferring your deposition of the adverse party until you have

---

[102] Pages 32–33.

seen the affidavit or affidavits with which he opposes your motion for summary judgment. You may also hope that the success of your motion will obviate discovery.

Much the same applies to other preliminary motions that you (or, for that matter, your opponent) may contemplate. If a motion stands a chance of disposing of all or part of the case, you may conclude that taking immediate depositions makes no sense. Even if the motion will lead only to clarification or amendment of the pleadings, waiting for the result before you take the opposing party's deposition may represent the wiser course.

Here is an example:

> Defense counsel in a private antitrust action brought by a group of fifteen wholesalers devoted many hours and thousands of dollars taking the depositions of plaintiffs and others, principally concerning a claim for price discrimination. After the action had been pending for almost a year, defendant moved to dismiss the claim for failure to state a cause of action. He based his motion on the face of plaintiffs' pleading, so the results of his discovery were of no use to him in the motion. The court granted defendant's motion.

How much better off attorney and client would have been in this case had counsel concentrated his energy from the start on the legal sufficiency of plaintiffs' complaint instead of hurrying to take the first deposition and then absorbing himself in a morass of factual complexities that time proved academic. His error of judgment, most of us know, was neither original nor unique.

The discussion and examples above provide no mechanical solution to the problem whether to strive for priority of deposition. They raise questions that can be asked in every such situation, questions whose answers will improve your chances of making the right decision.

b. Other Proceedings

Other discovery devices, such as interrogatories and discovery and inspection, may also pose problems of priority. Here, too, being first does not necessarily mean acting wisely.

In a case likely to involve voluminous documentary disclosure, a comprehensive set of interrogatories or notice of discovery and inspection may give your opponent ideas for an equally exhaustive counter-attack on your client's files.

In any action you may feel the need to serve interrogatories or conduct a discovery and inspection. You may, however, at the outset of the case not know enough about the matter to pose questions or demands both intelligent and comprehensive. It may then pay to wait and learn more about the case from the questions or demands that your adversary directs to you.

Acting precipitately in these situations may mean a less serious (surely a less expensive) error than when depositions are involved. Successive sets of interrogatories or notices of discovery and inspection are allowed far more readily than are successive depositions.

Letting your adversary move first in discovery proceedings other than depositions may, therefore, sometimes work to your advantage. You will always benefit from applying thought to your decisions in this area instead of proceeding by reflex action.

2. The Sequence of Your Own Proceedings

Making up your mind whether to seek priority of discovery as against your adversary does not end the matter. You must think about the order in which to launch your own discovery proceedings.

As we shall see, each type of discovery has its special advantages. Each has drawbacks. Once you decide that your case will benefit from resort to more than one type of proceeding, in what order would it be best to take them up?

Assume, for a start, a case in which both the testimony of live witnesses and physical evidence (books and records, for example) are going to play important parts. You wish to take the deposition of the adverse party. You realize that you cannot examine him effectively without first having reviewed the contents of his files or other physical evidence in his possession. Yet you lack the knowledge to draft a notice for discovery and inspection that you will feel sure qualifies as comprehensive and reasonably specific.

In such a situation, you should consider beginning your discovery by submitting interrogatories.[103] They, as we shall discuss further, provide a quick, cheap way to find out about background material without interrupting deposition questioning. Even in relatively uncomplicated cases, a party's discovery will often begin with interrogatories asking the opposing party to list the relevant evidence in its possession.

---

[103] See *Franchise Programs, Inc.* v. *Mr. Aqua Spray, Inc.*, 41 F.R.D. 172, 174 (S.D. N.Y. 1966).

In a routine personal injury action, for example, defendant's attorney might begin discovery with interrogatories seeking, in part, lists of:

1. plaintiff's medical bills;
2. any accident reports filed; and
3. documentary evidence of plaintiff's loss of income, etc.

Plaintiff's counsel might also begin with interrogatories. He would ask for enumerations of:

1. defendant's internal records of the accident;
2. its reports to insurance carriers;
3. photographs; and
4. witnesses' statements, etc.

In many situations, one should follow interrogatories with a notice or motion to discover, inspect and copy the material whose existence the answers to interrogatories has revealed. In jurisdictions where the interrogating party may require the attachment of documents to the answers to interrogatories,[104] one may be able to skip this procedure.

Taking the above step or steps before counsel takes depositions enables him to study beforehand the papers relevant to the depositions. The more complex the action, the more important it is to have time to study the documentary evidence before asking questions about its contents. Thus the right to require the production of papers and other things at the deposition will often provide an inadequate substitute for the earlier collection of material in the way outlined above.

Interrogatories, discovery and inspection (if necessary) and then the deposition, in that order, appear to form a logical sequence. But never come to regard this sequence as automatic. Circumstances will sometimes justify beginning by taking the opposing party's deposition. Oral questions about the contents of his files or similar background information may seem cumbersome and uneconomical as compared with written interrogatories, but a deposition gives you the party's own relatively spontaneous answers. Interrogatories will give you the product of his lawyer's draftsmanship.

On any subject, therefore, as to which you would like to catch a party more or less off-guard, taking his deposition first might be the better course. For example, a statute or rule may require that you give

---

104 For example, N.Y. Civil Practice Law and Rules, Section 3131. On the availability of this device in federal practice in the light of the 1970 amendments to Rules 33 and 34, see 4A MOORE'S FEDERAL PRACTICE ¶33.22.

an opposing party a copy of any statement he has made.[105] In a personal-injury case, you may have such a statement made by the injured party immediately after the accident, before he had retained counsel or perhaps even thought of suing. As defense counsel, you would like to take that person's deposition before having to supply a copy of his statement. The court may accommodate you.[106]

In some jurisdictions, statutes, rules or decisions will govern the sequence of your discovery proceedings. Certain discovery proceedings may not be available in some kinds of actions. We have remarked that such elements will figure in your choice of forum, whether you are plaintiff or defendant. They will necessarily also govern how you arrange the course of your discovery program.

3. Pre-Action or Pre-Complaint Discovery

a. To Frame a Pleading

In some jurisdictions you have the right to engage in some forms of discovery before an action is commenced. Where a plaintiff may commence an action by serving or filing a summons unaccompanied by a complaint,[107] discovery may be available after the action is technically begun, but before the drafting of the initial pleading. Overlooking the remedy, if available, of pre-action or pre-complaint discovery may cost you priceless evidence.

Pre-action or pre-complaint discovery consists of two kinds. It may give the discovering party the information he needs to frame a complaint or other pleading.[108] On the other hand, a potential litigant may in some jurisdictions engage in discovery, by deposition and sometimes by other means,[109] to preserve evidence that he fears will no longer be available once the action is commenced.[110] Either use normally requires a court order.

---

[105] Federal Rule 26(b)(3); N.Y. CPLR §3101(e).

[106] *Fernandes* v. *United Fruit Co.*, 50 F.R.D. 82, 84 (D. Md. 1970). Cf. *Bengiat* v. *State of N.Y.*, 45 Misc.2d 323, 256 N.Y.S.2d 876 (1965).

[107] See, *e.g.*, N.Y. CPLR §304; Pennsylvania R.C.P. 1007.

[108] Pennsylvania R.C.P., Rule 4007(a), for example, permits pre-complaint discovery by deposition if it will "substantially aid in the preparation of the pleadings." *Gross* v. *United Engineers & Constructors, Inc.*, 224 Pa. Super 233, 302 A.2d 370, 372 (1973); *Lapp* v. *Titus*, 224 Pa. Super 150, 302 A.2d 366, 369 (1973).

[109] Federal Rule 27(a)(3) empowers the court to allow pre-action discovery and inspection and physical or mental examinations. *Martin* v. *Reynolds Metals Corp.*, 297 F.2d 49 (9th Cir. 1961), holds that such relief can be granted independently of a deposition.

[110] Federal Rule 27(a)(1).

The first of the two purposes of pre-action discovery is probably the more difficult to obtain and the less common.[111] Suppose you think your client has a case. You need, however, more information, either from the contemplated defendant or from someone else, before you can draft a proper complaint. Getting court permission for such a deposition may be difficult. Among other things, you must usually show the judge that you are not just "shooting in the dark." You must prove that you have a claim on which you mean to sue and that you are not seeking to use discovery merely to decide whether or not to sue.[112]

Unfortunately, if you make a showing that you have a solid basis for an action, the court may decide that you already have enough facts to frame a complaint and so do not need a pre-action deposition.[113] Such an outcome will surprise no one familiar with the liberality of modern pleading requirements. An exception obtains under some codes that require the pleading of specific items in certain kinds of actions.

Where pre-action discovery is allowed, the sophisticated lawyer can turn to his own advantage the difficulty of getting permission for a deposition to help draft a complaint. Faced with a set of facts he thinks might be too sparse to support a complaint, he will move for a pre-action or pre-complaint deposition. He may realize what a poor chance he has of obtaining the required permission. He knows also that if a judge denies permission to take a deposition on the ground that plaintiff's attorney has enough facts to support a complaint, it will be difficult for the same judge or a colleague later to hold the pleading insufficient.

Plaintiff's counsel may feel pressure to begin his action promptly. He may forego pre-complaint discovery and take a chance on a possibly inadequate complaint. If his complaint is then dismissed for lack of necessary detail, he may get permission to engage in discovery for the purpose of preparing an amended complaint.[114]

---

[111] It may not be permissible at all in federal practice. See *Martin* v. *Reynolds Metals Corp.,* footnote 109, 297 F.2d at page 55.

[112] See *Williams* v. *Blount,* 14 N.C. App. 139, 187 S.E.2d 464 (1972); *Matter of Lewis,* 11 N.C. App. 541, 181 S.E.2d 806 (1971).

[113] *Vulcan Methods, Inc.* v. *Glubo,* 36 A.D.2d 773, 321 N.Y.S.2d 281 (1971), appeal dismissed, 29 N.Y.2d 710, 325 N.Y.S.2d 750 (1971).

[114] *Keely* v. *Price,* 27 Cal. App.3d 209, 103 Cal.Rptr 531 (1972); *Gonzalez* v. *School District of Phila.,* 8 Pa. Cmwlth. 130, 140, 301 A.2d 99, 105 (1973).

He may, on the other hand, learn that he should have resorted to discovery first.[115]

b. To Preserve Evidence

The second use of pre-action discovery involves the preservation of evidence. You may be contemplating an action, or you may have a client who expects to be sued. Your case will require the testimony of a witness who is available now, but who may not be available by the time you can start an action and take the witness's deposition.[116] Perhaps the witness is about to move, perhaps he is of advanced age or in failing health. If you can take his deposition now, you will avoid the risk of losing indispensable testimony forever. Perhaps other evidence to which you are now denied access may not be available when you need it. You should consider applying for permission to engage in discovery even though no action is pending.

Take this example:

> A manufacturer feared that cattle-raisers in its vicinity planned to sue it for damage to their livestock caused by alleged contaminants emanating from its plant. The manufacturer believed that it could accumulate evidence to defend the threatened action by testing the water, soil and vegetation on the cattle-raisers' property, examining live cattle and taking tissue and bone samples from the carcasses of dead cattle. To ascertain the source of these and other kinds of evidence, the manufacturer wished to take the deposition of one of the potential plaintiffs. After a hearing, a federal district court entered an order permitting the requested deposition and allowing the manufacturer to conduct the tests and examinations it desired. On appeal, the order was held a proper exercise of the court's power both "to preserve important testimony that might otherwise be lost" and to obtain other pre-action discovery under Rule 34 regardless whether a deposition was taken.[117]

---

[115] "However, plaintiff has no such right after filing an inadequately pleaded Complaint to cure the defects therein by subsequent discovery and deposition of the defendant." *Gross* v. *United Engineers & Constructors, Inc.*, footnote 108, 302 A.2d at page 372.

[116] *In re Sims*, 389 F.2d 148 (5th Cir. 1967); *Martin* v. *Reynolds Metals Co.*, 297 F.2d 49 (9th Cir. 1961). Remember that in federal practice a plaintiff may usually not take a deposition until 30 days after service of the summons and complaint. Federal Rule 30(a).

[117] *Martin* v. *Reynolds Metals Corp.*, footnote 116, 297 F.2d at pages 55–57.

To engage in pre-action discovery, your jurisdiction's procedure will probably require a petition, first served personally on your anticipated adversary, showing some or all of these elements:

1. Facts demonstrating that litigation is likely and that the necessary jurisdiction will obtain;
2. Factual reasons why you need this witness's testimony;
3. A summary of the facts to which he will testify; and
4. The facts that will make it impossible or difficult for you to take his deposition or put him on the stand after the action is begun.[118]

The recurrence of the words "facts" and "factual" in these paragraphs should guide your preparation of any affidavit or petition. You should concentrate, in preparing your petition, on the factual details supporting your application. You should not waste your own and the court's time on rhetoric denouncing the outrageous position your contemplated adversary has taken or elaborating on the violence that would be done to the cause of justice should you lose your case as the result of having been denied the evidence you seek.

As far as possible, you should, as in all situations, present your facts first-hand. For example, the reasons underlying a witness's expected unavailability would sound more convincing in an affidavit by him than on information and belief from you. Yet if the witness's failing health provides one of the reasons for your desire to take his deposition, let your papers include a physician's affidavit. That paper, incidentally, will usually be more candid and so more helpful if you obtain it yourself, without the witness's seeing it, than if he gets it from his doctor for you.

An application to engage in pre-action discovery may have strategic value. As potential litigation looms, each party seeks to demonstrate its determination to resort to suit if necessary and its confidence that the facts support its side of the controversy. What better, more vivid way to prove both points than to apply for leave to take the pre-action deposition of a key witness?

c. Opposing Pre-Action or Pre-Complaint Discovery

We have discussed some of the problems of pre-action discovery from the point of view of the party interested in discovery. The practising lawyer is just as apt to confront the situation where some

---

[118] See, e.g., Federal Rule 27.

other party to impending litigation wishes to engage in discovery before an action is contemplated.

One must think twice about opposing such an application on any ground. Resistance, whatever its stated grounds, may create an impression that disclosure or preservation of the facts will help the other side. That impression may do no harm at the time, but it may come back to haunt the opponent of pre-action discovery when the case comes to trial, particularly if the judge who hears the application presides at the trial.

Most of the grounds available to oppose a deposition in contemplation of an action have serious weaknesses. If you argue that the evidence to be elicited will be immaterial, hearsay or inadmissible for some other reason, you will be met with the principle, applicable in most jurisdictions, that inadmissibility does not bar discovery.[119] If you contend that the deposition will inconvenience the witness or jeopardize his health, the petitioner will answer that such a ground is for the witness to raise. You may dispute the thesis that the witness will not be available after commencement of the action. That objection has an obvious answer: taking his deposition ahead of time will do no harm.

In practical terms, your only real chance of thwarting a pre-action deposition rests in proving that the application does not satisfy procedural requirements. In a federal matter, for example, a showing that the applicant can, in fact, commence an action at once, should lead to denial of the application.[120]

Unless you can show that the party seeking the deposition does not qualify under the applicable statute or rules, or that the contemplated deposition threatens real prejudice to your client, you had better not oppose the deposition. Concentrate instead on preparing your cross-examination of the witness.

You may handle many cases before you confront a situation in which you can make profitable use of pre-action discovery. You will more likely recognize such an opportunity if you remember the two main purposes of the remedy, either to elicit facts needed to frame a pleading or to preserve material evidence. Keeping those functions in mind will also enable you to oppose pre-action discovery more selectively, more intelligently and more effectively.

---

[119] See discussion at pages 38–39.
[120] See, e.g., *In re Benjamin,* 52 F.R.D. 407 (E.D. La. 1971).

4. Completion of Discovery

By definition, discovery is a pre-trial device. Generally speaking, it must be completed before the trial begins.

Many courts, by rule or by pre-trial order, set a deadline for the completion of discovery. Exceptions normally require a showing of special circumstances, good cause or both.[121]

The right to discovery does not mean the right to postpone the trial forever. As the Supreme Court of Indiana said in a case where defendant in a condemnation suit filed a motion for discovery on the very day of the hearing:

> A party may not wait until the last possible moment to act, then rely upon the discovery rules and expect the court to halt its proceedings in order to accommodate his motion.

The trial court was upheld in its denial of defendant's motion.[122]

It takes hardly more than routine attention to applicable rules and to orders on file in your case to avoid such embarrassing and possibly dangerous oversights.

5. Discovery During Trial

Occasionally, and usually as the result of unforeseen occurrences, a court will allow discovery during a trial.[123] Specific requirements must be complied with to obtain such extraordinary relief. As would be expected, trial courts generally enjoy a wide area of discretion in allowing or refusing discovery during trial.[124]

This completes our survey of the considerations and problems involved in the general area of discovery. We turn next to the individual discovery devices. We shall begin with the most widely employed procedure, the deposition.

---

[121] *Bowen* v. *Fiore*, 42 A.D.2d 960, 347, N.Y.S.2d 749 (2d Dept. 1973).

[122] *Chustak* v. *Northern Indiana Public Service Co.*, 288 N.E.2d 149, 154 (Ind. 1972). See also *Klabunde* v. *Stanley*, 384 Mich. 276, 281–282, 181 N.W.2d 918, 920–921 (1970).

[123] See, e.g., New York Civil Practice Law and Rules Sections 3102(d) and 5223; *Wieneke* v. *Chalmers*, 73 N.M. 8, 385 P.2d 65 (1963).

[124] *Chustak* v. *Northern Ind. Public Service Co.*, footnote 122, 288 N.E.2d at pages 154–155; *Haynes* v. *Monroe Plumbing & Heating Co.*, 48 Mich. App. 707, 715–716, 211 N.W.2d 88, 93 (1973).

Chapter II

MAKING THE MOST
OF A DEPOSITION

A. PLANNING THE DEPOSITION

1. Taking Aim

a. The Range of Goals

Every experienced lawyer has seen some depositions handled with finesse and others bungled. Many of us have touched both extremes ourselves. What makes the difference between success and failure in a deposition?

We shall be talking now about the deposition of an opposing party or a neutral or unfriendly witness, usually someone whom you will not have had the chance to interview beforehand. A later chapter will deal with opposing counsel's deposition of your client or of a witness friendly to you.

Examining counsel should decide first of all what he wants from a deposition. Today broad discovery is taken for granted. Many lawyers thus take the other side's deposition more as a reflex action than as a planned stratagem. A deposition without defined goals loses much of its value.[1]

Without claiming to be all-inclusive, we may list the possible

---

[1] At least one jurisdiction, Illinois, recognizes two different kinds of depositions, those for discovery and those for use in evidence. The notice of deposition must state which kind is intended. Illinois Supreme Court Rule 212; *Slatten* v. *City of Chicago,* 12 Ill. App.3d 808, 813, 299 N.E.2d 442, 445 (1973).

objectives of the deposition of the opposing party or of a neutral
or hostile witness as one or more of the following:

1. To gain information, including the identity and location of
sources of evidence;

2. To preserve testimony for possible use during the trial;

3. To find out how much the person to be examined knows,
both about his own case and about yours;

4. To commit the party or witness to a version of the facts
from which he cannot later deviate so as to adapt to a changed
complexion of the case;

5. To confront the party to be examined with damaging evidence, or otherwise to show him the weaknesses in his case,
thereby inducing him to drop the case or make a settlement
favorable to examining counsel.

We shall review examples of these various purposes.

b. Getting the Facts

Let us consider an example of a deposition with the first of the
objectives listed above:

A small manufacturer sues a larger concern for breach of contract. Plaintiff supplied a component part for a complex data-
processing system devised and manufactured by defendant. The
defense is based on the failure of the completed system to pass
an inspection by the foreign government that contracted to buy it.
Defendant claims that the rejection arose from a weakness in
the component made by plaintiff. Plaintiff's attorney, in taking
the deposition of a representative of defendant, wishes to learn
everything he can about the dealings between defendant and the
foreign purchasing authorities. Plaintiff knows nothing of what
happened after it delivered the component to defendant. Its
attorney has no way other than discovery to find out if defendant's
contention has merit.

The outcome of such a case may hinge on what counsel succeeds
in learning from another party's employees and files.

c. Preserving Proof

Let us turn to a situation in which the attorney planning a deposition
might have the second listed objective.

In a personal-injury action, plaintiff's counsel decides to take the deposition of an eye-witness to a collision. He knows what the witness will say. He has no reason to fear that the witness will change or forget his version of the accident. He takes the deposition to make sure that whatever happens to the witness, his crucial testimony will be available at trial.

Plaintiff's attorney here is using the deposition for a classic purpose, the preservation of important testimony.

d. Exploration

Turning to the third possible purpose of a deposition, consider this case:

A discharged employee brings an action against his ex-employer for discrimination in violation of the Equal Employment Opportunity Act. Defense counsel knows that his case has its strengths and weaknesses. The latter include a recently retired personnel assistant. She, while still in defendant's employ, was inclined to make private statements about defendant's and her own skill at duping the authorities by hiring and retaining only token members of minority groups. Defendant's attorney believes that the retired assistant's utterances represent her own prejudices rather than her employer's policy or practice. He has some proof to back up his belief. He realizes nevertheless that if plaintiff knows of the former assistant's statements, defendant is in trouble. An objective in taking plaintiff's deposition is to find out how much the latter knows.

Here defendant's attorney will use the deposition to educate himself and thereby make a wiser evaluation of the case.

e. Pinning a Witness Down

To illustrate the fourth of our listed objectives in taking a deposition, assume this to be the case:

A corporation is accused of slandering an individual who had threatened suit over alleged theft of an idea. Defense counsel believes that plaintiff will rely on a remark by one Munoz, its former chief engineer. The remark was made at a meeting attended by plaintiff's lawyer and various of defendant's employees. If defendant's attorney is right about this, his client should prevail.

Munoz resigned long enough ago that his acts would be outside the statute of limitations. Counsel takes plaintiff's deposition in order to commit him to testimony that Munoz's remark is the only basis for his action.

Defendant's attorney here fears that unless he gets plaintiff committed under oath, the latter, upon realizing that he has no case, may be tempted to "recall" a more recent episode.

f. Disabusing the Witness

The fifth of our list of possible goals might come into play in a case like this:

Plaintiff in a personal-injury action has alleged a week's hospitalization followed by one month's confinement to bed at home. By means of intrepid investigatory work, defendant's attorney has purchased photographs of plaintiff dancing in a nightclub ten days after the accident. He has a witness to prove the date of the photographs. He takes plaintiff's deposition to confront him with the pictures and thereby inculcate a more realistic evaluation of the case.

Defendant's attorney in this situation has concluded that he will gain an advantage by revealing his hand in the hope of achieving a prompt, inexpensive resolution of the case.

g. The Need for a Choice

We have seen illustrations of five of the possible goals of a deposition. They comprise the most common purposes of taking pre-trial testimony. Your own experience may provide examples in which other goals have applied. Other such purposes will appear in examples cited in later pages of the present text. It suffices now to emphasize that the lawyer about to take a deposition should always determine his purpose.

Not that the choice will always be simple. One may have to plan varying strategies for different parts of one person's testimony. The objective of a deposition may expand or otherwise change as the questioning proceeds. Take, as an example:

In a personal-injury case, defendant's attorney is examining plaintiff. Examining counsel has evidence that his adversary has exaggerated his injuries. On the other hand, he is quite in the dark on several aspects of the issues of negligence. His goal with respect to topics related to liability will probably come closest to the first of the goals listed above, i.e., the gaining of information for examining counsel's benefit. When it comes to injuries and damages, however, his objective may be to commit plaintiff to the exaggerated version of his injuries so as to thwart any later attempt to adapt to defendant's contradictory proof.

You may ask why it is necessary at all to decide on a specific or even general goal in taking a deposition. Why not "play it by ear," simply asking questions and seeing what develops? That, to be sure, is one way to handle a deposition, and a common one. But the lawyer who wishes to make the most of a deposition cannot be satisfied with "getting by." He knows that capitalizing on the unique opportunities of a deposition requires exhaustive forethought. He knows too, that such forethought makes no sense if it does not include deliberation over the most fundamental question of all, namely, what the deposition can hope to achieve.

Among other benefits, singling out your purpose in taking a deposition will help you frame your questions and decide what approach you will take in posing those questions. That will be the next topic of this chapter.

2. Devising an Approach

Related to the determination of what you expect or hope to get from your deposition is determining the approach or strategy you will use to get it. How, in other words, should you treat the witness so as to achieve your desired result from the deposition? How should you handle such problems and opportunities as you are able to foresee? Here experience is the best teacher. A few observations may nevertheless help you gain from the successes and failures of others.

Your selection of the goal or goals of your deposition should take you a long way toward deciding the strategy of your examination. If, for example, you decide that your objective in the deposition will be to determine how much a hostile witness really knows about the strengths and weaknesses of your own or your adversary's case, you might think it best to assume the role of a friendly, sympathetic listener. You hope thereby to draw the witness into making admissions or revealing facts that might not come to light were he more on his guard. If, on the other hand, you decided that you wish mainly to commit the witness to the narrowest possible set of facts, you might think it wisest to assume a sterner role, hoping to impress the witness with the seriousness of the case and with the solemnity of his oath. There are, of course, many variations to these two basic techniques and many others as well. What is important is that you make up your mind, in advance if you can, what demeanor or style is going to do the most for you in a particular examination and how you should deal with specific situations likely to arise.

Knowing the witness helps immeasurably in deciding what approach to take in a deposition. That will be an advantage beyond your reach in most depositions where you are examining an adversary or a neutral or hostile witness. But even if you do not know the person or witness to be examined, you may know someone who does, namely, your own client. Most lawsuits, except in the personal-injury area, do not arise between strangers. The time you spend discussing the personality and the strengths and weaknesses of the person you intend to question will not be time wasted.

If you have no other way of learning about your deponent, you will have to do so during the deposition itself. This need may make it wise to keep an open mind about your strategy. To be sure, the matter should be thought out beforehand, but your conclusions should be tentative ones. During your preliminary questioning, particularly as you approach the principal issues of the litigation, observe the witness's conduct and demeanor. Ask yourself how sophisticated, how well-educated, and above all, how emotionally stable, he appears. How well does he understand your questions, not just in the literal sense but in terms of what you are really driving at? Is he short-tempered and apt to get exercised over the issues of the case, or will he more likely remain cool and composed regardless of how close your questioning gets to sensitive areas?

As a help in formulating this part of your deposition plan, here is a list of questions to ask yourself in preparation for, or if necessary, during, any deposition:

1. Should you appear, by silence and perhaps an occasional nod of the head, to accept the witness's version of the facts, no matter how outrageous you know it to be?

2. Would it, on the other hand, do more for your case to try to undermine the witness's self-confidence by indicating, in one way or

another, that you have reason (not necessarily to be disclosed) to doubt his story?

3. If the witness claims to have forgotten a particular event, are you going to try to refresh his recollection or let the record stand so that any revival of his memory at trial will appear suspicious?

4. If the person being examined makes a statement that you can disprove by documentary or photographic evidence, will you reveal his inaccuracy to him or let him remain in ignorance until the trial?

5. How will you deal with overt hostility on the witness's part, particularly if it takes the form of long, gratuitous tirades on the merits of the case?

6. How do you propose to deal with the opposite attitude, i.e., friendliness on the witness's part? Will you respond to it in kind, hoping thereby to win the witness's confidence, or will you display coolness in the hope of impressing the witness with the gravity of the situation?

A contract action illustrates the problem posed by the first two of the above questions:

> Plaintiff has charged defendant with breach of contract. His lawyer is taking the deposition of defendant's assistant director of purchases. The witness relates a conversation in which, he says, plaintiff's sales manager waived the alleged breach. Plaintiff's counsel knows that he may be able to "shake" this damaging story by pointing out inconsistencies with the witness's testimony earlier in the day. Having thought the matter out beforehand, he nevertheless resists the temptation to embarrass the witness. He realizes that he can exploit the contradiction more effectively at trial. He gives, therefore, every appearance of taking the testimony at face value.

Counsel in this situation has, of course, taken into account the possibility that the witness or his lawyer may notice and attempt to correct the inconsistency in reading the transcript of the deposition before signing it.

Let us consider an example of the type of problem posed by the fourth of our questions:

> An elderly lady has sued a stock-brokerage firm. She alleges that the executive in charge of her account caused her substantial losses by misusing his discretionary authority and "churning"

her account to enhance his own and the firm's income. Defense counsel has a handwritten letter from plaintiff, written a few months before the transactions of which she is complaining, at a time when market conditions were more favorable. Plaintiff's letter thanks and praises the account executive for his astute advice in making so many profitable trades and encourages him to "keep up the good work." Defense counsel feels safe in assuming that plaintiff, like most individuals, did not keep a copy of her handwritten letter. He ponders what to do.

We may envy defendant's attorney such a potent piece of evidence, but it does pose problems for him. He knows that if he shows the letter to plaintiff at her deposition for the purpose of authenticating it, he may discourage her and her attorney from continuing the action. This, of course, will save his client great expense. He realizes, on the other hand, that revealing this crucial exhibit at a preliminary stage may provide his adversary with time to explain it away or rebuild the case in some way not inconsistent with the letter. He must, therefore, consider withholding the document until he can confront plaintiff with it at trial.

The latter course of action also presents problems. First, if plaintiff dies or becomes incompetent before trial, defense counsel may fail to get the document into evidence. Secondly, plaintiff, even though she did not keep a copy of the letter, may remember it. She may, for all defense counsel knows, be prepared to explain it by, for example, saying that the account executive solicited it as a favor to help him keep his job in the face of a retrenchment then taking place at the firm. If defense counsel keeps the letter to himself until trial, he may thus receive an unpleasant surprise. Had he brought it out at plaintiff's deposition and heard her explanation, he might have decided not to use the letter or perhaps have conducted further factual research and developed a counter-explanation. The decision of what to do with so favorable a piece of evidence is not necessarily an easy one.

You can never foresee everything that will arise at a deposition and call for strategical and tactical decisions. What is more, you must retain some freedom of action to devise new strategies and tactics to cope with unexpected situations. Even so, the more you think out your approach to a deposition in advance, the better equipped you will be to make the decisions that will be required.

3. Studying the Terrain

The third rule in preparing for the deposition of an opposing party or a neutral or hostile witness calls for thorough knowledge of the background and subject-matter of the testimony to be taken. We are not talking now about preparation of the questioning itself. We will come to that. We are talking about the field of knowledge with which the deposition will be concerned.

If, for example, you are about to question a building contractor, you should learn all you can about the construction industry, not just about the project involved in your action. If you are going to take a doctor's deposition, you should know a great deal about medicine, as every first-rate personal-injury lawyer does anyway.

The rule under discussion does not apply just to the depositions of experts. If the witness to be questioned is the driver of a bus or semi-trailer involved in a collision, you should try to have some knowledge of the controls of such vehicles and the special skills and difficulties involved in driving them. One way to do this is to consult someone in the same occupation.

Your deposition may involve a particular geographic area or a segment of an industry or profession. If you are dealing with an automobile accident, you will wish to know everything about the site of the occurrence and its approaches, warning signs in the area, special visibility problems, the weather at the time, etc. In a medical malpractice suit, you should verse yourself thoroughly in the field involved, consulting not only authorative treatises, but also knowledgeable specialists.

Let us take a more specific example:

> In a products-failure case, you represent an executor suing the manufacturer of a piece of heavy construction equipment that rolled over and killed the decedent. You see that roll-bars would have prevented the death. You allege, therefore, a design defect. Before you take the manufacturers' deposition, you not only study all available literature on equipment of this kind, but, if possible, consult an expert as well. You brief yourself on what enlightened thinking in the field favors. You see if your expert can prepare at least a rough sketch that shows his concept of the kind of protection that the manufacturer should have provided.

You hope thereby to force the person whose deposition you
are taking to admit that the concept is feasible, that it is not
unheard-of and that it would have prevented the accident in suit.

Such admissions will surely strengthen your case for trial purposes.
They may lead to an early settlement.

Knowing as much as you can about background aspects of the
case will not just help you devise better questions. It will put you in a
better position to know whether you are getting truthful, candid
answers. This kind of preparation will also reflect itself in your own
self-confidence. You can be sure that the witness and opposing
counsel will be able to sense that. They will know, moreover, that
they are dealing with someone hard to take advantage of. This
can only redound to your benefit.

It helps to know the jargon of the field into which you are delving.
You may miss crucial evidence by not speaking the witness's language.
Take this example:

> Plaintiff's attorney in a treble-damage antitrust action took the
> deposition of one of defendant's veteran salesmen. Counsel had
> reason to believe that the salesman had made illegal arrangements
> with several of his customers, plaintiff's competitors. The witness
> denied any such deals. Plaintiff's attorney repeatedly asked the
> witness if he had prepared or submitted a "memorandum" of
> each visit he had made to any of the accounts in question. The
> salesman answered in the negative. Had counsel known that the
> salesman and his colleagues referred to their reports of visits to
> customers as "call reports" and that to them the word "memoran-
> dum" denoted something far more formal than the hasty hand-
> written notes they were accustomed to filing, he would not have
> emerged empty-handed from the deposition.

Yet it may sometimes be a wise strategy to conceal how much you
know about the subject-matter of the deposition. If the deponent
is one who you think might be tempted to exaggerate or lie, and if
you think it would be to your advantage to let him do so, in order
to discredit him later, you may well feign ignorance. Even then,
however, background preparation will be an asset in helping to tell
you right away just where and how far the witness has departed
from the truth.

Consider this example of the point just made:

Defense counsel was examining plaintiff in a personal-injury action. Plaintiff, a truck-driver, claimed to have been injured at defendant's factory when a stack of packing crates containing electrical equipment fell over and knocked him off a loading dock. To emphasize the force of the impact, plaintiff swore that the crates were stacked eight or ten high. Defense counsel had studied the site of the accident. He had interviewed the employees of his client's shipping department. He knew that because of their weight and strength and the type of lifting equipment available, the crates could not have been piled more than five high. He nevertheless feigned belief of plaintiff's story.

Without his background knowledge, defense counsel would not have realized the need to get plaintiff committed to the impossible set of facts.

If the dimensions of your case justify it, consider engaging professional help to give you any technical orientation that you need for an effective deposition. Your adversary may be able to discover the identity and even the views of an expert whom you expect to call as a witness, but that does not necessarily apply to one whom you hire for purposes of consultation.[2]

Knowing the case's factual and technical background is not enough. Immediately before the deposition, review your entire file exhaustively, paying particular attention to your adversary's pleadings and to any affidavits or other statements that he has made. If other depositions have been taken, read them too. These preparations are sure to help you. If nothing else, they will suggest questions or areas of examination that you might otherwise overlook.

4. Building Your Questions

a. Organize!

We turn to the fourth step in getting ready for a deposition. The watchword here consists of: *prepare your questions*. Never examine extemporaneously. If you do, you will probably forget something. You must, unless you are truly one lawyer in a million, question from an outline or notes.

Having an exhaustive, detailed outline will have benefits beyond

---

[2] See *Perry* v. *Darley & Co.,* 54 F.R.D. 278 (E.D. Wisc. 1971).

insuring that nothing slips your mind during the deposition. Let us list some of the other advantages.

You cannot be alert and perceptive during the deposition if while listening to one answer, your mind must be devising the next question. Observing the witness and assimilating what he says give you more than enough to do. A good outline lets you work full-time on those vital tasks.

The witness and opposing counsel will be favorably impressed if questions come one after the other without the pauses that with most of us characterize extemporaneous questioning. As we have pointed out and will touch on again, the respect of those across the table can help more than one's vanity.

Questioning that proceeds apace leaves an unscrupulous or opportunistic witness less time to contrive his answers. He will also have a harder time anticipating and avoiding inconsistencies in his testimony.

At some point or other in the deposition a new idea or an unexpected answer will send you off on a tangent. Your outline will help you find your way back to the point at which you departed from your prepared sequence of questions.

A well-organized outline will let you skip from topic to topic and back again without fear of omitting anything. However you proceed, you can check each item off as you cover it. This will avoid irksome repetitions, as well as omissions.

A well-prepared outline can save you money. Once you have all of your ideas for the deposition down on paper in organized form, you can begin eliminating points that seem superfluous or capable of being covered by some other discovery device. With no outline to work from, you will tend to go on and on in your questioning, always anxious that you will overlook something essential. An organized, planned deposition usually turns out to be a shorter and therefore a cheaper one.

These are some of the reasons why you should have an organized outline. Let us consider next how you should put it together and some of the things that should go into it .

In building an outline for your deposition, it is best to proceed logically. Follow a chronological order or some other system. That way you are less apt to omit something. In your questioning, as has been said, you may wish to skip around, shifting topics in a haphazard sequence. Such a technique makes no sense in preparing your outline.

As you prepare your outline, you should write out your important questions in advance, particularly those which you think you will wish to read into evidence. This can be a questionable practice at trial; reading prepared questions often sounds bad. At a deposition, however, you do not care how your questioning sounds. You care only how it looks when it is typed in transcript form.

Questions written out in advance can be studied and corrected in advance. If this precaution gets into evidence just one question and answer that would otherwise have been excluded, it will have been worthwhile.

b. The Indispensable Foundation

The preparation of an outline will help you in yet another way. It will lessen your chances of neglecting to lay a foundation for each question requiring it. If the time comes to read your deposition into evidence at the trial, a lenient judge may overlook flaws in the form of your questions. He knows, however, that he risks reversal by letting in evidence without a proper foundation. Procedural rules in most jurisdictions, as we shall see, require that objections to the form of questions be raised at the deposition but provide that other objections are deemed reserved until the time of trial.[3] Your adversary may, during a deposition, say nothing about questions lacking foundation. He leaves himself free on trial to object to the question. Then it may be too late to remedy the oversight.

A shrewd, experienced lawyer can often dupe a neophyte adversary by manifesting liberality during the discovery phase of the action. He seems unconcerned with such technicalities as authentication and laying a foundation. His grateful adversary takes the bait and neglects these apparently meaningless formalities. When the trial comes, the experienced practitioner changes his tune. He insists on every procedural refinement. He objects to every item of evidence not in perfect order. The beginner, having been led to dispense with what now turns out to be indispensable, finds much of his most important evidence excluded.

Your familiarity with the rules of evidence should obviate any extended discussion here of what we mean by laying a foundation. You should know, for example, that if you are asking a witness about what took place at a particular time or place, you must make sure that previous questions have shown him to have been in a position

---

[3] See, *e.g.*, Federal Rule 32(d)(3)(B).

to observe the occurrence. If you are seeking the details of a conversation, you must show by testimony that the witness was present.
You should also bring out when and where the talk took place and
who else was there. The rules of evidence as applied in many states
require that before a witness may give the details of a telephone conversation, it be established that the witness recognized the voice of
the other participant or had some other means of knowing with whom
he was speaking. Before the witness can identify someone else's
signature on a letter, you may have to show that he had previously
seen the person sign his name. Other examples will occur immediately
to anyone who knows the rules of evidence in his jurisdiction. Things
like these are what we mean by laying a proper foundation.

The deposition of an expert often calls for knowledge of how to lay
a proper foundation. If you are seeking to elicit an opinion, be careful
not to go beyond the area of the witness's established competence.[4]
Be careful also to base your questions only on facts in the record.
An appellate court in Pennsylvania, holding that an expert witness's
deposition had been properly received in evidence, said:

> The record shows that all of the facts necessary to support the
> witness's conclusion were contained in the deposition.[5]

c. The Rules of Evidence: Servant, Not Master

As you draft your outline, you will have the rules of evidence in
mind, but you will not let them inhibit your questioning. Remember
that although these rules control what ultimately gets into evidence,
they do not govern discovery. In discovery you may often inquire
beyond the bounds of admissible evidence.[6] You will not use this
freedom for the purpose of harassing your adversary, but you will
take advantage of it if that will help your case.

For example, in a personal-injury action the "collateral source"
rule may prevent defendant's attorney from offering evidence of
health-insurance or other payments made to reimburse plaintiff for
his medical expenses or loss of earnings. It does not follow that such
information lies beyond the scope of discovery. On the contrary,
the application forms and other records generated by such benefits

---

[4] *Williams* v. *Thomas Jefferson University*, 54 F.R.D. 615 (E.D. Pa. 1972).
[5] *Connelly Containers, Inc.* v. *Pennsylvania R.R.*, 222 Pa.Super. 7, 17, 292 A.2d
528, 533 (1972).
[6] See, e.g., Federal Rule 26(b).

may provide leads to evidence of the extent of the injuries, duration of disability, etc. Discovery, therefore may well be allowed.[7]

d. Some Ideas on a Handy Form

The physical form of your outline can be important. You have taken the time to draw it up. You have the right to demand of it fast, efficient service.

You do not, first of all, want to waste even seconds deciphering your own handwriting or trying to find your place. If the outline for a deposition is worth preparing, it is worth having typed. You will find in this regard that if your typist spaces the various topics or questions far apart on the page, they will leap to the eye instead of having to be searched for. Using solid capital letters helps in the same way. The less material you have on each page of your outline, the easier you will find it both to recognize your questions and to shift rapidly from topic to topic.

You may put your outline on loose-leaf pages or on index cards. Choose, in any event, a system that will enable you to reorganize or expand part of the outline with a minimum of retyping. Choose a system, too, whereby you can readily travel back and forth from section to section of the outline as your questioning proceeds.

5. Tips on Mechanical Details

a. Setting up the Deposition

We shall next review some of the procedural details necessary to preparing for a deposition. Each can be important in its way. Attention to detail rather than the seeming grand strokes often makes the difference between victory and defeat.

How does a lawyer arrange a deposition? Formal requirements do not usually involve much. Federal Rule 30(b)(1), for example, provides in part:

> A party desiring to take the deposition of any person upon oral examination shall give reasonable notice in writing to every other party to the action. The notice shall state the time and place for taking the deposition and the name and address of each person to be examined, if known, and, if the name is not

---

[7] *Reichert* v. *United States,* 51 F.R.D. 500, 502 (N.D. Calif. 1970).

known, a general description sufficient to identify him or the
particular class or group to which he belongs. . . .

A lawyer today often sets a deposition by merely telephoning his
adversary. Remember, however, that if the witness fails to show up,
or if other difficulties arise, and you must initiate enforcement
or punitive proceedings, it will stand you in good stead to
have a formal notice of deposition on record, together with proof
of service. So by all means make your arrangements with whatever
degree of informality prevails in your jurisdiction, but confirm the
arrangements with a written notice, just in case.

Your written notice should go to counsel for all parties who
have appeared in the action, not just to the attorney for the person
being examined. Should you wish some day to offer the deposition
testimony in evidence, it will be usable, with minor exceptions, only
against parties who knew of the deposition and had the opportunity
to attend.[8]

Postponements, too, should be confirmed in writing, either by formal
stipulation or by letter. It may turn out to be a good idea, incidentally,
in such instances to recite at whose request the adjournment is being
granted. Adjournments in which you merely acquiesce may return
to haunt you some day.[9]

The notice itself usually suffices to compel the attendance of a
party or a party's employee, officer or director for his deposition.[10]
Typical is Illinois Supreme Court Rule 204, which says:

> Service of notice of the taking of the deposition of a party or
> person who is currently an officer, director, or employee of a
> party is sufficient to require the appearance of the deponent
> and the production of any documents or tangible things listed
> in the notice.

If, however, you are to take the deposition of a non-party witness,
you will usually need a subpoena (probably accompanied by a check
for his statutory fee and mileage) served on the witness, as well as
notice to other parties.[11]

---

[8] *Ikerd* v. *Lapworth*, 435 F.2d 197, 205–206 (7th Cir. 1970); *Caldwell* v. *Stapleton*, 499 S.W.2d 640 (Tenn. App. 1973).

[9] *First Nat. Bank of Arizona* v. *Cities Service Co.*, 391 U.S. 253, 292, 88 S.Ct. 1575, 1594, 20 L.Ed.2d 569 (1968).

[10] See, e.g., *Marriott Homes, Inc.* v. *Hanson*, 50 F.R.D. 396, 399–400 (W.D. Mo. 1970); *Welter* v. *Welter*, 27 Ohio Misc. 44, 267 N.E.2d 442 (Ohio Com. Pl. 1971).

[11] Federal Rule 45(d)(1) provides for the issuance of a subpoena for the taking of a deposition. It also sets forth the procedure to follow in obtaining the subpoena.

A party's ex-employee must be dealt with as a non-party in that you must arrange his appearance by subpoena. This applies even if the witness was a party's employee at the time of the occurrence that gave rise to the litigation. Thus, if you were suing an employer for the negligence of its employee in driving a truck and wished to take the driver's deposition, and if since the accident the driver has left defendant's employ, you would have to serve a subpoena on the driver to procure his attendance at a deposition. It makes no difference that he was defendant's employee when the accident happened.[12]

You may trust a non-party witness to appear without the compulsion of a subpoena. Serve him with one anyway. If he fails for any reason to appear, your failure to have put him under subpoena may cost you your opponent's expenses in attending, perhaps even including a fee.[13] Similarly, if you postpone the deposition of a witness who is not a party, you must obtain his consent as well as that of other counsel.

b. Where to Hold Your Deposition [14]

As the attorney taking a deposition, you will usually have the right to specify the place where it will be held. For your own convenience you will probably prefer your own office, and this may be the custom in your area. If that is not suitable or permissible under local rules or tradition, consider holding the deposition at the office of the clerk of court, where facilities are sometimes available. Some court-reporting firms maintain examination rooms available to their clientele.

It is not a good idea when examining an adverse party to hold the proceedings in his lawyer's office. You do not wish to have the person being questioned feel too much at home. If, like most laymen, he has never taken part in a deposition before, strange surroundings may make him uneasy and so, you hope, more candid and spontaneous.

You should prefer a conference room or library for the conduct of the deposition. You do not wish your questioning interrupted by a telephone or visitors.

When one of the parties lives far away from where the action is

---

[12] *Dept. of Public Works* v. *Decatur Seaway Motor Express Co.,* 5 Ill. App.3d 28, 282 N.E.2d 517 (1972).

[13] See, e.g., Federal Rule 30(g)(2).

[14] A later section, at page 105, below, deals with depositions outside the jurisdictional limits of the court in which the action is pending.

pending, the question arises whether that party must journey to the forum for a deposition or whether counsel desiring the examination must do the travelling. The results of such disputes vary in the light of the circumstances prevailing in particular cases.

Often a remote plaintiff who has selected a forum must come there when his deposition is taken.[15] Exceptions to this principle obtain, for example, when the non-resident plaintiff has no real choice of forum.[16] Some courts have held that the proper place to take the deposition of a corporation through one of its officers is its place of business or the officer's residence.[17]

Most courts have discretion to decide who must do the travelling when a deposition is taken. This applies whether it be plaintiff, defendant or a witness who is to testify. Many elements, including relative ability to pay for the trip, enter into the determination.[18] Sometimes the party who seeks to take a deposition at a place remote from the forum must pay the cost of his opponent's attorney's attendance.[19]

c. When to Hold Your Deposition

Again, as examining attorney, you may set the hour at which a deposition will take place. You may wish to specify in your notice that the examination will continue from day to day until completed.

Elements of seeming triviality can be crucial in depositions as elsewhere. Strange as it may seem, setting a deposition for a morning hour sometimes produces a relatively unprepared witness. The attorney for the party to be examined may not bother to schedule a preparatory session with his client on the day before the deposition. If, on the other hand, you schedule the deposition for the afternoon, your adversary may be willing to spend the morning before, or at least the luncheon hour, preparing his client.

Observations like this do not mean that the prepared witness is necessarily perjurious. Nor do they mean, as many laymen suspect,

[15] *Hunter* v. *Riverside Community Hospital,* 58 F.R.D. 218 (E.D. Wisc. 1972); *Grey* v. *Continental Marketing Associates, Inc.,* 315 F. Supp. 826, 832 (N.D. Ga. 1970). Cases like *Lathem* v. *Lathem,* 42 A.D.2d 909, 347 N.Y.S.2d 733 (2d Dept. 1973), represent an attempt to achieve an equitable modification of this rule.

[16] *Hyam* v. *American Export Lines, Inc.,* 213 F.2d 221, 223 (2 Cir. 1954); *Kovalsky* v. *Avis Rent-A-Car, Inc.,* 48 F.R.D. 453, 454 (D. P.R. 1969); *Ellis Air Lines* v. *Bellanca Aircraft Corp.,* 17 F.R.D. 395, 396 (D. Del 1955); *Welter* v. *Welter,* footnote 10.

[17] *Buryan* v. *Max Factor & Co.,* 41 F.R.D. 330, 332 (S.D. N.Y. 1967), and cases cited.

[18] *Terry* v. *Modern Woodmen of America,* 57 F.R.D. 141, 144 (W.D. Mo. 1972): *Welter* v. *Welter,* footnote 10.

[19] See, e.g., *Meredith* v. *Gavin,* 51 F.R.D. 5 (W.D. Mo. 1970).

that the goal of an examining attorney is to catch adverse parties and witnesses off guard and trick them into admitting what is not so. Truth is rarely an absolute. The prepared witness may recite facts with perfect honesty, but his phraseology and emphasis will produce testimony favorable to his own rather than his questioner's side of the case. That explains why we prefer to have our own witnesses prepared and the other side's not prepared.

d. How to Record the Testimony

1. *Traditional Techniques*

Whether your jurisdiction's rules require it or not, you will probably wish a verbatim record of the deposition you are taking.[20] What method shall you use?

Independent court-reporting firms operate in every city. They offer the best solution to the problem of transcription. Your adversary may suggest saving money by using his secretary instead of a commercial reporter. You should decline such an offer, no matter how proficient the person in question may be at shorthand. In transcribing her notes, she may encounter an ambiguity or an otherwise dubious passage. She will surely consult her employer, whose recollection of the question or answer may differ from yours.

In a low-budget case, legitimate ways exist to save expense. If your adversary takes a deposition and engages a shorthand reporter, you are not required to order a copy of the transcript. You may not have to do so even if it is you who are taking the deposition. Federal Rule 30(c), for example, provides only that:

> If requested by one of the parties, the testimony shall be transcribed.

If some other party orders the testimony transcribed, you can read the transcript when it is filed in court. You may take your own tape recorder to the deposition and make an unofficial transcription. Lawyers sometimes do this anyway when they expect to have need for the testimony, e.g., to support or oppose a motion for summary judgment, before the court reporter is likely to have a typed transcript. If you make such an unofficial tape recording for your own use, do

---

[20] Federal Rule 30(c) says in part, "The [deposition] testimony shall be taken stenographically or recorded by any other means ordered. . . ." Illinois Supreme Court Rule 206(e) provides that the "testimony shall be taken stenographically or by sound recording device, unless the parties agree otherwise. . . ."

not count on being able to get it into evidence in lieu of the official stenographic transcript in the event, for example, the transcript is not ready in time for the trial.[21]

2. *Innovations: Sound Tape*

As electronic technology advances, and as court-reporters' fees mount, lawyers pay more and more attention to mechanical deposition testimony. Federal Rule 30(b)(4), by virtue of a 1970 amendment, permits recording of deposition testimony "by other than stenographic means." In view, however, of the uncertainties in the procedure, some of which are mentioned below, a court order is required.

Some lawyers distrust tape recordings. They can be "doctored," particularly through deletion. True, a dishonest court reporter can be corrupted, but the far greater risks involved in tampering with shorthand-recorded testimony appear to guarantee the virtual non-existence of that brand of chicanery.

District Judge Orrin Judd of Brooklyn permitted tape recording of a deposition in a civil case. He sought to eliminate the danger of tampering with the tape by directing that a duplicate original tape be filed in the clerk's office "as assurance of the authenticity" of the tape to be retained by the examining party. He imposed other conditions as well.[22]

As another source of misgivings about tape, most recording devices do not let the transcriber "sort out" the voices of two or more persons speaking at once. A skillful reporter can often do so. When the reporter does miss testimony for this or any other reason, he will interrupt the proceedings to straighten things out. A machine will not reveal the confusion until it is too late.

Background noise, such as coughing, the rustling of papers or the rearranging of a chair, can render passages of testimony inaudible. The participants often fail to realize this at the time.

The court reporter performs functions that a machine cannot duplicate. He administers the oath and certifies the accuracy of the transcript.[23] He may be needed if a question must be taken to court for a ruling. The mechanical or electronic recorder requires finding some-

---

[21] See *Carter* v. *Joseph Bancroft & Sons Co.,* 360 F. Supp. 1103, 1110 (E.D. Pa. 1973).

[22] *Buck* v. *Board of Education,* 16 F.R. Serv.2d 112 (E.D. N.Y. 1972).

[23] See, *e.g.,* Federal Rule 30(f)(1).

one else to do these chores. Counsel for a party, even if he is a notary public, may be ineligible.[24]

A federal judge in Chicago permitted the use of tape recorders for depositions in a class action under the antitrust laws.[25] He imposed a series of conditions, including:

> I.   Employment of an independent operator for the recording equipment;
> II.   Various technological safeguards, such as "duplicate original" tapes to prevent tampering, individual lavalier microphones, etc.; and
> III.   Allocation of costs in a fashion analogous to that traditionally employed in stenographically recorded depositions.

The opinion in this case deserves study by any attorney contemplating the use of sound recording equipment over another party's objection. So does Judge Frankel's opinion in a 1972 case in the Southern District of New York.[26]

Even if another party gets court permission to record a deposition electronically or by some other unconventional method, that does not necessarily end the matter. You may still have the right to use an "old-fashioned" shorthand reporter.[27]

3. Innovations: Videotape

Recent years have seen videotape come into use as a means of recording depositions.[28] It lets the trier of the facts see and hear the witness, rather than just have his words read by someone else.

---

[24] Federal Rule 28(c) disqualifies, among others, "a person who is . . . attorney or counsel of any of the parties, or is a relative or employee of such attorney or counsel. . . ."

[25] Austin, D. J., in *Kallen* v. *Nexus Corp.*, 54 F.R.D. 610 (N.D. Ill. 1972). See also the opinion of District Judge Denney in *Wescott* v. *Neeman*, 55 F.R.D. 257 (D. Neb. 1972).

[26] *Marlboro Products Corp.* v. *North American Philips Corp.*, 16 F.R. Serv.2d 302 (S.D. N.Y. 1972).

[27] See Federal Rule 30(b)(4).

[28] See, e.g., *State ex rel. Lucas* v. *Moss*, 498 S.W.2d 289 (Mo. 1973); and *State ex rel. Johnson* v. *Circuit Court*, 61 Wis.2d 1, 212 N.W.2d 1 (1972). For an early but comprehensive treatment of the use of videotape as a technique of recording depositions as well as trials, see Madden, *Illinois Pioneers Videotaping of Trials*, 55 ABA Journal 457 (1969). Cases on the subject are reviewed in *Rubino* v. *G. D. Searle & Co.*, 73 Misc.2d 447, 340 N.Y.S.2d 574 (1973). For a negative holding antedating the 1970 amendment to Federal Rule 30(b)(4), see *U.S. Steel Corp.* v. *United States*, 43 F.R.D. 447, 451 (S.D. N.Y. 1968).

The conventional transcript cannot show facial expressions. It cannot indicate pauses or reveal signs of nervousness. Videotaped testimony can bring out all of these elements almost as effectively as a personal appearance on the witness stand.

Videotape, moreover, can produce "close-ups" of objects such as photographs and X-rays, sometimes even more effectively than the witness on the stand. Finally, videotaping eliminates or reduces the deadly monotony that so often attends reading deposition testimony into a trial record.

This new technique may have disadvantages when compared to the conventional deposition. One of them is a somewhat greater cost. This may be justified in more substantial litigation, and the cost differential may diminish if, as seems likely, court reporters' rates continue to climb and additional entrants into the business liven competition in the videotape field.

Videotape offers broad opportunities for innovation in the taking of depositions. Take the case of a witness who must explain the functioning of a complex machine. If he can actually point to the controls and various parts of the apparatus, he will have an easier time testifying. The trier of the facts should find it correspondingly easier understanding the testimony. The same might apply to on-the-spot testimony concerning an accident or other occurrence. The use of maps, diagrams and sketches should become more meaningful.

One who pursues new ideas like this will proceed with caution or run the risk of regretting it. The court order by which a videotape or other unorthodox deposition is taken should go into detail. It should say precisely what will be done and who will do it. It should say whether the videotaping will supplement or replace the traditional shorthand recording of testimony.[29] If you plan to have the operator take close-up shots, say so in your order. If you can, work out an order to whose form your adversary will consent. If possible, stipulate that the tape may be received in evidence by being shown to the trier of the facts.

Videotaping shares with tape recording other possible disadvantages. One cannot go through a videotape to check or find an important point with the ease that one can in the case of a typewritten transcript. Some videotaping firms eliminate this handicap by supplying transcripts with the recording. More difficult to solve is the problem of how to introduce excerpts from videotaped testimony. The ever-present

---

29 See *State ex rel. Lucas* v. *Moss,* footnote 28.

possibility of mechanical failure may, if undetected, cause the loss of crucial evidence forever.

e. Who Should Attend the Deposition

When you take a deposition, is it better to do your work with only those present who must be? Is it, for example, wise to have one's client present while one takes the deposition of an adverse party? The rules of attendance vary from one jurisdiction to another.[30] They usually permit the presence of individual parties or the officers of corporate parties. This does not mean that such attendance is always a good idea.

Most lawyers exclude their clients from depositions. They say, for one thing, that it probably wastes the client's time. You may say that you need your client at your side to consult concerning the questioning. This may mean that you are not properly prepared. If the client knows anything about the subject-matter of the deposition, you should have acquired that knowledge yourself as a part of familiarizing yourself with the background of the case.

The presence of one's client at a deposition may dilute the control that examining counsel should have over the atmosphere as well as the actual course of the deposition. A client, having a personal stake in litigation, lacks the objectivity that a good lawyer brings to the most hotly contested case. By arguing or by reacting visibly to an answer that surprises or displeases him, a client attending a deposition may sabotage his lawyer's efforts to attain a helpful rapport with the party under examination. Examining counsel, anxious to prove his dedication to the cause, may in the presence of his client behave militantly or aggressively when the conciliatory demeanor that he would feel at liberty to affect were he alone would be more to his side's advantage.

For reasons of self-interest as well as of principle, you do not wish your own or your adversary's deposition disrupted. As one federal judge has said:

> The purpose of discovery is to provide an orderly, efficient and effective means for ascertaining the truth in order to expedite

---

[30] Federal Rule 26(c)(5), by empowering a court to order "that discovery be conducted with no one present except persons designated by the court," implies that in the absence of such an order discovery proceedings in federal actions are open to the public. A statute forbids exclusion of the public from depositions in equity suits brought by the United States under the antitrust laws, 15 U.S.C. §30. *United States* v. *Procter & Gamble Co.*, 356 U.S. 677, 683, 78 S.Ct. 983, 2 L.Ed.2d 1077, 1082 (1958).

a determination of the controversy on the merits. . . . That
purpose not only demands dignity, order and decorum, but also
unswerving attention to the business at hand.

The federal rules envision that discovery will be conducted
by skilled gentlemen of the bar, without wrangling and without the
intervention of the court. The vision is an unreal dream. . . .[31]

Having litigants present at a deposition does not often further the
attainment of this "unreal dream."

Every rule has its exceptions. Sometimes a client's presence can help.
Consider an example:

In a contract action between two corporations, plaintiff's attorney
was about to take the deposition of defendant's vice-president.
He learned from those in his client's organization who had dealt
with the prospective witness that the latter was basically honest
but not a forceful or strongminded type. The witness might,
plaintiff's counsel reasoned, be tempted to color facts as a result
of pressure from defendant's management. Plaintiff's attorney
decided to ask the four officers of plaintiff with whom the witness
was still on outwardly friendly terms, to attend the deposition.
They did so, with striking effect. The witness, subject as he may
have been to influence from his superiors, was even more strongly
influenced by the immediate presence of his four former associates.
He gave candid testimony that paved the way for a settlement
favorable to plaintiff.

We have concluded our discussion of preparing for and planning
the deposition. The stage is now set. We may consider how actually
to conduct the questioning.

B. TAKING THE DEPOSITION

1. Stipulations

a. A Word of Caution

A customary beginning to a deposition consists of the question,
"The usual stipulations?" asked by one counsel and answered with
a nod of the head by his adversary. The reporter sets down in the

---

[31] MacMahon, D. J., in *Harlem River Consumers Cooperative* v. *Associated
Grocers of Harlem, Inc.*, 54 F.R.D. 551, 553 (S.D. N.Y. 1972). The case involved
the taking of photographs at a deposition.

transcript his version of the "usual" stipulations. Examining this routine ritual may reveal it as unnecessary if not unwise.

Looking at a random selection of deposition transcripts will probably show you that each reporter had his own version of the so-called standard stipulations. If, then, you do not wish to commit yourself to undefined terms, you should actually read into the record any stipulations you decide to make.

First, however, let us ask whether most deposition stipulations are necessary or desirable. A review of your practice code may reveal that your routine stipulations deal with matters for which statute or rule already makes adequate provision or matters as to which nothing is to be gained by the kind of stipulation you have been making. Let us consider the subjects of some of the common stipulations.

b. Stipulations on Objections

Attorneys often stipulate at depositions that "Objections, except as to the form of questions, are reserved until the trial of the action. . . ." To the extent that such a stipulation paraphrases the words of a statute or rule, as it does in most jurisdictions,[32] the stipulation is merely redundant. To the extent that it lulls counsel into foregoing objections that should be made at the deposition, whether or not they are strictly necessary, it can do positive harm.

A stipulation preserving objections does not leave you free to ignore bad questions. The lawyer who, because he has "preserved objections," lets opposing counsel devastate a witness by improper questioning has made a mistake that is surely irremediable and may be fatal.

Where you have many parties represented at a deposition, another stipulation can be helpful. It provides, for example, in a case where plaintiff is suing a half dozen separately represented defendants, that an objection made by one defendant shall be deemed to have been made on behalf of all. The compulsion of some lawyers to make themselves conspicuous in every proceeding they attend sometimes renders such a stipulation more valuable in theory than in practice.

c. Stipulations on Signature of the Transcript

A prevalent stipulation provides for waiving the witness's signature to the transcript. This seems to have no advantage for anyone. Counsel

---

[32] The effect of sub-paragraphs (b) and (d)(3) of Federal Rule 32 is to preserve until the trial all objections to questions at a deposition except those relating to form, and objections to "errors of any kind which might be obviated, removed, or cured if promptly presented."

for the witness will want his client to have the opportunity to correct errors, typographical or otherwise, in the transcript. With signature waived, the other side may file or make use of the transcript before such corrections are made.[33]

Examining counsel, too, has an interest in having the transcript of a deposition signed. Notwithstanding the unconditional character or the good faith of a witness's waiver of signature, he can always make a later claim that he was quoted in error. Such a claim will have much less force if the witness has read and signed the transcript.

d. Miscellaneous Stipulations

Attorneys make other stipulations. They sometimes concern the certification, filing or other technical details of the deposition. Few such stipulations make sense in the light of practice provisions. Most are holdovers from earlier codes. For one thing, it may work to your advantage to have the deposition transcript on file in the clerk's office and thus readily available to the judge. You have nothing to gain from a stipulation waiving filing.

One stipulation can be helpful, at least in some jurisdictions. It permits the witness to sign and swear to his testimony before a notary public other than the one before whom he testifies. If the witness comes from a distance, and if local statute or rules do not make an appropriate provision, such a stipulation is imperative.

e. Stipulations of Fact

Your adversary may interrupt the deposition with an offer to save time by stipulating facts. Think his offer over before you accept it. You may be giving up a lot and gaining nothing.

Here is an example of such a mistake:

> In a patent case you are taking the deposition of an out-of-state expert for the purpose of preserving his testimony. As he begins to recite his educational background, opposing counsel interrupts to say, "We'll stipulate the witness's qualifications as an expert in organic chemistry." You feel relief at being able to get to the heart of the matter, *i.e.*, the witness's observations and opinions.

A moment's reflection should convince you to reject the offer. If your witness has any but the most meager qualifications, you will want

---

[33] See Federal Rule 30(e); *Rogers* v. *Roth*, 477 F.2d 1154, 1159 (10th Cir. 1973).

those qualifications on the record, not for the technical purpose of entitling the witness to express opinions but for the far more important purpose of adding weight to his opinions. By making his seemingly generous offer, your opponent is giving up nothing. He knows that you will qualify the witness anyway. He wants you to give up a great deal by stripping the expert testimony of the prestige that the witness's qualifications will lend that testimony.

Here is a more common example:

> As plaintiff's attorney, you are taking your own client's deposition in a personal-injury case. As you begin inquiring about events following the accident, defense counsel interposes:

>> Defendant will stipulate that plaintiff sustained all of the injuries listed in the bill of particulars and that he likewise underwent the hospitalization and other treatment set forth in the bill.

Here again you are being invited to give up something of value in exchange for nothing. You want the record to show all the details of the accident's consequences. No stipulation can take the place of your client's description of the pain and discomfort he went through. One of your biggest assets as plaintiff's lawyer is the human interest in the injuries. You want the trier of the facts to identify with plaintiff. The latter's word-by-word account of what he suffered will help achieve that important goal. Even if you plan to put the client on the stand at the trial anyway, a detailed recital of his injuries on the deposition transcript may help you gain a favorable settlement. Do not stipulate this asset away.

Some stipulations of fact may benefit both parties. Matters of time, weather, authenticity of documents or other incidental facts often fall within this category. We should all encourage the saving of time that can result. Before you make any factual stipulation, however, weigh with the greatest of care what you are giving up. If it exceeds what you are gaining, "No, thank you" must be your answer.

Keep in mind one precaution if you do decide to enter into a stipulation of fact. If what you are stipulating will help you, ask your adversary to agree not only to the facts, but also to their admissibility in evidence. Here is how you might word such a stipulation if you dictate it orally into the record of a deposition:

> MR. BERNSTEIN: May we stipulate, Mr. Morelli, that the witness, if asked the proper questions, would testify that he had

charge of the plaintiff's personal books and records for a period of approximately one year following April 25, 1971, that plaintiff's medical expenses as a result of the accident sustained on that date consisted solely of the items listed in Paragraph 19 of plaintiff's answers to interrogatories? And may we further stipulate that the contents of the preceding sentence of this stipulation may be received in evidence at the behest of either party without the laying of any further foundation?

MR. MORELLI: So stipulated.

Now if the facts to be stipulated redound to your opponent's advantage, you may not wish to be quite so generous. Let us assume this time that instead of dictating a stipulation to the court reporter, your adversary and you decide to sign a formal document. It might read:

> IT IS STIPULATED by the attorney for plaintiff and the attorneys for defendants that if any party to this action took the deposition of Arthur J. Burnham of 128 Foster Road, Allenville, Ohio, Mr. Burnham would testify that from January 1, 1965, to date he has occupied the positions of president and treasurer of Burnham Chalk Corp., that he is familiar with the books, records and files of that corporation and that those books, records and files contain no reference to any actual or purported rescission of the contract of May 19, 1969, referred to in Paragraphs 3, 4, 5 and 8 of the complaint in this action.
>
> IT IS FURTHER STIPULATED that the foregoing paragraph of this stipulation may be received in evidence on behalf of any party, as permitted by Federal Rule 32 [or other applicable statute or rule] and the rules of evidence, to the same extent as if the witness had actually so testified at a deposition.

As this example suggests, sometimes a stipulation can replace an entire deposition, not just particular items of testimony. A proposal to that effect should excite your suspicion all the more. You should agree to it only where the intended testimony covers subject matter of the most perfunctory and absolutely unchallenged character.

2. The Marking and Handling of Exhibits

The notice or subpoena with which you launch your deposition may require the witness to bring with him certain documents or other objects.[34] You may gain access to other papers because the witness

---

[34] Federal Rules 30(b)(5) and 45(d)(1).

uses them to refresh his recollection, even though you have not compelled their production at the deposition.[35] You may have papers or other items of your own about which to question the witness.

For one of the foregoing or other reasons, almost every deposition includes the marking of exhibits for identification. Some lawyers fail to perceive the point of this procedure and so do it improperly. This means wasted motion, and it can generate confusion in the record.

Marking an exhibit for identification has one purpose. Once the document or object has an identifying mark on it, along with the authenticating initials of the person marking it, anyone who reads the record can identify the item about which testimony is being given.

Say, for example, you are questioning a witness about a letter. Referring to it as "this letter" or even as "this letter of January 5, 1974," may be perfectly clear to you and to him at the time. It may, however, confuse someone who reads the transcript later. One never knows how many different letters were written on a given date, even between the same persons.

Say, however, that the court reporter has marked the letter "Defendant's Exhibit A" and signed his name or initials on it. If you, as examining counsel, always refer to the letter by that designation, the record will be clear.

More than just clarity may be at stake. You may be using the deposition to authenticate documents or other things. If on the trial you cannot prove that the item authenticated by the witness at the deposition is the same thing you are offering in evidence, you may have defeated the purpose of the deposition.

You should, therefore, have the document or object marked for identification before you begin your questioning about it. It makes no sense to engage in several pages of questioning about a paper or other item, as some attorneys do, and only then have it marked for identification. The intervening references remain ambiguous.

At depositions in most jurisdictions the court reporter handles the marking of exhibits for identification. In asking him to mark a document, you should describe it in detail. Here is a suitable formula for having a letter marked for identification:

> Mr. Reporter, I ask you to mark as Plaintiff's Exhibit 5 for identification this letter, two pages long, dated March 5, 1974, from Thomas Sayers to John C. Heenan, on the letterhead of defendant.

---

[35] *Cowen* v. *Hughes,* 509 P.2d 461 (Okl. 1973).

Or, if a physical object is involved:

> Mr. Reporter, please mark as Defendant's Exhibit G this sec-
> tion of fire hose, approximately 24 inches in length, bearing
> defendant's name and trade-mark and the serial number of
> NQ4318R.

Every subsequent reference to the document or thing should be by
its exhibit designation. Counsel should begin his questioning, for
example, by saying:

> Q. I hand you this letter of March 5, 1974, marked Plaintiff's
> Exhibit 5, and ask if that is your signature appearing toward the
> bottom of page 2?

The witness will have greater difficulty remembering this important
rule. It will be necessary to clarify his references from time to time.
For example:

> Q. When did you next talk to Mr. Heenan?
> A. About a week after I wrote this letter here.
> Q. Indicating Plaintiff's Exhibit 5?
> A. Right.

Marking exhibits for identification represents a simple but often
crucial procedure. If you understand what you are doing, you will
probably do it right.

Marking an exhibit for identification does not make it your client's
or your own property; it still belongs to whoever produced it at the
deposition. On the other hand, it is usually important that the exhibit
be kept available to the parties or to whoever else might have occasion
to read the deposition. In the case of documentary exhibits, it is not
uncommon to attach them to the transcript after copies have been
supplied to all parties.[36] The attorneys usually stipulate as to the
custody and care of other physical objects pending the trial.

3. The Questioning Itself

a. Watching

We come now to the actual questioning at a deposition. We have
emphasized the importance of a comprehensive outline to guide your
interrogation. We have pointed out the advisability of writing out in

---

[36] See Federal Rule 30(f)(1).

advance key questions, particularly on subjects that you expect to offer in evidence. We now take up some ideas that should make your questioning more productive.

If you are taking the deposition of an adversary or of an unfriendly or unknown witness, you will not be getting what you should from the proceedings unless you concentrate as much on the witness as on what he is saying. You should be forming an opinion of him as well as evaluating his testimony.

Your experience in cross-examination should have taught you how the weak points in a witness's story often reveal themselves. One advantage of a deposition is that you have no trier of the facts present. You can, therefore, probe for soft spots without the fear, always present in the courtroom, that a display of strength in an area where you hoped to find weakness will bolster the evidence you are trying to tear apart.

If the person testifying is worried about any part of what he has to say, his anxiety will betray him. It may do so by a change in his tone of voice, a sudden shifting of the eyes, or a nervous physical gesture such as raising the hand to the face. The witness, after having appeared relaxed and comfortable, may begin shifting in his seat, perhaps noticeably or perhaps almost imperceptibly, every time you touch on a particular topic. A human being has many ways of manifesting tension, and no sure way of concealing it. Part of your job in taking a deposition is to detect and interpret the anxieties of the party or witness you are questioning.

Let us consider an example:

An export agent sued a manufacturer for wrongfully terminating the contract of agency. The manufacturer counterclaimed on the ground that plaintiff had failed to remit certain amounts collected from customers for defendant's account. Defendant's attorney, taking the deposition of plaintiff's president, found the witness a forthright, apparently truthful person. He noticed that the witness looked his interrogator in the eye as he spoke. Counsel also noticed that on three separate occasions the witness's eyes dropped or moved away momentarily. After this had happened twice, the attorney realized that it coincided both times with the mention of a particular customer. The account in question appeared in order. Counsel, troubled by the minor aberration in the witness's behavior, nevertheless directed a further investigation. It revealed that his own bookkeeping staff had made an error and had understated the amount owing from the customer, the mention of whose name appeared to disturb plaintiff's president. Plaintiff had never called the error to defendant's attention, but merely retained the amount collected but not billed.

Defense counsel's alertness thus added a major item to the damages ultimately collected on the counterclaim.

Anxiety is not the only emotion that will reveal itself to the perceptive questioner. A witness may display relaxed self-confidence in speaking of an area of the case about which you think he should be quite sensitive. This may signal to you his ignorance of some evidence unfavorable to his side. You may decide to omit mention of this weak spot in his case and thereby avoid the risk of alerting him to it.

A witness, particularly one who is a party to the action, will often reveal anger over one or more aspects of the case. Astute counsel can turn this to his advantage in a number of ways. He may, as one course of action, wait until the trial and hope, by asking the right question at the right time, to treat the jury to the rarely flattering spectacle of a witness's losing his temper.

In the face of anger on a witness's part counsel may follow the more common practice of giving the witness free rein on the subject that provoked him. An experienced lawyer knows that what a party says in his deposition will rarely harm the other side. The very worst testimony under such circumstances will merely give warning of what would otherwise come as a surprise at the trial. The talkative witness, however, particularly under the stress of anger, may reveal something that he meant to conceal. More likely, he may say something in terms not the best calculated to further his view of the case.

The list of what can be learned by paying close attention to the deposition witness's demeanor is endless. One's skill at this game develops with experience. Even the beginner, if he appreciates the wealth of material often available, will find the practice rewarding.

b. Listening

Watching the witness is not enough. You must also be listening to what he says. At a deposition, no judge or jury is present. Examining counsel, busy as he is with so many things, is tempted to pay attention to the substance of the testimony he is eliciting. He may think that so long as the reporter gets it all down, he, the attorney, can safely content himself with studying the testimony afterwards. No competent trial lawyer should adopt this attitude.

However complex the subject-matter of the deposition, no matter how long the examination or how late the hour, you must pay close attention to the testimony throughout the examination. You should understand each answer fully. Whenever you do not, you should have the reporter read the answer aloud. If that does not help you, ask the witness to explain his answer. Digest, in other words, the testimony as it is given. Do not save it for some future study session.

The reasons for this practice hardly require explanation. You cannot, for one thing, know whether the witness has answered a question if you have not assimilated his answer. Also, the testimony you are eliciting should suggest new questions and new topics, items, that is, that did not occur to you in the preparation of your outline. If you do not grasp fully each answer as it comes, you may miss such supplemental points. You may likewise fail to catch inconsistencies or contradictions in the witness's testimony.

We have spoken of some of the things that you should be doing as the deposition proceeds. We might turn next to the questioning itself and ask how it can be conducted most effectively.

c. Some Effective Questioning Techniques

An earlier chapter dealt with the different strategies you may choose from as a questioner at a deposition. We shall deal now with specific techniques to be used in carrying out whichever of these strategies you adopt.

One principle applies to all questioning. The goal of the deposition is for counsel to elicit information from the witness. Inexperienced lawyers reverse that process. Their questioning technique, their reaction to the witness's answers and other aspects of their conduct reveal to opposing counsel what they think are the crucial parts of the case, what testimony disturbs and what pleases them. An even-tempered, impassive approach to the case as it unfolds from the witness's lips will serve your best interests.

An earlier section of this chapter stressed the value of an outline from which to pose questions. It was pointed out that to insure its being complete, the outline should usually be prepared in logical sequence. It bears repeating now that you need not do the questioning in the same sequence. On the contrary, skipping more or less at random from topic to topic may prove to be the undoing of the witness who has contrived his testimony and so must be constantly on the alert to keep his story straight.

In conducting his questioning, every lawyer knows enough to "speak for the record" and make sure that the witness does likewise. He will not refer to a document or other physical object without giving a brief description of it. If the witness nods or shakes his head instead of articulating an answer, counsel will come forth immediately with an explanation. If the witness estimates a distance as "about from here to the end of the room," counsel will clarify the record at once. We need not concern ourselves with such elementary points.

We must, however, discuss a related, often overlooked technique. It consists of making sure that an important segment of deposition testimony will stand on its own feet. To the extent that you plan to use the deposition as evidence, you should do your best to construct any important part of the testimony so that you can read it into evidence without complicated cross-references to other parts of the transcript.

Let us cite an example:

> Plaintiff's attorney in a breach-of-contract action was questioning defendant's employee about a certain letter. The original of the document was missing, and counsel was doing his questioning from a carbon copy. He was trying to establish that the letter had never been signed, but represented a draft that had been thought unsuitable and so discarded. The witness was reluctant to concede the point. Questioning on it continued for several pages of transcript. Finally, counsel managed to elicit from the witness:
>
> **Q.** And as far as you know, it was never signed at all, was it?
>
> **A.** That's right.

Unfortunately, the document had last been specifically identified a number of pages earlier. In the intervening pages, reference had been made to other documents. The crucial admission, therefore, lacked clarity. The explanation required at trial to gain its admission in evidence detracted from the effect of the testimony.

The difficulty could have been avoided if the key question had read:

> **Q.** And as far as you know, this letter of July 20, 1974, marked Plaintiff's Exhibit 4 for identification, was never signed at all, was it?

The art of building a proper record has many aspects. It includes making note of any significant events that do not appear as part of a question or answer. For example, if a witness consults a paper or book before or during one of his answers examining counsel should say something like this:

> The record will show that the witness referred to [designation of paper or book] before giving his last answer.

If the item that the witness consulted has been marked for identification, it should be designated by its exhibit number. If not, it should be referred to simply as "a paper" or some other appropriate term, as specific as possible. Counsel taking the deposition should then ask to see the unmarked item. If the request is granted, the item should be marked for identification, no matter how trivial it seems. The witness or his attorney, of course, may turn down the request. That, however, can be embarrassing, and it will at least have the effect of curtailing references to extraneous material in the future.

Examining counsel should deal likewise with any occurrence out of the ordinary. The witness's attorney, for example, may be communicating with his client by passing him notes, pointing to a document or notation, etc. It will do you no harm to get that on the record in terms such as these:

> Mr. Osborne, your attorney seems to be trying to call your attention to something he's written on his note pad. Would you like a brief adjournment so that you may confer with him?

Again, a statement like this, if it does nothing else, should prevent a recurrence of the conduct to which attention has been called.

Let us turn next to some errors common in the taking of depositions. You must, for one thing, always be sure to give the witness time to finish each of his answers. Lawyers with any deposition experience at all need no list of the practical considerations that make it imperative to observe this courtesy.

Each time you read the transcript of a deposition that you yourself have taken, watch out for repetitious mannerisms that mar the technique of many examining attorneys. Such habits as beginning question after question with the word "Now," or repeating (or, worse yet, trying to summarize or paraphrase) each answer after it has been given tend to catch the eye or ear of anyone reading or listening to the reading of the transcript, particularly if the reader or listener is a lawyer or judge himself. They dilute the attention that should be paid to the substance of the testimony. Apart from that, they brand the questioner as an amateur.

4. Coping with the Other Side's Objections

However skillfully conceived and carefully framed your questions at a deposition may be, they will not please your adversary. He will interpose objections. He may do so in good faith, or he may wish merely to show his client, when the latter reads the transcript, that he, the attorney, knows the rules of evidence and is earning his fee.

Be that as it may, a few simple rules will help you deal with your opponent's objections. You will have two goals in mind in this respect. You do not wish objections to interfere with the legitimate purpose of your deposition. You do not wish to let them consume unnecessary time.

The other side's objections will fall into two broad categories. Counsel may state his objection and let his client answer anyway. That will preserve the objection until you or someone else tries to read the question and answer into evidence during the trial. Then the judge can rule on the objection.

Your adversary, on the other hand, may object to your question and instruct his client not to answer it. That poses a more immediate problem.

To begin, try to understand each objection made to your questions. If counsel does not state his grounds, ask him what they are unless they are obvious.

Knowing the reason or reasons behind an objection can help you in at least two ways. First, it may enable you to correct any deficiency in your question and thereby eliminate the objection. A statement of the grounds for the objection may, on the other hand, reveal to you (and later to the judge) that the objection lacks merit.

Secondly, be aware of and rely on whatever statute, rule or case law governs objections to deposition questions in your jurisdiction. Know, for example, that in a deposition in a federal case, according to Federal Rule 30(c):

Evidence objected to shall be taken subject to the objections.

Lawyers in many areas ignore this clause and corresponding provisions in state practice codes. Even so, reciting such a provision at the right time may improve the record for purposes of any judicial hearing that results from an instruction not to answer one or more of your questions. It may also, although less commonly, persuade the objecting lawyer that he is taking an untenable position and thereby risking embarrassment in the event the matter comes before a judge.

Once opposing counsel has instructed his client not to answer a question, a precaution may be advisable. That is to ask the witness if he in fact refuses to answer the question. This will perfect your record for purposes of any motion to compel an answer. If the procedure becomes time-consuming because of the number of such instructions, you may ask your adversary and his client to stipulate that unless the witness speaks up to the contrary, he will be deemed to have followed all instructions not to answer questions. (It is probably wisest not to suggest such a stipulation at the outset of the deposition. Why give your adversary ideas?)

If opposing counsel persists in instructing his client not to answer your question or questions, you can get help only from a judge or someone to whom the judge has properly delegated authority for that purpose. In federal practice, the prescribed procedure is to move under Federal Rule 37(a)(2) for an order compelling an answer or answers. In many jurisdictions, including some federal districts, it is customary to visit a judge in chambers to obtain his rulings on questions to which objection has been made.

Say that opposing counsel has instructed his client not to answer one of your questions. Should you interrupt the proceedings then and there to obtain an immediate ruling from a judge? In federal practice, Rule 37(a)(2) gives you, as examining counsel, two choices. You may adjourn the deposition to make a motion to compel an answer to your question. As the alternative, you may defer such a motion until your examination is completed. Which route should you select?

The practicalities usually dictate waiting until the questioning is completed. That way multiple trips to the courthouse will be avoided if more than one objection arises. Later questions and answers may solve the problems posed by some or all of the objections. Finally, time plus cooling of tempers may have diminished the importance of issues raised in the heat of battle.

If you must seek enforcement from a judge, you should be able to present to the judge the actual wording of the question or questions objected to. Most court reporters will supply you with the text of individual questions for this purpose. You can make the reporter's job easier by notifying him of your request at or immediately after the interposition of the objection. This will save him a long hunt through his notes.

You must, we emphasized, avoid letting objections either interfere with your attaining the goals of your deposition or consume unwarranted time. The suggestions above should help you achieve that objective.

5. Adjournments and Other Interruptions

Lawyers learn not to overlook the significance of any phase of a deposition. That includes such routine matters as adjournments, recesses and other interruptions.

The typical deposition begins in the morning. If the questioning is not completed by noon, a recess of an hour or so will be had for lunch. The participants may agree to a short recess in the middle of each half-day session.[37] It may become necessary to adjourn the proceedings to a future date, either because the subject-matter requires additional time or because the witness must search his files or make other inquiries before questioning can continue.

Skilled counsel will not let these interruptions jeopardize the achievement of his goals in taking the deposition. He will not use them to gain an unfair advantage over the witness or to inconvenience his adversary. He will merely see that they do not serve as devices to prejudice his case.

Keep one thing in mind. Any interruption in the deposition is likely to occasion a conference between the witness and his lawyer. That is, of course, not improper. If, however, a revision in testimony follows such a talk, examining counsel may be suspicious as well as disappointed. A few basic safeguards can diminish the likelihood of such occurrences.

Take as an example:

In an action for slander, a discharged employee claimed that his ex-employer had wrongfully accused him of theft. The alleged

---

[37] Always keep the court reporter's comfort in mind. He or she is expending more physical effort than anyone else at the deposition.

defamation had occurred at a joint union-management hearing over the employee's discharge. Under applicable substantive law, the employer's statements enjoyed a qualified privilege. The employee, that is, had to prove malice in order to recover.

Defendant's attorney began questioning plaintiff in the morning. He elicited a detailed account of the hearing. This testimony showed that defendant's representatives at the hearing had acted with restraint and had presented evidence of the alleged theft without a trace of animosity or vindictiveness. Pleased over having foreclosed any possible proof of malice, defense counsel suggested an adjournment for lunch.

After the luncheon recess, the questioning turned to a different cause of action. When the time came for plaintiff's attorney to cross-examine his client, he asked plaintiff if he had omitted anything from that morning's testimony concerning the discharge hearing. Plaintiff answered that he had. He proceeded to tell of how one of defendant's employees, the key witness to the theft, had come up to him, plaintiff, in the hearing room. The employee said, according to plaintiff, that at last his chance had come to "get" plaintiff as he had been itching to do for years. He added, said plaintiff, that he only regretted that he could not have plaintiff sent to prison as well as fired.

Defense counsel suspected that plaintiff's belated recollection of this incident had been inspired by a lunchtime warning that the case was about to be lost for want of proof of malice. Defendant's attorney consoled himself with the thought that the record would reveal the contrived character of this crucial addition to the testimony. Reviewing the transcript, however, showed him that although he had questioned plaintiff at length about the hearing, he had neglected to ask one or two closing questions such as:

Q. Now have you told us absolutely everything that you remember happening at the hearing?

Q. Did Mr. Atkins or Mr. O'Leary say anything to you or to the group generally that you have not testified about this morning?

Had he taken these precautions, counsel might have prevented the repair job attempted later in the day. He would at least have detracted greatly from its plausibility.

Another simple technique can dilute the effectiveness of the revisions of testimony that sometimes follow the interruption of a deposition. It involves simply asking the witness, upon resumption of the session, whether during the recess he conferred with his attorney. The contents of any such conversation will be privileged, but not the fact of the conference itself. A forthright question about it may make the witness leery of changing or supplementing his previous testimony in any way.

Some attorneys follow such a question with the inquiry whether the witness can think of anything in the previous session's testimony that was inaccurate or incomplete. This tactic compels the witness to change his story, if he is going to do it, in a context suggestive of connivance. It may further throw the witness off balance by raising the subject of a change of testimony at an unexpected point in the proceedings. A witness bent on a contrived modification of his testimony will find it harder under such circumstances to go through with his plan.

Preventive measures are always superior to remedies. You should, therefore, try to plan your questioning with a view to reducing the chances of revisions of testimony by afterthought. Try to complete your questioning concerning a particular episode or transaction at one sitting. You should conclude, as defendant's attorney neglected to do in the illustrative example above, with a series of questions designed to "freeze" the testimony as representing the witness's total recollection of the subject under inquiry. If you do not think that time will let you finish your questioning on a crucial topic before a recess, stay off that subject entirely until after you reconvene.

You should feel free to consult other counsel in advance about the hour of the luncheon recess, how late into the afternoon the deposition should continue, etc. Such foresight may spare you painful doubts over a colleague's motives in interrupting your questioning to suggest a luncheon recess or an adjournment for the day just as you are about to "nail down" a vital point of evidence.

When a deposition extends over a number of days, the participants sometimes do not reconvene until after the court reporter has transcribed and distributed the transcript of the previous session. Many practitioners begin adjourned sessions under such circumstances with the question whether the witness has read his earlier testimony and, if he has, whether he has found any errors or any items on which his testimony was incomplete. Besides making revisions of testimony more difficult, questions of this sort will tell you how much of an advantage your own review of the previous testimony has given you over the witness. If you suspect him of having falsified matters at the earlier session, you can feel more confident of your chances of catching him up in an inconsistency if he has not reviewed what he said before.

At the commencement of an adjourned session, many lawyers make sure that the witness understands that he remains under oath even though the oath is not repeated. Perhaps asking him if his attorney has so advised him accomplishes the job somewhat more courteously. Be that as it may, getting this assurance will keep a captious witness from contending that since no one bothered to swear him in at the beginning of the adjourned session, he thought that he was free to say what he pleased.

One or two additional points deserve mention. We have discussed how to handle the witness's talks with his attorney during any recess or adjournment. It is a good idea, too, to ask him upon reconvening whether he has, since the last session, talked about any aspect of the case with anyone else. If he has, you should ask for full details, since no privilege will apply. Such questioning will not often elicit material of great value. Nevertheless it usually takes the witness by surprise. It may thereby make him more cautious about trying to deceive his interrogator.

A witness will sometimes ask to confer with his attorney before answering a question. This is permissible, at least in most jurisdictions, and usually unavoidable. The fact of the consultation, however, should appear on the record. If the request itself is made off the record, examining counsel, before resuming his questioning, should say something like this:

> The record will please show that the witness has just conferred with Mr. Brevard.

If the talk has lasted more than a minute or two, counsel might add "for approximately —— minutes" to his statement.

The remarks above show you how the scheduling and timing of your questioning can help you get the most out of a deposition. You are engaged primarily in research into facts. You should make every legitimate effort to be sure that the facts you collect are the true ones.

6. Cross-Examination by Your Adversary

If you expect to use your deposition on trial, you have an interest in seeing that other counsel have the opportunity to question the witness. If the court deems the deposition incomplete because this oppor-

tunity was not accorded, you may have trouble getting the testimony
into evidence.[38]

Be sure, therefore, that you terminate the deposition by asking
counsel for every other party present whether he has any questions.
Do this on the record. If you must adjourn a deposition without having
completed your own questioning, consider offering the other attorneys
the chance to pose questions, out of turn, before the adjournment.
This tactic makes particular sense where a factor such as the witness's
health or personal plans raises the question when, if ever, the adjourned session will be held. A party's acquiescence in an adjournment
that turns out to deprive him of the right of cross-examination may
doom his effort to suppress the deposition.[39]

C. FINAL DETAILS: CORRECTION, SIGNATURE
AND FILING

We have discussed the wisdom of waiving signature of the transcript.[40] If you have not made such a waiver, the witness has the right to
review and, if necessary, correct his testimony.[41] As examining counsel, you in that case have details left that should be attended to with
care.

You should submit the transcript to the witness for correction and
signature. As a matter of professional ethics and courtesy, you should
do this through his attorney. If the transcript is not signed, you may
find it impossible to use at the trial.[42]

Should the party or witness fail or refuse to sign the transcript, you
have an alternative. Federal Rule 30(e) provides, for example:

> If the deposition is not signed by the witness within 30 days of
> its submission to him, the officer [before whom the deposition is

---

[38] Federal Rule 30(c). The failure to complete a deposition for reasons of death,
disability, etc., may but does not necessarily bar its receipt in evidence. *Derewecki* v.
Pennsylvania R. Co., 353 F.2d 436, 442–443 (3d Cir. 1965); *U.S. Steel Corp.* v.
United States, 43 F.R.D. 447, 449 (S.D. N.Y. 1968); *Smith* v. *Kalavity*, 515 P.2d
473, 476 (Colo. App. 1973).

[39] *Continental Can Co.* v. *Crown Cork & Seal, Inc.*, 39 F.R.D. 354, 356 (E.D.
Pa. 1965).

[40] Pages 87–88.

[41] Federal Rule 30(e); *Rogers* v. *Roth*, footnote 33.

[42] *Bernstein* v. *Brenner*, 51 F.R.D. 9 (D.C. D.C. 1970), discusses the criteria
governing the use or suppression of a completed but unsigned deposition. See also,
e.g., *Crabtree* v. *Measday*, 85 N.M. 20, 508 P.2d 1317, 1323 (1973), cert. den., 85
N.M. 5, 508 P.2d 1302 (1973); *Bell* v. *Linehan*, 500 S.W.2d 228 (Tex. Civ. App.
1973).

taken] shall sign it and state on the record the fact . . . of the refusal to sign together with the reason, if any, given therefor; and the deposition may then be used as fully as though signed. . . .

Study the corrections that the witness has made in his transcript. Enter all of them, even the most insignificant, in your own copy. If any corrections do not materially conform to applicable rules, or if they change the testimony to an extent making further inquiry of the witness necessary,[43] you should take action promptly by moving either to suppress all or part of the deposition, or for leave to resume your questioning. Waiting until the trial to take advantage of what you consider improper or suspicious changes in the transcript by commenting on them to the jury may cause you serious trouble.[44]

Be sure to file the original transcript if your procedural rules so require or permit.[45] This will make it available to the judge at the time of trial. The transcript can also be readily used to support or oppose motions and other pre-trial proceedings.

Omission of procedural details such as signing and filing may be waived by failing to make a timely objection.[46] You will be better off in most cases, however, if you attend to these details than if you dispense with them in the hope that your opponent will take the same casual attitude.

This completes our review of the steps necessary and advisable in taking the deposition of an opposing party or an unfriendly or neutral witness. Before we turn to the problems that arise when other counsel take the deposition of someone on your side, let us consider a relatively rare but nonetheless important type of deposition, the one that you must take outside your own jurisdiction.

D. KNOWING ABOUT EXTRATERRITORIAL DEPOSITIONS

Sometimes the needs of a case call for discovery, usually in the form of a deposition, in another jurisdiction. It may be a question of another state in the United States or a foreign country. Such proceedings will

---

[43] *Allen & Co.* v. *Occidental Petroleum Corp.*, 49 F.R.D. 337, 341 (S.D. N.Y. 1970); *Erstad* v. *Curtis Bay Towing Co.*, 28 F.R.D. 583 (D. Md. 1961).

[44] *Rogers* v. *Roth*, footnote 33.

[45] Federal Rule 30(f) prescribes a detailed procedure, often ignored in practice, for filing and giving notice of filing the transcript of a deposition. Filing is nevertheless desirable for the reasons given in the text.

[46] Federal Rule 32(d)(4); *Trade Development Bank* v. *Continental Ins. Co.*, 469 F.2d 35, 44–46 (2 Cir. 1972); *Kawietzke* v. *Rarich*, 198 F. Supp. 841 (E.D. Pa. 1961). As to waiver of the failure to sign a deposition see *Crabtree* v. *Measday*, footnote 42.

involve basically the same skills as those you will employ at home. The distinctions and problems are essentially technical.

To begin, discovery outside your jurisdiction may not be necessary. If the court in which your action is pending has or can obtain jurisdiction over a person or other legal entity, whether party or not, it can use its power to compel the production of persons or things located outside the state or nation but subject to the control or direction of the entity within its jurisdiction. As a distinguished federal judge explained years ago:

> The force of a subpoena for production of documentary evidence generally reaches all documents under the control of the person or corporation ordered to produce, saving questions of privilege and unreasonableness, and it makes no difference that a particular document is kept at a place beyond the territorial jurisdiction of the court that issues the subpoena. The test is one of control, not of location.[47]

Do not, therefore, resort to the often expensive and always complex devices available for extraterritorial discovery until you make sure they are necessary.

Remember also that a federal court has a qualified subpoena power over "a national or resident of the United States who is in a foreign country. . . ."[48] Use of this authority in a civil action may present obvious enforcement problems.

Because of the expense and inconvenience involved in taking testimony in an area remote to the forum, parties in this situation often make use of written questions rather than oral examination.[49] That technique has many of the advantages and disadvantages of written interrogatories, to be considered in a later chapter. Many of the suggestions made concerning interrogatories apply with equal validity to depositions by written questions.

In a federal case, you will have no procedural difficulties taking a deposition anywhere within the United States. When it comes to proceedings abroad, you will be subject to Federal Rules 28(b), which provides in part:

> In a foreign country, depositions may be taken (1) on notice before a person authorized to administer oaths in the place in

---

[47] Patterson, D. J., in In re *Harris,* 27 F. Supp. 480, 481 (S.D. N.Y. 1939).
[48] 28 U.S.C. §1783.
[49] See, *e.g.,* Federal Rule 31.

which the examination is held, either by the law thereof or by the law of the United States, or (2) before a person commissioned by the court, and a person so commissioned shall have the power by virtue of his commission to administer any necessary oath and take testimony, or (3) pursuant to a letter rogatory.

State codes have similar provisions.[50] In the case of a state action, however, the extraterritorial procedure must be resorted to whenever one engages in discovery in another state, as well as in another country.

Stipulations of counsel provide the most common means of taking depositions outside the jurisdiction. That desirable procedure requires the cooperation both of other counsel and of the witness whose testimony is sought. If such cooperation obtains, and if the contemplated proceedings do not conflict with local law, a deposition outside the jurisdiction may take place in much the same way as a regular examination in home territory.

What must one do if someone concerned with the proposed deposition withholds cooperation? The first of the three techniques listed in the federal provision quoted above involves "notice." That, in a federal case, suffices to validate the deposition as to other parties. It will not, however, compel the appearance of an unwilling witness outside the jurisdiction. For that purpose, you must resort to one of two procedures, the commission or letters rogatory.

A commission, for present purposes, consists of a local court's appointment of an official in another jurisdiction to preside at a deposition in the latter area. Inasmuch as the commission has no extraterritorial effect itself, a court or other authority where the proceeding is to be held must honor the commission and implement it by issuing its own authorization for the deposition. This will take the form of or include a subpoena or corresponding process to apply compulsion to the witness whose testimony is sought.

Some foreign nations, notably Switzerland and certain Eastern European countries, prohibit the taking of depositions in their territory for use elsewhere where a foreign state has appointed the presiding officer.[51] To take a deposition in such a nation, you must use letters rogatory.

Letters rogatory consist of a request that a foreign state appoint an officer of its own to take testimony for use in a tribunal of the re-

[50] See, e.g., Illinois Supreme Court Rule 205(b) and (c); 8 Ann. Laws Mass. 233, §41; Pennsylvania Rules of Civil Procedure, Rule 4015(b). N.Y. CPLR 3108 and 3113(a)(2) and (3).

[51] See 4 MOORE'S FEDERAL PRACTICE ¶28.01[6].

questing country. The request depends upon comity for implementation. Diplomatic considerations may consequently complicate use of this procedure.[52]

Our federal government, most or all of our states and most foreign nations have established procedures for effectuating commissions, letters rogatory, or both, issued by other jurisdictions.[53]

A deposition outside your jurisdiction will probably involve testimony of exceptional importance. If it did not, you would not go to the unusual bother of arranging it. Such a proceeding usually involves extraordinary expense. You thus have two reasons to take special care not to let a procedural imperfection jeopardize the usefulness of the testimony you are seeking.

Remember in this regard that you must comply with two not necessarily consistent sets of statutes or rules, those of your own jurisdiction and those of the place where the deposition is to be held. Make sure, for example, that the commission or other credentials you obtain from your own court will satisfy the authority that must give them effect. Make sure likewise that the procedure followed in the other jurisdiction will not bar the use of your deposition at home.

Depositions in some foreign states, for example, are not taken under oath. In some nations the reporter paraphrases or summarizes the testimony rather than recording it verbatim.[54] If you cannot be sure that your courts allow the receipt in evidence of testimony taken under any such unorthodox (to lawyers of the United States, that is) circumstances, consider such means as having the proceedings held before a U. S. Consular official or engaging a private shorthand stenographer instead of an official court reporter. Stipulating the admissibility of testimony taken abroad usually provides the easiest solution to problems of this sort.

Particularly if you are concerned with taking testimony in a foreign nation, you must take special precautions to avoid infringing local law. You do not, for example, wish to travel to Switzerland to take a deposition by stipulation or commission and discover there that you may be violating a Swiss statute. A substantial case may justify retaining counsel in the foreign state for assistance in this regard. Indeed, attorneys often do that when they merely take a domestic out-of-state deposition

---

[52] See, *e.g., The Signe,* 37 F. Supp. 819 (E.D. La. 1941).

[53] See, *e.g.,* 28 U.S.C. §1782; Federal Rules 37(e) and 45(e)(2); and Calif. Code of Civil Procedure §2023.

[54] A provision in Federal Rule 28(b) eliminates the two cited possibilities as barriers to the use of a foreign deposition taken pursuant to letters rogatory.

in a state action. If your matter does not have dimensions appropriate to such aid, consider making inquiries of the consulate of the nation where your deposition will take place. Then check whatever information and advice you receive with the United States Consul in the foreign state. You will usually find both sources accustomed to inquiries on the subject of extraterritorial depositions.

Your repertory of discovery techniques must include many diverse skills. If you lack a familiarity with what you must do to arrange discovery in an area beyond the reach of your own court's direct power, you cannot fully exploit the advantages that discovery confers on today's litigant.

Chapter III

HANDLING THE DEPOSITION OF YOUR OWN CLIENT OR WITNESS WISELY

A. SELECTION OF THE SPOKESMAN

We shall take up the opposite of the situation with which we have been dealing. We shall assume now that another lawyer wishes to take the deposition of your client.

If you represent a corporation or other organization, you may have the problem *in limine* of selecting the person who is to appear on its behalf. Some jurisdictions reserve this choice to the party whose deposition is to be taken, not to examining counsel. Federal Rule 30(b) (6) provides:

> A party may in his notice and in a subpoena name as the deponent a public or private corporation or a partnership or association or governmental agency and describe with reasonable particularity the matters on which examination is requested. In that event, the organization so named shall designate one or more officers, directors, or managing agents, or other persons who consent to testify on its behalf, and may set forth, for each person designated, the matters on which he will testify. A subpoena shall advise a nonparty organization of its duty to make such a designation. The persons so designated shall testify as to matters known or reasonably available to the organization. This subdivision (b) (6) does not preclude taking a deposition by any other procedure authorized in these rules.

This provision, added by 1970 amendment, appears to supplement rather than replace the prior federal practice whereby the examining party might designate an officer or managing agent to appear on behalf of the corporation.[1]

What criteria will govern your selection of a spokesman? First of all, you will pick someone knowledgeable, someone who knows the subject-matter of the proposed examination. If you abuse your right of selection by producing a witness with inadequate knowledge, you may forfeit that right and be forced to produce someone named by the court, perhaps on nomination by your adversary.[2]

Say, however, that you have a choice among two or more knowledgeable witnesses. This makes your job more difficult, but you will be facing the problem that every lawyer encounters when he must select a witness. You want, in brief:

> Someone astute enough to understand the questions he is asked and to perceive what motivates opposing counsel to ask them;
> Someone articulate enough to phrase answers that will read well when transcribed;
> Someone resourceful enough to phrase what he says so as to make the best of the strengths of your case and to de-emphasize its weaknesses to the extent legitimately possible; and
> Someone of character, a witness who will speak the truth and whose phraseology and tone of voice will manifest his candor and accuracy.

Every experienced lawyer has opinions about what occupational groups make relatively good or poor witnesses. Some say that salesmen, experienced as they are in voicing their ideas in persuasive terms and in coming up with extemporaneous answers to customers' questions, generally make better witnesses than, say, scientists. The latter, they say, tend to be introverted and to qualify or hedge their utterances in a constant effort to attain an unexceptionable precision of expression. Any dozen lawyers picked at random will probably give twelve different theories on this subject. Your own notions may be as good as any of them.

If you are acquainted with a potential witness, especially if you have seen him in action, you have a head start. If not, perhaps he has had prior experience in court. You may then be able to find out from

---

[1] *Terry* v. *Modern Woodmen of America*, 57 F.R.D. 141 (W.D. Mo. 1972).

[2] See, e.g., *Stettner* v. *Twin Double TV, Inc.*, 34 A.D.2d 924, 311 N.Y.S.2d 646 (1970).

an attorney in the earlier case or from the transcript of a deposition, how he performed. Time spent in exhaustive research on this matter before you select a deposition spokesman for the organization you represent will not be wasted.

Not a moment's doubt should attend the question who selects the spokesman. The job is too important to be left to anyone else. You must make the selection and be responsible for its success or failure. If you let the client tell you whom to produce in its name, you are failing it and not living up to what should be your own professional standards.

B. PREPARATION: THE WITNESS

1. General Preparation

a. Know the Ground Rules

Preparing a witness [3] for his deposition requires a generous amount of the lawyer's most precious commodity, time. No matter how simple the case and how sophisticated the witness, counsel must allocate hours to his preparation.

Appendix A[4] consists of a checklist of items you will wish to go over as you prepare someone for a deposition. We shall discuss here the reasons for the items on that list.

To you, depositions are old hat. To your witness, they probably stand as a mysterious unknown. Your preparatory session with the witness should begin, therefore, with an elementary exposition of who is going to be present at the proceedings and what is going to happen. Explain the purpose of the deposition and what use may be made of the transcript.

In your preliminary talk with the witness, be sure you cover all eventualities. Tell him that you may object to a question and then let him answer it anyway. This will probably strike him as ridiculous unless you explain it. Make it clear also that if you direct him not to answer a question to which you have objected, he should follow your advice no matter how outraged opposing counsel seems and no matter how harmless the question seems to him, the witness.

Whoever the witness may be, you must establish that you, not

---

[3] The word here is used to designate any person who testifies, including a party.
[4] Pages 282–284.

he, are in charge of the deposition. This may be difficult, especially if the witness is president of your firm's biggest client. It may be even more difficult if you are dealing with an experienced professional expert witness, someone who knows the subject-matter of the case and who may have been in court more than you have. You must, nevertheless, in one way or another, make it plain that you are the boss. If, as sometimes happens, the witness feels free to overrule your instructions not to answer a question, you are not doing your job as his lawyer.

Explain to the witness that you may cross-examine him when your opponent has finished his questioning. You may use this explanation to justify the advice, recommended below, that the witness not worry about volunteering testimony that he thinks helpful to your side of the case. Tell him that if any such material is overlooked, you, as the lawyer, can bring it out on cross-examination.

To make sure of omitting nothing, you might divide your preparation of the witness into two main parts. Concentrate first on advice that has to do with depositions generally, that is, the kind of advice you would give regardless of the subject-matter of the action. After you have completed this area, turn to the facts and the issues of your particular case.

This dual approach will let you prepare an approach to the first, general part of your preparation which can be used again and again. Once you have drawn up a check-list for this part of your preparatory talk, you can file it away and use it each time you prepare someone for his deposition. You will thereby enlarge the time you have available for preparation on the subject-matter of the deposition.

Some explanatory comments follow on the kind of check-list that you might draw up for the first part of your preparatory talk with a prospective deposition witness.

b. Tell the Truth

This direction, which should come first, need not be put in moral terms. Rather deal with it as legal advice. As you know, but as the witness may not, he will do far better in his testimony if he can concentrate on accuracy rather than on avoiding inconsistencies in a fabricated story. It will likewise bolster the witness's respect for and confidence in you if you convince him that you take the oath seriously and expect him to do the same.

This is a good point at which to advise the witness not to deny having spoken to you before the deposition. Tell him that your preliminary interview is entirely proper and that it is senseless not to acknowledge it.

Although truthfulness comes first in giving deposition testimony, the witness you represent should not let himself be intimidated by opposing counsel's insinuations or accusations of perjury. Tell the witness that having answered one or more questions to the best of his honest ability, he should see through such scare tactics as:

Do you realize you're testifying under oath?
        or
Is that really your sworn testimony?

Explain to the witness that he owes a duty to obey his oath. If he meets that duty, the displeasure of opposing counsel should not concern him.

c. Answer the Question

An art that few witnesses master unaided is that of giving a responsive answer to even a simple question. Accustomed to the undisciplined character of informal conversation, the typical witness views a question as a cue to start talking on a subject and to continue until someone interrupts him or his train of thought ends. You must teach him to give exactly what is called for and not a bit more.

Here is where it helps to explain the true character and purpose of the deposition. The uninitiated layman views it as a preliminary trial. He thinks it his duty to get in as much favorable evidence as he can. You must cure him of this notion. Emphasize that the proceeding is actually intended to enable the other side to gain evidence and that generally speaking, any information, helpful or not, that is not asked for, should not be given. As an Illinois court has said:

There is no burden on the party giving a discovery deposition to produce all the evidence he may have.[5]

We have noted that it will put the witness at ease to tell him that you can remedy any omissions by cross-examination.

d. Stick to Facts

Normal conversational habits cause the inexperienced witness to sprinkle his testimony with "I assume," "I suppose," "I must have,"

---

[5] *Wegener* v. *Anna*, 11 Ill. App.3d 316, 319, 296 N.E.2d 589, 591 (1973).

"I probably" and the like. You must warn him beforehand that his oath and the rules of evidence forbid him to speculate or infer. He must stick to what he knows.

This sort of problem occurs when a witness is shown a letter bearing what appears to be his signature. The witness may be a businessman who writes hundreds of letters every year, and the letter in question is several years old. If the witness has no specific recollection of the letter, but recognizes his signature, the letterhead, the dictation symbol or some other extrinsic feature, his inclination is to say, "I must have written it," "I assume I did," "I'm sure I wrote it" or something similar. You should warn him that unless he actually recalls writing the document, the only truthful answer is, "I don't remember."

That answer, incidentally, is one about which many witnesses feel guilty. A clever examining attorney can cause uneasiness by manifesting, subtly or not, a measure of suspicious incredulity after a series of his questions have, perhaps by his own design, elicited admissions of a failure of recollection. The witness's attorney should issue advance warning that an imperfect, even a poor memory should embarrass no one. He should caution the witness not to feel that he somehow owes examining counsel an answer after having failed him a number of times. He should do his best with each question as it comes.

Every lawyer has difficulty convincing witnesses to recite facts that they have observed with their senses and not to take for granted what they have learned second-hand. One good way to get this important message across is to point out that in day-to-day conversation, where such short-cuts are permissible, one is not speaking under oath. That context, you must explain, demands a higher standard of accuracy.

This rule does have what appear to be exceptions. First, the witness may properly be asked to report conversations with others. This will mean hearsay testimony. Tell the witness that in answering questions of this kind, he should make plain that he is reporting what someone told him, not what he saw or heard himself.

A second exception to the rule arises when a deposition witness is asked for his opinion. You, of course, may object to such a question. If you allow it, the witness should again be under instructions to let his answer show that it contains a conclusion, not actually observed facts.

e. Remember Who's Who

Some experienced counsel show great skill at winning the confidence, even the friendship of the person whose deposition they are taking. They accomplish this by understanding nods of the head, friendly smiles and other indications of interest and belief. Counsel's manifestations of sympathy do not show up in the transcript. The admissions that he often elicits do.

If successful, this kind of strategem can result in the witness's pouring out his heart to the sympathetic listener across the table. He may even manifest annoyance at his own attorney's interfering objections. This juxtaposition of roles can cause disaster.

A properly prepared witness will not fall into this trap. His attorney will have told him to keep constantly in mind that interrogating counsel, no matter how friendly he appears, has but one goal. He wants facts or admissions that serve his client's purposes.

A witness, particularly if inexperienced, will tend to follow a pattern as the deposition proceeds. He will be nervous to begin. He will gradually overcome this initial tension and begin to relax. What he thought would be an ordeal turns out to be not so bad after all. As the session wears on, he finds himself actually enjoying being the center of attention. Those present are hanging on his every word. He is discussing subjects or events about which he knows more than anyone else in attendance. It is only human for him to begin to feel pleased with himself.

The properly prepared witness recognizes this change in attitude as a danger sign. Counsel has told him that so long as he is nervous he is on guard. That is how he should remain until the deposition is over.

f. Play It Straight

Counsel preparing someone for a deposition should urge him to avoid humor, no matter how receptive his audience may appear. A clever quip, particularly in a facetious vein, may cause laughter when uttered. When seen, however, in the black-and-white of the transcript page, which does not show the twinkle of the eye or wry smile with which it is spoken, the remark may devastate your case.

Consider this example:

> In an action alleging the faulty manufacture of a large quantity
> of consumer goods, plaintiff's attorney was taking the deposition

of one of defendant's employees. He questioned the witness about the manufacturing process. That process culminated in an inspection at the end of an assembly line, from which the product was carried off to be packaged. Plaintiff's attorney brought out that the inspector could leave his post, while the manufacturing process continued. He then asked, with a smile:

> **Q.** In other words, the final inspector could go off somewhere for a cup of coffee and the stuff would keep coming right through, is that right?

The witness, apparently anxious to sustain the friendly atmosphere, replied with a grin and philosophical shake of the head:

> **A.** Well, you know, I've often accused him of doing just that.

Everyone laughed except defense counsel, but the humorous context did not show up in the transcript. It was necessary to prepare an affidavit of correction, explaining that the witness had been joking and that in fact if the inspector left his station, the release of his foot from a pedal would cause his section of the assembly line to stop.

It is not always so easy to repair the damage caused by a witness's pride in his sense of humor, as this illustration shows:

> A salesman sued to collect commissions from his former employer. Plaintiff's attorney was taking the deposition of defendant's sales manager. The principal issue of the case was the amount owing to plaintiff at the time of his resignation. Counsel confronted the witness with a discrepancy between two figures that had been represented to plaintiff as the amount due him. The apparent inconsistency baffled the witness, accustomed as he was to letting subordinates trouble themselves with such details. In an effort to relieve the embarrassed silence, he shook his head, grinned and said:
>
> > Well, I suppose that's what he gets for relying on our figures.

Humor, as this anecdote shows, comes in handy as a means of relaxing tension. It has no place at a deposition.

g. Keep Your Temper

A lawyer learns, like a psychologist, that the human mind cannot work efficiently when charged with emotion. The client or witness about to undergo a deposition must be reminded of this.

We have seen what it can do to let examining counsel beguile the witness into a spirit of cooperative comradeship. Permitting the opposite to happen can do just as much harm.

We all, when angry, say things that we later regret, things that we do not really mean. No one who is under oath and whose every word is being recorded can afford such outbursts. He needs, moreover, every ounce of his mental energy to study each question asked him and each answer that he gives.

The best way to keep a witness from falling prey to anger that may prove self-destructive is to explain that examining counsel may well try to provoke him. The witness whom you have put actively on guard against the loss of his own temper has a head start toward making the best of whatever confronts him at the deposition.

Counsel can help further with the problem by setting a good example. Some lawyers, conscious of the cynicism of clients over friendliness between supposedly opposing lawyers, go out of their way to pick quarrels with their adversaries whenever a client is present. The deposition provides a common forum for this immature tactic. The astute attorney needs no one to tell him why he should avoid such behavior.

h. Some Final Points

Here, in conclusion, is a list of seemingly trivial but sometimes vital points to go over with a witness about to have his deposition taken. None of them requires explanation or justification.

1. Some persons, particularly in relatively formal statements, persist in using "we" when they mean "I." Point this out before the deposition; if the error occurs anyway, correct it at once.

2. The court reporter cannot record an answer given as the shake or nod of the head rather than as a word.

3. A party witness should not give opposing counsel any information "off the record." Talk at recesses, in the corridors, etc. should be confined to the weather, sports, etc.

4. Watch out for tricks. If examining counsel picks up a piece of paper and asks, for example, if you made a written statement right after the accident, do not automatically conclude that you did and that he has the statement.

5. Make sure you finish your answer. You may have to insist on this right. If examining counsel cuts you off, before you have finished an answer, do not start your answer to his new question until you have gone back and finished the interrupted one.

Your experience at depositions will enable you to lengthen this list of pointers. Be sure that every witness you prepare for deposition testimony gets the benefit of what you have learned from earlier proceedings.

2. Specific Preparation

a. Understanding the Case

We have been speaking up to now of aspects of your general preparation of a deposition witness. We have dealt with the kind of advice that will apply as much to one case as to the next. You will also wish to prepare your witness for the specific subject-matter on which you expect him to be questioned. This phase of preparation provides a test of the patience and dedication to detail that distinguish the superior lawyer from his colleagues.

Begin by explaining what the case is all about. Set forth, in terms understandable to a layman, what you are contending. Tell him what your adversary seeks to establish. Summarize the evidence on both sides. Make sure your witness understands the case. Make sure also that he understands where he fits in. Tell him what you hope to prove through him and what use the other side wants to make of his testimony.

Giving your witness this education or indoctrination will have important benefits. It will, first of all, improve his chances of making a good witness. He will cope much better with hostile questions if he knows what is behind them. All his answers are apt to be better if he has in mind your evidentiary goals.

You should tell the witness as part of his preparation why you are spending time explaining the case to him. Stress how much better he will be able to handle questions if he understands what purpose lies behind them. Similarly, warn him to be especially on his guard when he encounters questions without understanding what his interrogator hopes to prove by them.

Here is an example:

> The general contractor sued the manufacturer of building materials for alleged structural defects in a new office building. Plaintiff's attorney was about to take the deposition of an employee of defendant who had sold the materials to a subcontractor. Before the deposition began, defense counsel, in preparing the

witness, told him that plaintiff's attorney would try to establish a principal-agent relationship between the manufacturer and the subcontractor. He explained that this would help plaintiff attribute the subcontractor's errors to defendant. He pointed out that he, defense counsel, hoped to prove that the relationship was no more than that of buyer and seller. He summarized the evidence tending to support both contentions. As a result, the employee-witness, although sticking to the truth, phrased his testimony in a way that ultimately brought victory to his side.

Taking a client or a friendly witness into your confidence has another valuable by-product. The better he understands your case, the more he is apt to take your side. Once you have instilled a spirit of partisanship in someone, you know that he will work harder in preparation and do better in his testimony. A hard-fought lawsuit, even at the deposition stage, generates a spirit of camaraderie like that which develops among fighting men in combat. You want to take legitimate advantage of this phenomenon. To do so, you must, among other things, make sure that all concerned understand your case and how you propose to win it.

This does not mean encouraging witnesses to distort facts for you. On the contrary, enlisting participants on your side requires showing them that you intend to fight hard but fair. A witness can tell the truth in more ways than one. Whatever the facts may be, they can usually be related either in a way that will benefit your case or in a way that will harm it. Both ways will be truthful. Anyone who considers himself on your side will do his best to give truthful evidence in a way that will do you the most good or the least harm.

b. The Client's Candor

Just as you owe your client an analysis of the case and an appraisal of your own and the other side's strategy, he owes you absolute candor. If he has failed you in this respect, his deposition may reveal the default to your joint sorrow.

Clients tend to conceal unfavorable facts from their lawyers. For whatever psychological or other reason, the initial interview concerning a litigated matter commonly consists of the client's trying to convince counsel that he has a just cause. Too often this includes playing down or actually concealing unfavorable evidence.

As lawyers, we have difficulty understanding why a client thinks he must "sell" his case to his own counsel. We all, however, know that he does think so.

You should have tried in your initial interview to convince your client that he must tell you all, the bitter with the sweet. If you have succeeded, fine. If you have not, or if you are not sure, the pre-deposition conference may be your last chance to avoid disastrous consequences. You must convince your client that however damaging a fact may seem to him, concealing it from you will make it worse.

Proper timing can improve the chances that this advice will take effect. If you stress the importance of candor at the close of your interview, or even after it has begun, you are implying that your client may not have been honest with you. You are putting him in a position of having to confess his concealment or distortion of facts. If, on the other hand, you give him the advice at the outset of your talk, he can follow it, even if it means changing the version he gave you some time ago, at your initial interview, with far less embarrassment.

A subtle form of flattery may help extract the truth from your client. Tell him that although you have ideas of what the opposition will try to prove, you can never be sure how correct or complete your theory is. Ask him to give you any ideas, no matter how far-fetched they may strike him, of what your adversary's version of the facts will be. This again may enable your client to save face by giving you, in the guise of the other side's contentions, facts that contradict what he himself has said.

c. Knowing the Evidence

The person whose deposition is about to be taken must, as we have seen, understand the case. It is just as important that he know the evidence thoroughly.

Your review of the facts with the prospective witness should be as comprehensive as you can make it. You will show him and discuss with him each and every document that might be used to question him. You should also go over any other papers that might refresh his recollection or help him understand any of the evidence.

The best technique to use in reviewing facts with a prospective deposition witness is to let him do as much of the talking as possible. Ask him questions about the facts you are going over instead of just telling him what they mean. As you hear him expressing ideas in his own words, you can tactfully correct any errors that he makes and suggest better ways of expressing what he has to say. You will also be more likely to maintain his attention by letting him talk instead of forcing him to listen constantly to you.

Never forget to go over with the witness all relevant material that is already of record. This includes previous depositions, affidavits, etc. You should point out that you are not trying to alter or adjust the witness's version of the facts to harmonize with what anyone else has said or might say. Emphasize that if his recollection varies from what someone else has said or written, under oath or not, his duty is to speak what he believes to be the truth. Tell him that any contradiction between his testimony and someone else's will be less apt to confuse him if he knows about it in advance.

Your preparation should include information about the personality, competence and tactics of the lawyer who will be doing the questioning. Best of all, let the witness read the transcript of a deposition that this lawyer has taken, in another case if necessary. First explain to him what counsel was trying to bring out or establish in that case. The witness can then see how his interrogator works toward an objective.

The task just suggested will be easy if you have dealt before with the practitioner in question. If you have not, and if you cannot consult anyone who has, you might substitute a review of typical devices used at depositions. We have mentioned some of these in previous pages. Your own experience will add items to the list.

Some practice questions will help the witness get ready for the deposition. Some lawyers use a tape recorder for this purpose. It enables them to play the practice testimony back and point out to the witness his strengths and weaknesses.

To conclude pre-deposition preparation, try asking your client whether he feels absolutely ready in all respects to testify. Leave enough time so that if the question is answered in the negative or with any qualification, you can go over whatever needs further work. Then, just to test yourself, ask the witness after the deposition whether he now thinks that he was adequately prepared. Whether his answer pleases you or not, it is sure to help you. It will at least show you mistakes to avoid or deficiencies to correct.

C. PREPARATION: YOU, THE LAWYER

In anticipation of the deposition of your client or a friendly witness, you have much to do in getting the deponent ready. You must do some preparation as well on your own. In fact, the best lawyers prepare as earnestly and as exhaustively for a deposition as they do for trial.

Before you speak to the witness, you should go through your file with the greatest care. Study each pleading, each set of motion papers and, above all, the transcript of each deposition that has already been taken. If the case has involved interrogatories or other proceedings of any kind, you should review all related papers. Even your correspondence file deserves meticulous study.

If your case turns on extensive documentary evidence, you will want to go over every item. Your review will not be limited to documents in the other side's possession. You must dig into everything that can conceivably equip you to prepare the witness for his examination or protect his interests at the deposition itself. In one way or another, however, you will sort out, in your mind or on paper, the evidence known to your adversary as distinguished from that in your file but not yet revealed.

Lawyers have devised various systems for the latter purpose. In cases at all complicated, some practitioners draft an outline, either as a narrative account or as a list of documents interspersed with references to depositions and other sources. They underline in red the evidence known to their opponent. Such a tool, of course, is of little use if it is not brought regularly up to date.

All these preparations will help you prepare your client or witness for his deposition. When that job is done, you have further work to do.

For one thing, you should make sure that you have a grasp of the substantive law on which your case will turn. Reread the leading cases in the field and make a careful check of the advance sheets. If you can find a recent article in the field, by all means read it.

This review of the law will stand you in good stead in at least two ways. First, it will give you insight into the point behind examining counsel's questions. You may say that in most cases your adversary will not have made a special study of the law and therefore you need not do so in order to cope with him. If, however, you set your standards of preparation according to the median of competence that you encounter, you will not make full use of your talents.

An exhaustive review of the substantive law will help you in another way. For tactical reasons to be explained later in this chapter, you will wish to make whatever objections are necessary at the deposition in terms as persuasive as possible. Knowing the substantive law will enable you to excell in this regard.

Finally, right before the deposition, you should reread the statute and rules governing pre-trial discovery. If yours is a federal case, read, preferably in an annotated version, Federal Rules 26 through 30, 32 and 37. You may or may not find something that had slipped your mind. You can be sure in either event that from this review you will gain a greater degree of competence and confidence to deal with the procedural details that will inevitably arise.

So much for preparations. The deposition is at last about to begin. We must turn our attention to what you, as counsel for the person being examined, should do while the proceedings are taking place.

D. YOUR PART IN THE DEPOSITION

1. The First Rule: Participate

Some lawyers look on attending a deposition as counsel to the party being questioned as an opportunity for a few hours' freedom from responsibility, the chance to watch someone else do the work for a change. Such professional laziness represents outright abdication. The lawyer representing the witness plays a part just as important as that of the attorney posing the questions.

One principle governs all others when it comes to representing a deponent. The rule is, *participate*. Play an active role.

How can one do this? In a number of ways. First, by raising legitimate objections. Secondly, by instructing or advising the witness when that becomes necessary, as for example in situations of this kind, where Attorney Watson represented the plaintiff, Lofski, who was being questioned by defense counsel:

> Q. When did you next have occasion to speak with Mr. Schulman?
> A. At the next meeting of our dealers' association in Toledo.
> Q. And how much time elapsed between the conversation you've just told us about and that dealers' association meeting in Toledo?
> A. Not more than a couple of weeks, I would guess.
>   MR. WATSON: I instruct the witness not to guess. Mr. Lofski, give your best recollection. If you don't remember, say just that.
> A. Well then, I don't really remember how long it was.

Many opportunities to take part in the deposition, rather than just listen to it, will present themselves. You can ask the reporter to read back a question that you did not hear or understand. If examining counsel starts to show your client a document, you can hand the latter your own copy of the paper. You can instruct the witness to read the entire paper before he answers any questions about it. You can ask for the spelling of names or unusual terms that arise in the questioning.

What, you may ask, is the point to all of these trivial interruptions and interjections? In fact, they are not trivial at all. They serve more than one purpose.

Remember that the witness is new at all this. He is bewildered and nervous. He needs your help. You cannot give it to him by suggesting answers, but you can prove that you are alert and on the job, protecting his interests. By correcting his tactical mistakes, you show him that even if he forgets some of the lessons that you taught him in your preparatory session, you are still there to remind him.

Your active part in the deposition will have another helpful effect. Examining counsel, we have seen, will be trying to build a *rapport* between himself and the witness. He wants to establish a confidential dialogue. He hopes that the witness will thereby reveal more than he would otherwise. Your interruptions will interfere with this process.

Tactics such as these must be legitimate ones. You must not raise spurious objections or interrupt for the sake of interrupting. You should not harass your adversary or seek to communicate answers to the witness. Your participation in the deposition should be active and persistent. It should also be fair.

We have mentioned objections as one of the proper ways in which the attorney for the person being questioned can make his presence known, take an active part in the deposition. We shall go next into the subject of objections more thoroughly.

2. Your Objections

As attorney for the party whose deposition is being taken, you have the right to object to questions. This applies even when you represent a witness who is not a party.[6] What rules should guide you in making the best use of this right?

We must first distinguish between different kinds of objections. We may draw a distinction in either of two ways.

First, we may categorize objections according to what effect you give them. You may object to a question and instruct the witness not

---

[6] See, e.g., *Stokes* v. *Lorain Journal Co.*, 26 Ohio Misc. 219, 266 N.E.2d 857, 861 (Ohio Com. Pls. 1970).

to answer, or you may allow him to answer notwithstanding your objection.[7]

We may also classify objections according to whether they go to the form of a particular question or to its substance. In some jurisdictions you waive an objection to the form of a question unless you make it when the question is asked.[8] All other objections are preserved until the trial even though not mentioned at the deposition.[9]

Let us take a practical look at the first distinction. When should one instruct one's client not to answer an objectionable question? When should one just make the objection and let the question be answered?

Common sense calls for directing a witness not to answer a question as rarely as possible. Each such instruction, if adhered to, will require a judge's attention, since you must assume that your adversary will move to compel answers.[10] If you prompt too many refusals to answer questions, you will appear to be obstructing the examination.

At least nine out of ten, perhaps 99 out of 100, objections will serve their purpose if you just put them on the record and raise them again when your adversary tries to read the offending question into evidence. Do not waste the potent weapon of a refusal to answer by using it where you do not need it. In general, this will mean directing a refusal to answer only when your client or his case will be materially damaged by the mere disclosure of a fact, not just by its later receipt in evidence.

Consider this example:

> Assume an action by a manufacturer's representative against the manufacturer whose products the representative once sold. Plaintiff claims breach of contract between the two parties. At the deposition of defendant's general manager, plaintiff's counsel asks for the details of defendant's arrangement with the representative whom defendant engaged to replace plaintiff. Defense counsel perceives no relevance whatever to the question. He objects. Because, however, disclosure of this arrangement will do his client no harm, he tells the witness to answer the questions anyway.

---

[7] Federal Rule 30(c), however, provides simply that "Evidence objected to shall be taken subject to the objections." This at least implies that counsel has no right to instruct his witness not to answer an objectionable question.

[8] See, e.g., Federal Rule 32(d)(3)(B) and New York Civil Practice Law and Rules, 3115(b).

[9] Federal Rule 32(d)(3)(A) and New York Civil Practice Law and Rules, Rule 3115(a).

[10] See *Heldmann* v. *Johnson*, 51 F.R.D. 3 (E.D. Wisc. 1970).

Then plaintiff's attorney begins asking about details of the manufacturing process. This, too, is irrelevant to the case. Defense counsel objects again. This time, however, he tells his client not to answer. He knows that plaintiff now represents one of defendant's competitors and that disclosure of the irrelevant information will cause harm whether or not it gets into evidence.

Questions of privilege sometimes provide the occasion for advising a witness to refuse to answer a deposition question.[11] Counsel for a witness knows that he can exclude most improper material from evidence at the trial, no matter what is revealed at a deposition. When it comes to his client's talks with him, however, he fears that failing to do everything possible to prevent such disclosure, even at the deposition, may be deemed a waiver of the privilege.

As noted above,[12] Federal Rule 30(c) implies that even objectionable questions must be answered at a deposition. Federal Rule 26(b)(1), however, limits discovery to "any matter, not privileged, which is relevant to the subject matter involved in the pending action." Federal Rule 30(d), moreover, gives the objecting party the right to demand suspension of the deposition while he moves to terminate or limit the examination on the ground that it is being conducted in bad faith or so as "unreasonably to annoy, embarrass, or oppress the deponent or party."

Does it follow that a witness, on advice of counsel, may refuse to answer a privileged or irrelevant question on the ground that it falls outside the realm of permissible discovery and thus is not subject to Rule 30(c), or on the ground that the revelation of privileged matter will unreasonably "annoy, embarrass or oppress" him? And must he risk contempt charges if his attorney believes that an order by a judge to answer the question is erroneous? In some jurisdictions, the prerogative writs may solve the dilemma of counsel who must decide whether to subject himself or his client to a charge of contempt or risk waiving a privilege by obeying a discovery order that he considers improper.[13]

The direction not to answer questions can, in any event, be used as a tool to keep a deposition within proper bounds. Take this case as an example:

---

[11] *Insurance Co. of North America* v. *Steigler*, 300 A.2d 16, 19 (Del. Super 1972), affd., 306 A.2d 742 (1973).

[12] Footnote 7.

[13] See, e.g., *Roberts* v. *Superior Court*, 9 Cal.3d 330, 107 Cal. Rptr. 309, 508 P.2d 309 (1973).

An inventor is suing an engineering firm for misappropriation of a claimed invention. At plaintiff's deposition, defendant's attorney begins going into the history of each of plaintiff's many previous inventions. Plaintiff's counsel recognizes this as a plain delaying tactic which, if pursued, will prolong the deposition indefinitely. He tells his client not to answer further questions.

We classified objections, you will remember, in yet another way, as to whether they went to the form or to the substance of a given question. Objections to the first category must often be made at the time, we pointed out, or they are waived. Those within the second category may be automatically preserved until trial even if not mentioned at the deposition.[14]

Does it follow that one should object to errors of form and remain silent in the fact of all other improper questions? It does not. Several reasons weigh in favor of voicing an objection at the deposition whenever it arises, whether or not the objection is necessary to avoid a waiver.

The distinction between objections to the form and to the substance of questions is not always clear. Most authorities would agree that a leading question raises an objection as to form.[15] Hearsay, on the other hand, has been held an objection of substance, i.e., one not waived by failure to voice it at the deposition.[16] In between those two examples lie many debatable points. How about, for example, an improperly phrased hypothetical question? [17] Or a question such as:

> **Q.** Did Mr. Gregory tell his partner about the meeting of April 9?

instead of:

> **Q.** Did you hear Mr. Gregory tell his partner about the meeting of April 9?

You have usually but a few seconds to decide whether to make an objection. You may need more time than that to resolve the subtle

---

[14] See, e.g., Federal Rule 32(d)(3)(B); Illinois Supreme Court Rule 211(c).

[15] *Elyria-Lorain Broadcasting Co.* v. *Lorain Journal Co.*, 298 F.2d 356, 360 (6 Cir. 1961).

[16] *Johnson* v. *Nationwide Ins. Co.*, 276 F.2d 574, 578–579 (4th Cir. 1960); *Grewe* v. *Mount Clemens General Hospital*, 47 Mich. App. 111, 209 N.W.2d 309 (1973); *Wynder* v. *Lonergan*, 286 N.E.2d 413, 415 (Ind. App. 1972).

[17] *Richmond Gas Corp.* v. *Reeves*, 302 N.E.2d 795, 808 (Ind. App. 1973).

distinction between "form" and "substance." A snap decision may mean the admission or exclusion of important evidence. In case of the slightest doubt, then, voice your objection.

Another factor argues for making an objection at the deposition even though it will be preserved anyway. Once on the record, your objection remains visible. You have eliminated the chance of forgetting to interpose it in the haste and tension of the courtroom. Moreover, the judge or anyone else who reads the deposition transcript before the trial, e.g., in the course of considering a motion for summary judgment, will see the objection. If you have merely made a note, mental or physical, of it, the objection might not occur to another reader of the transcript.

Finally, we saw in an earlier section that valid objections serve an ancillary purpose. They involve you in the proceeding. They prove to your client that you are alert and ready to battle for his interests. Objections present you as knowing your way around at a proceeding that probably mystifies your client. They help disrupt any *rapport* that examining counsel seeks to establish with the witness. They tend otherwise to throw him off his stride.

The best rule, then, would seem to be to raise every legitimate objection at a deposition, even though not all are necessary to preserve the point for trial. In contrast to your extremely conservative use of instructions to refuse to answer questions, be reasonably liberal about voicing your objections.

How should you interpose objections? Should you merely state the objection as tersely as possible, or should you point out the grounds on which it rests? Should you go even further and make a brief argument supporting your objection?

The middle ground appears to present the best answer to the question. If you merely say "I object," or something equally uninformative, you can, to be sure, explain your objection at the trial. Anyone, however, including a judge, who reads the transcript before trial may not take the time to analyze the question to determine the validity of your objection and may conclude in haste that you are being frivolous. This danger increases in direct proportion to the number of objections that you make.

Failure to express the grounds of your objections exposes you to the charge of depriving your adversary of opportunity to remedy his error. This may cause your objection to be deemed waived. As Federal Rule 32(d)(3)(B) provides in part:

> . . . errors of any kind which might be obviated, removed or
> cured if promptly presented, are waived unless reasonable ob-
> jection thereto is made at the taking of the deposition.

Remember, in this regard, the general principle of evidence that a
court will overrule an objection made in general terms (without a
statement of grounds, that is) if the question under attack is supportable on any theory.[18]

A brief statement of the grounds for your objection will usually
suffice. Arguing the point at length will probably get you nowhere.
It will waste your time and tend to distract your attention from the
important business at hand.

We have seen that as counsel for a party or witness you should,
in objecting to the examiner's questions, use as sparingly as possible
any right you may have to direct your client not to answer. You
should generally voice all objections whether or not they will be preserved anyway. Finally, it is wise to state the reasons for an objection
but not to embark upon a full-fledged argument of the point.

3. To Cross-Examine or Not?

As your adversary takes the deposition of your client or of a witness,
you must be making up your mind whether to cross-examine. Your
decision may not seem crucial at the time, but it will likely have
important repercussions.

The term "cross-examine," strictly speaking represents a misnomer
in this context. A lawyer does not really cross-examine his own client
after his adversary has questioned him. And since one does not make
a non-party his own witness by taking his deposition, opposing counsel
cannot accurately be said to be cross-examining such a person either.

Be that as it may, cross-examination in the context of a deposition
means questioning a party or witness after other counsel has completed the questioning for which he instigated the deposition. Statutes
and case law use this definition, and we shall do so here.[19]

We are talking about something more than just nomenclature.
Cross-examination at trial means first and foremost the right to ask
leading questions. At a deposition that right may be defined or

---

[18] WIGMORE, EVIDENCE (3d Ed. 1940) §18 and cases cited, 1972 Pocket Supplement
96–99.

[19] See, e.g., Federal Rule 30(c).

circumscribed by statute or rule. Federal Rule 43(b), for example, at least until its abrogation by the proposed Federal Rules of Evidence, as applied to depositions by Rule 30(c), entitled one to ask leading questions of an "unwilling or hostile witness" or of an opposing party or its officer, director, employee or managing agent. It follows that one might not properly lead a witness, be he party or not, outside that category. It would seem strange indeed for a court to allow counsel to ask leading questions of his own client merely because he did so at his adversary's deposition of the client.

The moral is clear. When cross-examining any person on your side at a deposition, phrase your questions as you would for direct examination. Conversely, when the lawyer on the other side is cross-examining, be sure to express your objections to any leading questions. Your failure to do so will probably waive those objections. Leading questions, we have pointed out, provide the one classification that undebatably falls within the imperfectly defined category of matters of form.

We have yet to confront the basic question whether to cross-examine or not. We can safely say, to begin, that if your opponent's questioning has created an ambiguity or misimpression that redounds to the detriment of your case, you run a risk by not clearing it up on cross-examination.

A simple example illustrates the point:

> In an action by the occupant of a car against the driver-owner for injuries sustained when a streetcar struck the automobile at an intersection, defense counsel took the deposition of a third occupant of the car. Examining counsel adduced testimony that the streetcar's lights had not been on and that the witness had not seen the streetcar until almost the moment of impact. As the record stood at the close of direct examination, this testimony ended to negate the defendant driver's alleged negligence.
>
> Plaintiff's counsel, having interviewed the witness soon after the accident, knew that although the witness had in fact not seen the streetcar until the very last second, he had heard the clanging of its bell as the automobile driven by defendant approached the intersection. He brought this out on cross-examination of the witness.

Under other circumstances, plaintiff's counsel might prefer not to bring the helpful evidence out until the trial. With the witness's principal testimony already recorded, however, and in light of the ever-present possibility that circumstances might intervene to make the witness unavailable at trial, plaintiff's attorney could hardly afford to risk the receipt in evidence of the devastating principal evidence without recording the life-saving amplification.

In deliberating, then, over the question whether to cross-examine, you will keep in mind that:

1. You can never be sure that the person whom your adversary has examined will be available for trial.

2. If for any reason he is not, his direct testimony may be admissible. Your excuse that you waived cross-examination without having foreseen the unforseeable will do you no good.

With the major reservation explained above (the virtual imperative of clearing up ambiguities or misimpressions in view of the possibility of the witness's unavailability at trial), your decision on cross-examination will almost parallel the decision whether to take a deposition at all. You will, to put it briefly, ask yourself questions such as:

1. Is there some fact or facts not brought out on direct that I wish to learn from this witness?

2. Do I wish to commit him or "pin him down" more precisely than did the direct examiner?

3. Does my case require that I preserve for the trial some fact or facts not adduced by my adversary?

As a general rule, your cross-examination will cover only those areas that satisfy one or more of these needs. Remember also the salient advantage of the deposition, namely, the safety with which one may ask questions without any idea what the answers may be. You can exploit this advantage on cross-examination at a deposition as well as on direct. For example:

Defendant is taking the deposition of a supposedly neutral witness in an action for fraud in the sale of a retail business. He establishes the witness's presence at a conversation between plaintiff and defendant. He elicits the details of that conversation as evidence tending to disprove the alleged fraud. He turns the witness over to plaintiff's attorney. The latter conceives of several possible flaws in the witness's apparently airtight story. Without any idea what answers will be forthcoming, he feels free to ask on cross-examination:

a. Whether the witness has any connection, business or personal, that might bias him in defendant's favor;

b. Whether he has an interest in the outcome of the litigation;

c. How he happened to be present at a confidential business discussion between two other persons and whether records such as his appointment book and expense account confirm his presence; and

d. Why he cooperated in defendant's taking of his deposition after having refused plaintiff's attorney even a brief, informal interview.

Asking such questions on cross-examination during the trial would present risks. An adroit, well-prepared witness could give answers that would only strengthen the impact of his direct testimony. At the deposition the risks of such "shots in the dark" on the cross-examiner's part are far fewer.

Likewise, the prolonged exploratory cross-examination, while never a commendable and rarely a worthwhile tactic, will probably be far less a disaster on deposition than at trial. Indeed, astute counsel sometimes use an apparently pointless, meandering deposition cross-examination to disguise just one or two key questions.

We can mention one more reason to cross-examine at a deposition. If your opponent is taking your client's deposition, you know that come what may, he will be able to read passages from it into evidence at the trial. If he is examining a witness, he may be or may not be able to do so. If he does so in either case, you will have the right to read passages from the transcript that he uses.[20] Your cross-examination at the deposition will not prevent his offering in evidence whatever he finds helpful in the testimony, be it impeachment of your side's version or damaging admissions. You can, if you plan ahead, promptly offset the damaging effect of the testimony he selects by making sure that the transcript contains something helpful to your case. This might cause you to cross-examine concerning a topic not otherwise worth exploring. As an example:

In an action for defamation plaintiff's attorney, to show malice, takes the deposition of a witness who observed a violent quarrel between the parties. Defense counsel realizes that if this testimony is read to the jury, some of the statements attributed to his client will carry weight. He decides, therefore, to bring out on cross-examination the witness's knowledge of the truth of some of the allegedly defamatory statements. He does this even though he

---

[20] Federal Rule 32(a)(4); *Rogers* v. *Roth*, footnote 33, Chapter II. See discussion at pages 155–156.

expects to have at the trial far more effective evidence to the same effect. He calculates that at the trial he can immediately soften the impact of otherwise possibly devastating testimony.

We shall point out that one usually need not wait until the presentation of one's own case to read into evidence parts of a deposition from which one's adversary has offered selections.

Law is an exacting and an exciting profession because exactly the same problem never arises twice. The decision whether or not to cross-examine at a deposition will in each case depend on different sets of pros and cons. The wise lawyer knows what to look for on both sides of the ledger. That knowledge increases the chances that his decision will be the right one.

4. Reviewing and Correcting the Transcript

When opposing counsel has taken the deposition of your client or of a witness on your side, your approach to the details of correction and signature will differ from that to be followed when you play the part of examining counsel. These details can still be of crucial importance.

The witness will usually have the right to make substantive corrections in his testimony as well as to rectify mistakes in transcription and typographical errors, provided, of course, he has not waived signature of the transcript.[21] He will also, at least if you represent him, probably be able to consult with you privately about corrections he wishes to make.[22]

Begin, therefore, by reading the transcript carefully. Make precise note of every discrepancy, actual or apparent inaccuracy, and reporting or typographical error. You will wish to point these out to the deponent when you submit the transcript for his study and signature. It is wise to do this by letter. Counsel for the other side may be entitled to find out whether a given correction originated with you or with the witness.[23] It may spare you embarrassment if under such circumstances you are able to produce a letter containing a passage like this:

---

[21] Federal Rule 30(e); Calif. Code of Civil Procedure §2019(e); *Rogers* v. *Roth,* footnote 33, Chapter II; *Allen & Co.* v. *Occidental Petroleum Corp.,* 49 F.R.D. 337, 340 (S.D. N.Y. 1970).

[22] *Erstad* v. *Curtis Bay Towing Co.,* 28 F.R.D. 583, 584 (D. Md. 1961).

[23] *Ibid.*

> If you do not agree with any or all of the possible corrections I have pointed out, you should disregard them. Remember that the deposition testimony represents your sworn account of the facts. It must, therefore, be accurate and truthful to the best of your knowledge and recollection.

The procedural rules governing your deposition may prescribe the manner in which corrections are to be made. They may require an explanation of any corrections.[24] The practice prevails in some jurisdictions of appending to the transcript an affidavit of the witness setting forth and explaining his corrections. Such an affidavit might begin thus:

> 1. Plaintiff's attorney in this case took my deposition in his office on May 17, 1974. I have read the transcript of my testimony, consisting of 118 numbered pages. I wish to make the corrections listed below before signing my testimony.

It is a good idea to conclude the affidavit with a passage such as:

> 18. My signature of the transcript is to be deemed subject to the foregoing corrections.

To avoid overlooking any corrections of the transcript, some attorneys bind the affidavit of corrections as a physical part of the transcript. As an added precaution, one might have typed across the top margin of each page as to which a correction has been made:

> See affidavit of correction following page 118.

In some jurisdictions, it is permissible to make corrections by simply crossing out the mistaken word or words and entering the proper version in the witness's handwriting. Care should be taken, if this is done, to draw merely a single line through the erroneous words. Other counsel may have the right to introduce in evidence the original as well as the corrected testimony.[25] Obliteration instead of just lining out will look suspicious.

---

[24] See, e.g., Federal Rule 30(e). It provides incidentally, that corrections and explanations are to be entered on the transcript "by the officer" before whom the deposition was taken. This provision is widely disregarded in at least some areas.

[25] *Usiak* v. *N.Y. Tank Barge Co.*, 299 F.2d 808, 810 (2 Cir. 1962).

E. OPPOSING OR LIMITING A DEPOSITION

1. Outright Opposition

Up to now this chapter has assumed that you have consented to another party's plans for a deposition. What of the situation where you wish to prevent the taking of your client's or someone else's deposition or at least to limit its scope or force a change in its time or place?

If you plan to oppose a deposition altogether, you have a hard job. The climate of judicial opinion today favors full disclosure before trial, almost at any cost. The judge who considers your application to vacate a notice of deposition or a subpoena will be strongly inclined to turn you down. You may argue that a deposition will inflict hardship or inconvenience. The judge may then modify the notice, but he will want to let the facts come out.

You may base your application to quash a deposition on the lack of knowledge of the person to be deposed. The judge will probably reason that the witness can just as well appear anyway and let examining counsel satisfy himself that no relevant information is available.

Generally speaking, you may not have a deposition or other discovery proceeding cancelled on the ground that questions will come up which your client has the right to refuse to answer because of a privilege. If you make such an attempt, you will probably be told to wait and assert the privilege as specific questions arise.[26]

Situations nevertheless occur in which you must do what you can to prevent a deposition from taking place. A corporate client may tell you that it cannot spare its factory manager for the undetermined length of time it will take to elicit his testimony. You cannot brush off such a plea, if made in good faith, without an earnest effort to get the contemplated witness excused. The same goes for the individual client who tells you that taking a day off for a deposition will disrupt long-standing plans and needlessly cost him and others time and expense. Keeping in mind a few suggestions will improve your chances of success in such instances.

---

[26] *In re Turner*, 309 F.2d 69, 71 (2 Cir. 1962); *Guy* v. *Abdulla*, 58 F.R.D. 1 (N.D. Ohio 1973); *Insurance Co. of North America* v. *Steigler*, 300 A.2d 16 (Del. Super., 1972), affd. 306 A.2d 742 (1973) and cases cited.

If you are to have any chance at all of getting a deposition called off by a court, you must first of all know what you are doing. Study the procedural rules that apply and the cases decided under them. If, in a federal case, you label your application "motion to quash" or something like that, the judge will see that you are merely groping for some half-forgotten common-law principle. If, on the other hand, you head your papers "Motion for Protective Order" and sub-head them "Rule 26(c), Federal Rules of Civil Procedure," you will show the judge he is dealing with someone who knows his rights. You will also be pointing out that specific, written authority exists for the granting of the relief you are requesting. This will give you the good start that you need.

Your knowledge of the procedural aspects of the situation should extend beyond nomenclature. Be aware of all the requirements and all the consequences of your application. Does, for example, the making of your motion automatically stay the proceeding you are challenging,[27] or must you take some further action to postpone the deposition until the court has made its ruling?

As another essential preliminary, you must demonstrate that you know what you have to prove to get what you want. If, as in federal practice, the rules require you to show that canceling the deposition is necessary "to protect a party or person from annoyance, embarrassment, oppression, or undue burden or expense," then mention that standard repeatedly and tailor your entire factual showing to it. Your motion itself should state its grounds in the exact words of the applicable statute or rule.

A motion, for example, in federal practice might begin:

> Plaintiff moves the Court, pursuant to Rule 26(c) of the Federal Rules of Civil Procedure, for a protective order that the deposition of John C. Heenan not be held on the grounds that such an order is necessary to protect both plaintiff and said John C. Heenan from annoyance, embarrassment, oppression and undue burden and expense in that. . . .

If your application rests on less than all of the grounds given in the rule (e.g., on undue burden and expense, but not on annoyance, embarrassment or oppression), you should limit your statement accordingly. You do not wish to let the judge think that you are merely rattling off the words of the rule mechanically.

---

[27] See, e.g., N.Y. CPLR §3103(b); Pennsylvania R.C.P., Rule 4013.

You should, as another preliminary step, brief yourself on the case law that applies to your situation. Suppose that in your jurisdiction courts have held that the type of objection you have in mind should be made at the deposition itself rather than by moving in advance against the notice of deposition. If you come to court unaware of such precedents, your adversary may easily defeat your application. If you are aware of the precedents, you at least have the chance to study them and perhaps distinguish your situation. If the case law is with you, you will, of course, wish to make use of it. Even if your application does not involve a real question of law, it may help you to call to the judge's attention at least one reported decision illustrating the granting of the same kind of relief.

You will rarely if ever get a deposition called off by a judge on technical grounds. You should avoid creating the impression that that is what you are trying to do. You must nevertheless know exactly what standards govern the effort you are making. Your function as a lawyer is to demonstrate how the facts of your situation satisfy those standards.

What sort of factual proof must you assemble in support of your motion to have a deposition set aside? In all likelihood your first job will be to draft a motion and at least one supporting affidavit. Let us consider a few of the ways in which you can make these papers more effective.

The affidavit or affidavits supporting your motion will work better if you make them both factual and first-hand. Do not insert long passages expressing outrage over the high-handed, unfair tactics of the other side. Save that for your brief or your oral argument. Use the affidavit to set out facts that make the deposition objectionable. Show those facts by the person most knowledgeable on the subject. Affidavits or statements of counsel, no matter how earnest, do not count for much in proceedings of this kind. "Information and belief" diminishes the effectiveness of any proof.

To be convincing, each of your affidavits should use the kind of language that one would expect from the person signing it. As an accommodation to those involved and to save time and insure accuracy, you will probably wish to draft the affidavits yourself, having first obtained the facts from each of your affiants. The judge will take it for granted that you composed each affidavit. You need not remind him of that fact by scattering legalisms like "whereas," "hereinabove," and "whatsoever," throughout what purports to be a layman's sworn statement.

You cannot hope to have a deposition cancelled unless you advance grounds of substance. You will rarely succeed without demonstrating two things. You must prove, first, that annulling the deposition will not deprive any party of evidence. You must show, secondly, that holding the deposition will bring about a real hardship or some other harm, not just inconvenience. You must, to repeat, make that showing through facts, not through argumentative discourses on your adversary's unreasonableness. Point out, in the most specific, concrete terms you can muster, the precise nature of the harm that will result from the taking of the deposition. If a loss of income is threatened, say how much and show why. If a deposition will endanger a party's or a witness's health, tell the court exactly what is wrong with him, and do it preferably through a doctor.[28]

If you can show that some person or class of persons other than the witness himself will suffer in the event the deposition is allowed to go forward, by all means do so. Do it, if you can, by an affidavit or proof in other form from the person or a member of the class of persons likely to be affected. This will show the court that you are not acting merely out of selfish motives. For example:

> Plaintiff's attorney is challenging the deposition of a scientist who expects to be in the jurisdiction for only a short time. He needs all that time to prepare and present an address to the convention of an international learned society. To support his motion, plaintiff's lawyer decides to obtain the affidavit of an official of the society. Such a person, counsel realizes, can say more convincingly (and perhaps with less immodesty) than the witness that the latter's absence will frustrate the entire purpose of the meeting. An affidavit of the proposed witness himself shows why his stay in the jurisdiction cannot reasonably be prolonged to accommodate the attorney who wishes to examine him. It shows also why the court's cancellation of the deposition will not deprive the court and the parties of relevant evidence.

One mistake must always be avoided. Do not say or imply that anyone's work or position is more important than the court's. Even if you are trying to set aside the deposition of a public official or the head of a giant corporation, do not say anything that could be taken as an assertion that his time is too valuable for him to bother with giving testimony. To the judge who will decide your motion,

[28] *Grotrian, Helfferich, Schulz, Th. Steinweg Nachf.* v. *Steinway & Sons,* 54 F.R.D. 280 (S.D. N.Y. 1971).

the business of his court is the most important in the world. If you even hint that any other activity has a higher priority, he may seize the opportunity to prove you wrong.

Another way to help overcome the difficulties involved in a motion to set aside a deposition is to convince the court that you really care about the outcome. To do this, include every possible supporting item in your papers. If your rules permit you to file a brief or memorandum in support of your motion, do not fail to do so. Do not waive oral argument unless you must. Convince the court that a genuine crisis is at hand and that grave injustice will be done if your application is denied. Only an all-out effort on your part can quell the judge's inevitable suspicion that you wish merely to harass the other side or that your real concern is over the possible disclosure of evidence harmful to your case.

On the subject of a brief to support your motion, we have spoken of the wisdom of pointing out precedent for the granting of the type of relief you wish the court to award you. You might also give thought to including a section on any questions of substantive law that may help you. Perhaps you can demonstrate that the only area in which your client is competent to testify has no relevance to the issues. Perhaps he can only testify to transactions outside the statute of limitations. His knowledge may be limited to matters that are unnecessary or superfluous as elements of either side's case.

In moving against a deposition, you have a basic question of strategy to decide. Are you going to present the judge with a choice other than those of simply granting or denying your motion? You might, for example, suggest that although a deposition of the person in question would be pointless and prejudicial at any time, it would do somewhat less harm if held later in the year or perhaps at a different place. Presenting such a compromise solution may diminish the chances of outright defeat, but it also reduces the likelihood of getting the result that you really want. As we have mentioned, the judge will be strongly disposed to find some way to avoid vacating the deposition altogether. If, therefore, you decide to leave open an "escape route," you should make sure to emphasize that it, too, would be unnecessary and unfair, but less so than the deposition as originally scheduled.

The lawyer who sets out to have a proposed deposition cancelled has chosen a difficult assignment. The pages above give some ideas how to reduce the steep odds against success in such an endeavor.

2. Modification or Limitation

If your goal is to modify a notice of deposition rather than vacate it outright, your chances of success are better. You should take this into account when deciding what kind of relief to go after.

Most of the suggestions advanced in our discussion of how to challenge a deposition outright apply to the problem of seeking modification or limitation. The proof supporting your motion will be factual and first-hand, not argumentative or derivative. You will show your knowledge of the legal standard you are trying to satisfy. You will point out the availability of the relief that you desire. You will show that compliance with your adversary's notice of deposition or subpoena as it stands will effect true hardship or some other substantive evil and that the modification you seek will not extinguish or conceal relevant evidence or otherwise prejudice the interests of justice. If you are trying to limit the scope of a deposition, you will avail yourself of substantive law to show that what you are trying to eliminate is not germane to any issue of the case.

We mentioned earlier the problem whether examining counsel must travel to the witness's location or the witness must come to the lawyer when the two are a distance apart.[29] This issue may provide the most frequent background for motions seeking to modify notices of deposition. As our discussion above pointed out, the judge in such a situation has broad discretion. This provides the practitioner with the opportunity to present exhaustive first-hand factual detail in support of a motion to change the place of his client's deposition.

One or two other considerations will come into play when you attempt to modify a notice of deposition. You should show the court, in detail, that you have made efforts to obtain the desired modification by informal request of the attorney who wishes to hold the deposition. Point out when and how you communicated with him and state the reasons that he gave for turning down your request. If someone other than you conducted the negotiations, include an affidavit from him or explain why you have not done so.

The law's dedication to full, uninhibited pre-trial disclosure does not always suit our interests. The astute lawyer, therefore, knows how to oppose the various types of discovery as well as how to make the most of their use.

---

[29] See discussion at pages 79–80.

Chapter IV

PUTTING THE DEPOSITION TO USE

A. INDISPENSABLE PREPARATION

1. The All-Important Summary

Often a deposition serves its own purpose. It provides the taker with information. Sometimes, however, counsel wishes to make further use of the testimony he has obtained. That further use will most commonly arise at trial.

You cannot make use of a deposition for any purpose unless you know its contents. You must also, especially if you expect to use the deposition at trial, be able to find what you want quickly and surely. Preparing a careful summary of the transcript provides the best means to both ends. Drudgery though this may be, it will help make your deposition worth the time and effort you put into preparing for and taking it.

Summarizing a deposition makes sure that you know and understand what is in the transcript. You cannot condense what you do not grasp. Once you comprehend a fact or an idea well enough to put it in other words, it will likely remain with you. Often, this makes it a good idea to do your summarizing a relatively short time before trial. On the other hand, a deposition summary has so many other useful purposes not directly related to the trial (e.g., in preparing for other depositions) that the circumstances of a given case may dictate its preparation much earlier.

Some experienced lawyers, even when they have competent junior counsel available, prefer to do their own summarizing. They thereby make certain not only that the job is done exactly as they wish, but also that counsel in charge of the case has all of the deposition testimony firmly in mind.

If you work carefully and skillfully, you should have no trouble boiling ten pages of testimony down to one page of summary. You will use your own system of abbreviations and symbols. The more drastically you shorten individual names and words without sacrificing comprehensibility, the more compact a tool you will have.

A properly summarized deposition can serve several valuable functions. It provides a handy way for others to read the substance of the testimony. The question-and-answer form of a deposition poses difficulties for the lay reader. The witness himself should read his deposition testimony in its entirety, word-for-word, before he testifies at trial. Others, however, who must familiarize themselves with the testimony, such as fellow witnesses, co-counsel, etc., can use your summary to advantage.

2. The Index and Other Tools

A careful summary will have put you well on the way to converting a deposition transcript into a useful courtroom weapon. You can take other steps toward the same end.

An index can enhance the utility of even a summarized deposition. Like the summary, it will help you find what you want in a hurry. It need not be elaborate. The roughest outline, with page numbers indicated opposite each entry, will often prove a precious time-saver. Here is a sample index to a deposition in a personal-injury action:

Preliminary	1–3
Before accident	4–5
Collision	6
Aftermath and ambulance	7–9
Hospital	10–14
Other medical	15–21
Workmen's comp. proceeding	22–23
Statement to adjuster	24
Accident report	25–26

As an additional way to improve the usefulness of a deposition you expect to need at trial, consider a proper marking of the transcript. To avoid embarrassing pauses while you leaf through the transcript and select passages for use, you should indicate either by underlining or marginal symbols:

    1. The specific questions and answers that you wish to read into evidence for your client;

    2. Those questions and answers that you wish to read in the event your adversary omits them in his reading into the record;

    3. Questions and answers likely to be helpful in impeachment; and

    4. Questions to which you wish to object and answers which you wish to move to strike in the event of their use by opposing counsel.

Some lawyers use different colored pencils for these four kinds of markings. This technique can save you still more precious trial time and show the judge and other counsel that you are an efficient, well-prepared practitioner. All of these time-saving devices likewise deprive the hostile witness of time to think his way out of any tight spots into which your cross-examination has put him.

Finally, it can sometimes help your use of a deposition to make copies of pages containing testimony that you expect to use. If, for example, you arrange your proposed exhibits and other trial materials according to subject-matter or witness, you can make sure that you will have needed deposition testimony where you want it when you want it.

B. USE AT THE TRIAL

1. Something to Keep in Mind

As this discussion proceeds, we shall see both the strengths and weaknesses of deposition testimony used at trial. We might first cite a consideration that you may neglect to take into account in the turmoil that reigns when you are making trial decisions. Remember that using the deposition at trial may improve your chances, if you prevail in the action, of recovering the expense of the deposition as taxable costs.[1]

2. Choosing a Use

a. The Choices

We know that filing the deposition does not make it a part of the record for purposes of the trial. Before the trier of the facts may

---

[1] *Sperry Rand Corp.* v. *A-T-O, Inc.,* 16 F.R. Serv.2d 1360, 1366 (E.D. Va. 1973). See also authorities cited at footnotes 9 and 10, Chapter I.

consider anything in a deposition, counsel must take action to get it into evidence.[2]

In most jurisdictions, a deposition may be used on trial in one or both of two different ways. Counsel may use the transcript to impeach a witness, just as he may avail himself of any prior inconsistent statement. He may, on the other hand, use the deposition testimony as his own evidence. The latter right usually exists only as to the testimony of an adverse party or that of a non-party witness who is not available to testify at the trial.[3] A party's deposition testimony, when offered by an opposing party, is admissible in federal practice and in some states even though the party attends the trial.[4] Receiving in evidence the deposition of a non-party witness who is available to testify in person may, in contrast, constitute reversible error.[5]

The use of deposition testimony for impeachment, and its use as evidence each has its own advantages. Each in turn also presents its own problems.

You will often be able to use a deposition in either or both of the two ways. If the party or witness says something at trial that contradicts his deposition, should you impeach him on cross-examination, or should you read his earlier testimony into the record as evidence itself? Would it be best to do both? No sensible lawyer will form an absolute rule to govern such situations. He will consider, each time the question comes up, the pros and cons of all courses of action open to him.

b. The Advantage of Impeachment

Impeaching a witness by his deposition testimony has an obvious advantage. It immediately counteracts the witness's trial testimony before the trier of the facts has had time to assimilate it. If a witness in a commercial action sits on the stand and says under oath that

---

[2] *Salsman* v. *Witt*, 466 F.2d 76 (10 Cir. 1972).

[3] In federal practice, sub-paragraph (1) of Rule 32(a) permits the use of a deposition for impeachment. Sub-paragraphs (2) and (3) govern its use as evidence. See also, e.g., *Zimmerman* v. *Safeway Stores, Inc.*, 133 App. D.C. 342, 345, 410 F.2d 1041, 1044 (1969); and *Karrigan* v. *Nazareth Convent & Academy, Inc.*, 212 Kans. 44, 48, 510 P.2d 190, 194 (1973).

[4] *Pursche* v. *Atlas Scraper & Engineering Co.*, 300 F.2d 467, 488 (9 Cir. 1961), *cert. denied*, 371 U.S. 911, 83 S.Ct. 251, 9 L.Ed.2d 170 (1962), reh. denied, 371 U.S. 959, 83 S.Ct. 499, 9 L.Ed.2d 507 (1963); *Van Ornum* v. *Otter Tail Power Co.*, 210 N.W.2d 188, 195 (N.D. 1973); *Sun Cab Co.* v. *Carter*, 14 Md. App. 395, 402, 287 A.2d 73, 77 (1972). If the adverse party is a corporation or association, the witness whose testimony is sought to be used must usually be an officer or "managing agent." Federal Rule 30(b)(6); *Phelps* v. *Magnavox Co.*, 497 S.W.2d 898 (Tenn. App. 1972).

[5] *Childress* v. *Jubelt*, 45 Mich. App. 181, 205 N.W.2d 889 (1973).

he took a full hour to discuss with your client the delivery clause of a sales contract, and if on the same morning you show that he swore a year earlier that he did not spend more than fifteen minutes negotiating the entire contract, the judge or jury may discount his entire testimony. If you wait until a day or two later, when it is your turn to present evidence, and merely read the contradictory testimony into the record, you may appear to be picking flaws in an account which has solidified into a plausible rendition of the facts.

Confronting a witness on the spot with a documented contradiction to his testimony generally has a more dramatic and potent effect than disproving it, however categorically, later. The contradiction can produce visible confusion, sometimes outright consternation, on the witness's part. In a Maryland case, for example:

> Plaintiff, suing for damages arising out of a collision at an intersection, testified that at the time of the accident it was dark and he had his lights on. Defense counsel read passages from plaintiff's deposition claiming that it was not dark and his lights were not on. Asked on the stand which was true, plaintiff answered in part:
>
> > Well, let me say it was—when that question was asked I had my lights on, but as I have stated when I get extremely upset the reason for that answer that he just read is when I get extremely upset I tighten the muscles on each side, also in back of my head. I become so upset that I become frightened and then the people and the faces in front of me they become unreal and all I see is a bunch of noise and all and they are doing is yelling and all and all I want to do is run and when you ask me and I cannot give you—I lose all line of thought and I am not responsible for what comes out of me . . .[6]

Not every use of deposition testimony for impeachment produces such vivid results. In most cases, however, if properly used, it can be effective.

c. Negative Factors

Impeachment does have a corresponding disadvantage. It gives the witness an opportunity to explain the inconsistency or repair the damage. He may claim to have misunderstood the question asked

---

[6] *Sun Cab Co.* v. *Carter,* footnote 4, 14 Md. App. at page 401, 287 A.2d at page 76.

him at trial, or he may introduce some new element that purports to reconcile the apparently conflicting versions. For example:

> The witness to an automobile accident emphasized at the trial plaintiff's display of anguish and suffering after the accident. Defense counsel confronted him with his deposition testimony stating that plaintiff said nothing and made no sound upon the witness's arrival on the scene. The witness explained that he interpreted the deposition question as applying to the immediate aftermath of the collision, when plaintiff appeared numb with shock, but that it was after he had begun to come to his senses that he began complaining of severe pain. He added that it was the latter period that he was testifying to on the trial.

Such a reconciliation may sound far-fetched. Triers of the facts, we all know, sometimes go far to believe evidence supporting the side on which their sympathies lie.

Using a deposition for impeachment does not normally entitle the other side to offer portions of the transcript in evidence. This, we shall see, is a consequence of using the deposition as evidence. Impeachment by deposition, however, even when it is not the witness's own, may have that consequence if, for example, the court finds you to have created a misleading effect by your selections from the transcript or to have "opened the door" to areas dealt with elsewhere in the deposition testimony.[7] This possibility justifies a review of your rules of evidence before using for impeachment purposes material from a deposition transcript that contains things likely to help your adversary.

d. Pros and Cons of the Deposition as Evidence

We are reviewing the factors to weigh in the decision whether to use your deposition for impeachment purposes or as evidence for your client. We come now to the factors that come into play in evaluating the latter use.

Say that defense counsel in the hypothetical automobile-accident case above decides not to confront the witness with his contradictory deposition testimony. He waits instead for his turn to present evidence and reads the witness's earlier version into the record as part of his

---

[7] See opinion of DeBruler, J., in *Indianapolis Newspapers, Inc.* v. *Fields,* 254 Ind. 219, 266, 259 N.E.2d 651, 673 (1970), *cert. denied,* 400 U.S. 930, 91 S.Ct. 187, 27 L.E.2d 190 (1970).

own case.[8] This stratagem might leave him free to stress the contradiction to the court or jury in his summation without having to worry about an explanation by the witness on redirect. True, the witness might be put on the stand to explain the inconsistency as part of plaintiff's case in rebuttal. But if the deposition testimony is offered inconspicuously, the contradiction may not register on plaintiff's counsel's mind. Indeed, artful counsel may, particularly in a complex case, "bury" a contradictory item deep in a long mass of tedious testimony. He hopes in doing so that the helpful matter will go unnoticed until he can exploit it on summation. Then again plaintiff's attorney, even if he does perceive the contradiction, may conclude that rebuttal will only underline the discrepancy between the two versions. The rebuttal explanation, in any event, will be no more effective, and probably much less effective than an explanation on redirect, immediately following the impeachment.

Using the deposition as evidence rather than as impeachment, when you have a choice between the two, has one plain disadvantage. Putting deposition testimony into evidence gives other parties broad rights to read into the record other passages from the same transcript. This they may not be able to do if you use the deposition merely for impeachment purposes.

Take a look, for example, at the applicable federal provision, Rule 32(a)(4). It says:

> If only part of a deposition is offered in evidence by a party,
> an adverse party may require him to introduce any other part
> which ought in fairness to be considered with the part introduced,
> and any party may introduce any other parts.

Note that this applies when someone offers part of a deposition "in evidence." We shall discuss the breadth of the rights which this and corresponding provisions in state practice confer. Remember for now that when you can choose between using a deposition to impeach on the one hand and offering it in evidence on the other, you may be doing your opponent a favor by picking the latter alternative.

If you do not use a deposition as evidence, it may not be admissible at all. You will usually be the only one who can initiate the use of an adverse party's deposition as evidence. If you refrain from putting the deposition into evidence, no one else can. True, the party may

---

[8] Counsel would have this option if the witness were a party to the action. If not, and if the witness were present at the trial, the deposition could normally be used only for impeachment.

take the stand and testify to the same effect, but that will be subject to cross-examination. Deposition testimony stands as read.

Conversely, if the deposition testimony is of a kind that your adversary will be able to read into evidence anyway, you will not be opening it up by making the first use of it. The testimony, for example, might be that of a witness unavailable for trial. You know that no matter what you do, your adversary will use those parts that help him. You reason that you might as well gain what advantage you can from the passages that favor your side.

e. Governing Criteria

We see that counsel having deposition testimony in conflict with what has been said from the witness stand must weigh several factors before deciding whether to use the contradictory testimony as impeachment or as part of his own case. He might pose the problem by asking himself these questions:

1. How acute is the contradiction between the trial and the deposition testimony? Is it so fundamental that any explanation from the stand is bound to appear contrived, or is it a relatively superficial inconsistency that the witness can easily reconcile in credible terms?

2. What sort of witness am I dealing with? Will he be flustered or paralyzed by disclosure of the contradiction, or will it merely challenge his ingenuity?

3. How is the trier of the facts reacting to this witness? Will impeachment appear to be a petty effort to catch up an honest but possibly confused witness and thereby generate sympathy, or is it more apt to provide the court or jury with the grounds they are looking for to reject inherently suspicious testimony?

4. How important is the contradiction to the substantive merits of the case? Will its disclosure "blow the case open," or will it merely point up a flaw in the evidence against my client? (If the former, the contradiction might better be presented by way of impeachment; if the latter, as opposing evidence.)

f. Helping a Speedy Decision

As happens so often in litigation, counsel may have a few short minutes to make the decision, upon which so much can hang, whether to use the deposition as impeachment or as evidence. He can offset the handicap of this time pressure by properly preparing the deposition before trial. The paragraphs below will show why this is so.

This chapter has stressed the absolute necessity of summarizing every deposition. It has pointed out other ways, notably the preparation of an index and marking the transcript, to make the deposition a useful tool. Having a deposition in the shape to do the most good in the courtroom requires at least one further step.

A careful rereading of the transcript provides help that nothing else can match. You should do this as close as possible to the time that you expect the witness to take the stand. Ideally your review should take place the night before or during the luncheon recess preceding the witness's appearance. If the deposition is too long to permit this step, at least read your summary again. Whichever you do, you will find that the tension of trial will cause items to stick in your memory and be available when you need them.

We have talked about deciding whether to use the deposition of an opposing party or his witness for impeachment or as your own evidence. We have also discussed preparing the transcript for the one use or the other. We shall turn next to some techniques of making the most of first one use and then the other.

3. Effective Impeachment

a. Going About It

Impeaching a witness by means of his own deposition differs only slightly from impeachment by any other prior inconsistent statement. Depending on the rules of evidence in your jurisdiction, your procedure in impeachment via deposition testimony will consist of the usual steps, namely:

> 1. Setting the stage by establishing and emphasizing the trial testimony that you propose to discredit;
> 2. Asking the witness if he did not appear on a stated date at a specified place and testify under oath by deposition; and
> 3. Asking him if he recalls the question and answer (which of course you must read) that establish the contradiction.

You may think it best to drop the matter there and let the judge or jurors draw their own conclusions. Your tactics in this situation will depend in part on the overall strategy of your cross-examination. Do not, however, overlook some of the special advantages that deposition testimony provides as a weapon of impeachment.

b. Capitalizing on Special Advantages

Following the three steps outlined above treats deposition testimony like any other prior inconsistent statement. The deposition may permit counsel to make much more of a contradiction.

First, in the case of a deposition the prior inconsistent testimony was given under oath. Judges, of course, know this, but in a jury case counsel should emphasize it. He can do so either by asking the witness (probably the better way) or by means of a permissible explanation to the jury. Sometimes a cross-examiner can underscore an inconsistency of the kind we are discussing by a question like this:

> Now, Mr. Osborne, will you tell the jury why, eighteen months ago, which was less than a year after your visit to defendant's office in Pittsburgh, you were willing to swear that you conferred with Mr. McLaughlin on that occasion, and yet today, when you were again under oath, you deny that any such conference took place.

Another question of the same type consists of:

> Mr. Bernstein, what happened in the six months since your deposition was taken to cause you to change your sworn testimony?

One never asks a question like this if the witness has a chance of coming up with a plausible explanation of the conflict in his two versions. In such a case the sworn character of the deposition testimony can be effectively emphasized to the jury in summation.

The deposition's second advantage over much prior inconsistent material used for impeachment lies in the witness's right to read and correct the transcript before signing it. This makes it difficult for the witness under impeachment to contend that he misunderstood the question or that the reporter misquoted him. A previous chapter has suggested that examining counsel can make this feature of deposition testimony even more secure by pointing out to the witness during the deposition that he will have the right to read his testimony and make substantive as well as typographical corrections.

An adverse party's deposition has a third advantage over most impeachment material. The party made his statements while represented by counsel and presumably after preparation. Again, astute counsel will bring out during the deposition the fact (although of course not the content) of an adverse party's prior consultation with counsel. If the witness then gratuitously blurts out that his lawyer told him to tell the truth, so much the better for impeachment purposes. Questioning of this sort can turn such unsolicited matter to the cross-examiner's advantage:

> **Q.** Mr. Reilly, one thing I don't understand. You testified at your deposition that you had spoken beforehand with your lawyer, Mr. Raggio, didn't you?
> **A.** Yes, I did.
> **Q.** And you added, did you not, that Mr. Raggio had instructed you to tell the truth?
> **A.** Yes.
> **Q.** I suppose that before you appeared on the stand today you again conferred with Mr. Raggio?
> **A.** That's right.
> **Q.** Did he again tell you to tell the truth?
> **A.** Yes, he did.
> **Q.** Well then tell me, Mr. Reilly, why at your deposition did you follow Mr. Raggio's advice to tell the truth by swearing that you remembered talking to a policeman right after the accident, and yet today you followed the same advice by swearing that you remember nothing whatsoever until you regained consciousness in the ambulance?

Once more, counsel must decide whether to give the witness this chance to explain away the contradiction or to save it for emphasis on summation. Whichever course he pursues, the fact of the witness's representation by counsel at the deposition will add weight to the prior inconsistent statement and thereby serve to inflict greater damage on the trial testimony under attack.

4. Using the Deposition as Evidence

a. The View from the Bench

As lawyers, we base the decision whether or not to use a deposition at trial on what it will do for the case. We must also remember and take into account what the judge is apt to think from his objective point of view. The court will not like to see counsel who has two or more ways of proving a point using a method that the law considers the less desirable.

This applies to depositions. Courts have always preferred flesh-and-blood testimony. As Circuit Judge Learned Hand said decades ago:

> The deposition has always been, and still is, treated as a substitute, a second-best, not to be used when the original is at hand.[9]

Therefore, when you can choose between using deposition testimony and putting the same witness on the stand, the possibility of having to explain your resort to the former should figure in your decision.

b. Security: An Advantage to Exploit

The lawyer who decides to use part or all of a deposition as evidence should appreciate its several important advantages over "live" testimony. But it also has weaknesses. Awareness of both the assets and liabilities of this kind of proof, together with forethought, will help emphasize the former and compensate for the latter.

Deposition testimony's one undebatable strength lies in its certainty. No lawyer knows the exact words that a "live" witness, no matter how well prepared, will utter in answer to a given question. He always knows precisely what a deposition will bring out.

This asset of deposition testimony leads some lawyers to prefer it to "live" testimony when seeking to establish a crucial point. Choosing between proof already down in black and white on the one hand and the unpredictable utterances of a friendly but weak (or an unfriendly and tricky) witness on the other, particularly if one's case hinges on the point, can be difficult. The difficulty is aggravated by the principal liability of deposition testimony, next to be discussed.

c. Dullness; a Handicap to Surmount

Reading "canned" questions and answers from a transcript means presenting evidence in the most lifeless way conceivable. Deposition testimony, regardless of how carefully the jury is instructed beforehand, lacks the reality of words emanating from a witness's mouth. It strikes any listener as cut and dried, lacking the suspense and spon-

---

[9] *Napier* v. *Bossard*, 102 F.2d 467, 469 (2d Cir. 1939). For more recent expressions of the same view, see *Salsman* v. *Witt*, footnote 2, 466 F.2d at page 79; *Akers* v. *Norfolk & W. Ry.*, 378 F.2d 78, 79 (4th Cir. 1967); *Bacon* v. *John Hancock Mutual Life Ins. Co.*, 317 F. Supp. 302, 304 (D. Md. 1970).

taneity of face-to-face confrontation between lawyer and witness. Above all, deposition testimony is tedious. After having read more than half a dozen questions and answers, counsel is lucky if half his audience is still paying attention.

How offset this handicap? Many experienced lawyers try to follow these three rules in using deposition testimony as evidence:

>   1. Do not read testimony into the record as monologue. Have an assistant or someone else read the answers in response to your reading of the questions. Most judges will permit this and will let the person reading the answers sit on the witness stand.
>   2. Offer deposition testimony in small doses. In most cases, you will be using a deposition to establish a number of relatively brief evidentiary points. If you can avoid it, do not string them all together, but intersperse them between "live" witnesses.
>   3. Where possible, read disposition testimony into the record in the morning, when minds are fresher.

d. Availability; Another Strength to Take Advantage of

This brings us to the second great advantage of deposition testimony, its flexibility. The deposition transcript is always available. Unforeseen emergencies, traffic jams and the weather cannot keep it from the courtroom. Few things exasperate a trial judge more than a lull in the proceedings. If a witness fails to show up on time, or if you finish a part of your proof ahead of schedule, you can, if prepared, fill in the vacant time with the reading of deposition testimony.

Occasionally a shrewd practitioner can exploit this flexibility of deposition testimony to the detriment of his adversary. Say that your opponent, in the midst of presenting his case, finds himself confronted with an unexpected lull. If he is hapless (or inept) enough to have to ask for an adjournment because of it, you can sometimes offer to make use of the otherwise vacant time by reading in deposition testimony out of turn. Your adversary, especially if flustered by whatever turn of events disrupted his schedule, may see consenting to your proposal as a means of redeeming himself in the judge's eyes.

We have seen how the relatively few, simple rules on the use of depositions at trial have broad strategic and tactical ramifications. Nothing that has been pointed out is likely by itself to win or lose a case. Each point mentioned has value in the trial lawyer's determination of how best to use this important category of evidence.

5. The Rights of Opposing Counsel

a. Your Deposition Evidence

In most jurisdictions, reading part of a deposition into evidence entitles opposing counsel to read in other parts.[10] Never use passages from a deposition as evidence without taking this right into account. Conversely, counsel whose opponent reads deposition testimony into evidence should remain alert to the rights that this confers on him.

We are assuming now that you have made the decision to read into evidence portions of a deposition from which your opponent is likely also to read passages. We discussed above the factors that should go into that decision.

You can often do at least one thing to diminish the effectiveness of passages of deposition testimony that you expect opposing counsel to use. You can steal his thunder by reading those passages into evidence yourself. They may sound less harmful coming from you than from your opponent. Take this example:

> A wholesaler sues a retailer for the price of goods sold and delivered. The retailer's principal defense is breach of warranty. Plaintiff's counsel took the deposition of one of defendant's branch managers to authenticate business records showing that only a small fraction of the products delivered, principally kitchen utensils, proved defective or damaged. On cross-examination at the deposition defense counsel led the witness into pages of detailed description of the defects in the few damaged shipments. At trial, plaintiff's counsel fears that if he read the brief statistical evidence that he elicited, his adversary will repeat his performance and divert the jury's attention with a list of details whose very number will tend to suggest that a great volume of defects is involved. To guard against this possibility, plaintiff's lawyer decides to begin by reading some of the material elicited by defense counsel. Having catalogued the troubles that the retailer encountered, he puts them in proper perspective by then showing that they made up only an insignificant fraction of the business involved.

---

10 See, e.g., Federal Rule 32(a)(4), quoted at pp. 147–149. See also *Rogers v. Roth*, footnote 33, Chapter II; Illinois Supreme Court Rule 212(c); Pennsylvania Rules of Civil Procedure, Rule 4020(a)(4).

The effect created by plaintiff's tactic redounds to his client's benefit, especially in contrast to what would have resulted had he let defense counsel undermine the statistical evidence with the more attention-getting proof of the defects.

b. Your Adversary's Deposition Evidence

If your opponent reads deposition testimony into evidence, you want to make the most of the rights and opportunities made available to you. Study the applicable statute or rule,[11] and consider what it lets you do.

To begin, you may not have to wait until your part of the case to read from the deposition. Your opponent, by reading from a deposition, may give you a chance to get or regain the attention of the trier of the facts out of your normal turn.[12]

This can prove a special advantage if your practice does not require that what you read from the deposition have anything to do with what your adversary has read. Interrupting your opponent's case by reading material helpful to your side, particularly if it has nothing to do with what he has been trying to prove, may throw him off his stride. It may divert the court's or jury's attention to matters that you would prefer them to concentrate on.

As attorney for a party against whom deposition testimony is being read, you wish to press all proper objections. The deposition has the advantage of letting you know beforehand what questions and answers are available for use against you. On important points, therefore, your objections should be well thought out and supported. A short memorandum of law can sometimes help eliminate potentially decisive proof against your client. So, we have pointed out, can marking the transcript in a way that will prevent your overlooking any valid objections.

We have covered the steps involved in preparing for and taking the deposition of an adverse party or an unfriendly or neutral witness. We have reviewed what should be done when another party takes your client's deposition. We have gone over the use of the deposition at trial, from the standpoint both of the party making such use and that of his adversary. We are ready to take up other discovery devices that can serve as alternatives or supplements to the deposition.

---

[11] The provision applicable to federal practice appears at pp. 147–149.

[12] *Westinghouse Electric Corp.* v. *Wray Equipment Corp.*, 286 F.2d 491, 493–494 (1st Cir. 1961), *cert. denied*, 366 U.S. 929, 81 S. Ct. 1650, 6 L.E.2d 388 (1961).

Chapter V

HELP FROM DISCOVERY
AND INSPECTION

A. INTRODUCTION

We shall now consider "discovery" in the sense of obtaining specific, concrete material either from other parties to the litigation or from outsiders. Our topic is defined for purposes of federal practice as:

> . . . production of documents or things or permission to enter upon land or other property, for inspection and other purposes.[1]

In this chapter we shall be talking for the most part about cases involving documentary evidence. That is what discovery and inspection usually involves. One must not forget, however, that this procedure likewise applies to physical objects. Indeed, the outcome of a lawsuit may often turn on one party's ability or inability to examine properly a crucial piece of physical evidence. Remember, therefore, as we proceed that observations concerning "papers" or "documents" often apply with equal validity to other objects.

We have mentioned previously [2] and will discuss briefly again [3] that in some jurisdictions, including the federal courts, the party seeking discovery and inspection merely serves a notice on his adversary. In others, a court order is required. The two procedures have both distinctions and common problems.

---

[1] Federal Rule 26(a). Rule 34(a) sets forth a more comprehensive definition.
[2] See footnotes 78–80, Chapter I.
[3] See page 162.

B. KNOW THE LIMITATIONS OF DISCOVERY AND INSPECTION

1. Are You Getting Everything?

Today discovery and inspection plays a role in all but the simplest litigation. The importance of that role requires no explanation. Because, however, discovery and inspection offers a short-cut that may tempt the lawyer to forego more expensive or time-consuming remedies such as depositions and interrogatories, the dangers of relying exclusively on discovery and inspection merit consideration.

First of all, if you examine a file or group of files, scanty or voluminous, without preliminary or subsequent interrogatories or deposition testimony, you can never be sure that you are getting everything. You may trust your adversary implicitly. He may tell you in good faith that he believes that the files he turns over for your review are complete. Do you, however, trust his client? You probably do not even know him. If he is caught in litigation that may cost or gain him a fortune, are you sure that he, unrestrained by legal ethics, can resist the temptation to "edit" or "purify" his files by removing damaging material before he turns the files over to his own lawyer? Questioning a party under oath, orally or in writing, may not eliminate all possibility of chicanery, but it certainly reduces it. Interrogatories or deposition questions about the completeness of a file, moreover, will foreclose the surprise appearance of a documentary exhibit that turns up only at trial, perhaps with an explanation of having been missing as the result of "misfiling."

This is not to say that gaps in the material you get on discovery and inspection necessarily result from deliberate deception. Carelessness and natural human oversight are your real enemies. Particularly if your adversary is a large organization, a municipality or business corporation, for example, you must realize that its facade of efficiency may conceal chaos, at least in record-keeping. Here are some of the questions that discovery and inspection, if unaccompanied by other discovery devices, leaves unanswered:

1. A file turned over for your discovery and inspection may be complete, but how, if you have no one knowledgeable to question, can you be sure that it is the only file?

2. In the organization opposing you does each division, de-

partment or bureau have its own filing system, or is there a central repository?

3. Who turned the papers over to opposing counsel, and how much does he know about the filing system?

4. If the subject-matter of your action requires the opposing party to extract material from a number of different files, was the searching job given to someone of reasonable competence, and what were that person's instructions?

Without the answers to these and many other questions, you can never know that the material turned over to you is all there is to be found. You cannot get those answers without a deposition or interrogatories.

Even if your notice or motion for discovery and inspection produces all relevant papers, it does not follow that you have elicited all pertinent information. The most routine communication can be deceptively incomplete. The writer of a letter, for any one of many reasons, puts down what he has to record or what he wants to record, not necessarily everything there is to record. A business meeting, for example, may consume several hours. A participant may "summarize" it or "confirm" its outcome in a one-page letter or memorandum. That one page, to be sure, contains what its author believes to constitute the essence of the meeting. It may not contain what is important to your case. That you can obtain only by questioning.

2. Are You Getting the Truth?

Even assuming that you get everything, discovery and inspection unsupported by other procedures has limitations. Just one of them may cripple the prosecution or defense of your action.

Take as an example a "typical" business letter. It bears a date, the names of its addressee, author, and perhaps those of the recipients of carbon copies. It probably contains a caption and either appears on a letterhead or shows a written return address. Human nature, which includes in all of us a measure of laziness, tempts one to take this convenient source of information at face value. Experience teaches every competent lawyer to show skepticism.

Always remember one fact: letters are not written under oath. An infinite variety of motives may cause a correspondent to distort or color facts, exaggerate, omit material or tell an outright lie. It is easy to reason that in day-to-day life letters composed "in the regular course of business," customarily set forth accurate versions of their subject-matter. Such a philosophy overlooks the tensions, conflicts and emotions that dominate even routine life. Persons at every level of business and government protect themselves and their jobs by emphasizing their successes and glossing over their failures. Many a subordinate tries, consciously or otherwise, to make his position, or his influence over his superiors, seem more important than appearances indicate. Any of the resulting distortions can give you, as a lawyer, a false version of crucial facts unless you dig beneath the surface of the written word. You can do that only by deposition or interrogatories.

Take an example from a non-legal field. Every employer considering a job applicant knows better than to take a glowing letter of recommendation at face value. When one fires an employee, be it for incompetence or even dishonesty, one often feels obliged to atone in part for the dismissal by giving the dismissed person a good start toward a new job. The equivalent of *caveat emptor* therefore warns others to take a former employer's recommendation with a grain of salt. That is only one ready example of the kind of inaccuracy to be found in routine correspondence.

Remember, too, that a letter can be written *ante litem motam* and still be egregiously self-serving. Take this case:

> A publisher was being sued by an author for copyright infringement. A letter from defendant's files, written by one of its executives to the complaining author's agent over a year before suit was filed, began:
>
> > As I said in our conversation yesterday, a reading of [*Name of the allegedly infringing work*] convinced me, as I am sure it would any fair reader, that the occasional, incidental similarities between it and Mr. [Plaintiff]'s manuscript could only have resulted from pure coincidence.
>
> Had plaintiff's attorney relied on discovery and inspection alone, he would have considered this document worthless to his case. By taking the executive's deposition and through other research, he learned that in the conversation of the previous day the writer of the letter had conceded that similarities between the two works were "astonishing" and made him "suspicious." He had written the letter upon realizing what harm his oral admissions might do.

Limiting your pre-trial preparation means taking the written word at face value. Think carefully before you risk handicapping your case by so broad an assumption.

3. What Else Are You Missing?

It hardly seems necessary to labor the point by citing other aspects in which a letter, memorandum, or other communication can mislead counsel or deprive him of valuable evidence if he relies on discovery and inspection alone. Let us simply list some of the other shortcomings:

> 1.   As an outsider, the lawyer may not be able to "read between the lines" of a written instrument. Skillful questioning, especially by deposition, should bring out implications, insinuations, or innuendos of significance to the litigation.
>
> 2.   The writing you examine may have been only a draft, never sent. Even if final, it may have been corrected by a later telephone or personal conversation. Questioning its author or someone else connected with the letter will remove these doubts.
>
> 3.   One cannot always tell by the bare perusal of a letter or memorandum whether its ostensible author actually signed or even dictated it. The stenographer's symbol is not necessarily conclusive in this respect.
>
> 4.   A deposition or interrogatories enables you to make sure you have seen all copies of a document. This can be crucial, in view of the frequent appearance of marginal notations, corrections and the like on many business and official papers.

We may close our discussion by mentioning two practical considerations that can make discovery and inspection by itself an inadequate proceeding. We have mentioned that most letters, memoranda and other written instruments are not written under oath. This deprives them of one of the key values of both depositions and interrogatories, that of committing a party or witness to particular facts. As an example:

> A letter written by defendant's executive vice-president showed him to have been "out-of-town" on the day he claimed to have participated in a conversation with plaintiff. When plaintiff's attorney came upon this letter in the course of discovery and inspec-

tion, he thought that he had won his case. On trial, however, the vice-president testified that the "out-of-town" statement was untrue. He had it to cover his embarrassment over not having written an overdue letter sooner. His expense records confirmed his trial testimony.

Had the deposition of this witness been taken, one of two things would have happened. Either he would have committed himself to the "out-of-town" story, making his later explanation impossible, or plaintiff's counsel would have learned of the explanation much earlier, avoiding the unpleasant surprise at trial.

Finally, your discovery of a written communication does not necessarily make it admissible in evidence. You may need answers to interrogatories or deposition testimony to authenticate the papers turned over to you.

Our discussion of discovery and inspection has begun on a negative note. We have warned that this remedy cannot do the job alone. No one, however, will deny that in many cases discovery and inspection is essential to proper preparation. We shall consider next how to use this remedy so as to make the most of it.

C. SKIP THE FORMALITIES?

In some jurisdictions, the party wishing to conduct discovery and inspection must make a motion and obtain a court order.[4] In others, he merely serves a notice.[5] Under the motion procedure, the party seeking discovery must usually make an affirmative showing of "good cause." [6] The notice procedure sometimes requires the other party, if he objects, to take the initiative of enlisting judicial intervention.[7] Thus the notice procedure makes the discovering party's job easier. Either procedure, however, creates special opportunities and special problems.

---

[4] See, e.g., Connecticut Practice Book, §168; 12 Okl. Stats. Ann. §548; and the other sources cited at footnote 80, Chapter I.

[5] Federal practice now belongs in this category. Rule 34, as amended, begins, "Any party may serve on any other party a request. . . ."

[6] The Oklahoma statute cited in footnote 4 so provides.

[7] N.Y. CPLR Rules 3120 and 3122 provide an example of this approach, although failure to comply with Rule 3122's requirement of moving for a protective order against an objectionable notice may be waived. *Handel* v. *Handel*, 26 N.Y.2d 853, 258 N.E.2d 94 (1970). In federal practice, the objecting party need merely serve a response setting forth his objections. The discovering party must then apply under Rule 37(a) for an order compelling discovery. Federal Rule 34(b).

As discovery has broadened and become a matter of course in most actions, lawyers have adopted short-cuts in availing themselves of discovery devices. Orders and notices have often given way to stipulations and even to casual, oral understandings. One must commend the saving in time that informality often generates, as one must praise the professional spirit that enables practitioners to dispense with procedural technicalities. However, one should still not forget that formalities have their purpose. Their wholesale elimination can cause trouble.

In discovery and inspection, some lawyers make a "cards on the table" approach. Counsel proposes to his adversary that each side voluntarily turn over to the other all relevant files for inspection and copying. No notice or order is used. The respective perusals of files take place at the convenience of the attorneys involved.

Such a technique has advantages. The proposer displays a position of strength by proving that he has nothing to hide. Indeed, he may make the offer in the hope that his opponent will turn it down so that he, at an opportune moment, may mention to the court that he had tried to obviate procedural wrangling by proposing "all-out" discovery by both sides. The principal advantage to the informal approach, however, lies in its saving in time. As we shall see, drafting a proper notice or motion and order for discovery takes careful thought and likely a number of hours. The temptation to finesse this exacting work must always be strong. Caution is nevertheless in order.

Informality's greatest drawback in discovery and inspection is its uncertainty. The casual exchange of files leaves the participating lawyer with no sure way of knowing whether his opposite number has in fact shown him, as promised, "everything." True, documents can be withheld in formal discovery and inspection proceedings too, but disobedience of an order of notice for discovery can lead to specific sanctions. A judge might well frown on an attorney's breach of the understanding underlying an informal exchange of files, but it is difficult to conceive what action he could take to punish it.

If, for example, your adversary were to offer in evidence at trial a document that you had never seen before but which came within the terms of an order or notice for discovery, you would have a potent objection to its admissibility.[8] If, on the other hand, the failure to show you the paper beforehand violated nothing more than a vaguely phrased understanding, your position would be weaker.

---

[8] See discussion at pages 271–274.

Factors other than willful concealment may create this kind of problem. An informal exchange of files will necessarily be limited to "relevant" material. Your adversary may quite legitimately take, with respect to his client's files, a narrower view of "relevancy" than you would take in drafting an order of notice. Much the same goes for questions of privilege, which can sometimes be as close as those of relevance. Total informality leaves each side free to exclude unilaterally any material that it deems outside the bounds of proper discovery.

A sensible compromise between utter informality and procedural perfectionism is not difficult to devise. A voluntary exchange of material, confirmed by a written stipulation, might provide some of the benefits of both systems. Such a stipulation might set forth terms more general than those required of a notice or motion for discovery and yet protect both parties from the other's omissions or exclusions. Instead of a stipulation, a letter might do the job just as well.

As yet another technique, the lawyer engaging in an informal inspection might follow it by writing his adversary a letter listing the items shown to him and asking whether they compromise all of the writings within certain stated categories. The express or implied representation might not supply grounds for court sanctions, but it would provide the author of the letter with a persuasive objection to the receipt in evidence of any writing not disclosed.

Much depends on the person with whom one is dealing in a given situation. Lawyers who have opposed each other for years, who know that they will encounter each other many more times, may have developed a degree of mutual trust that makes the totally informal approach the only sound one for them. If, on the other hand, you do not know your adversary well, erring on the side of caution may turn out to be the sensible course.

Finally, do not let informality in discovery and inspection lead you to neglect the details that will be necesary to get the discovered material into evidence. Your adversary may be candid and open-handed when it comes to turning over papers from his client's files. He may turn into a stickler for every technicality when you try to get the material into evidence. You may think that you have won your case when in an informal exchange of files you receive a memorandum that proves a vital point. Let us assume, however, that the memorandum, although found in the files of the other party, was written by an outsider. You still have a job to do authenticating the document, laying a proper foundation for its admission and fitting it within an exception to the hearsay rule. Do not count on opposing counsel's providing the same cooperation in those regards that he showed in placing the paper in your hands. He may have hoped that by generating an atmosphere of liberality and informality he would lull you into overlooking details as important in their way as the evidence.

In all probability, then, you will wish to draw up some sort of papers to implement your discovery and inspection. This task will present you with problems as well as with opportunities.

D. LAYING THE GROUNDWORK

1. Working for Specificity

Successful discovery and inspection calls for more than just drafting the necessary notice or motion. The practitioner makes advance preparations for the proceeding, just as he does for other phases of the litigation.

The draftsman looking ahead to the framing of papers for discovery and inspection will have two goals relevant here. First, he wishes his discovery notice or motion to be so precise and specific that neither his adversary nor the court can fail to perceive what he has in mind. We shall discuss below why this specificity is desirable and in some situations imperative. Counsel seeks also to have his designation of the material to be discovered broad enough so that no possible evidence will escape him. That goal requires no explanation or justification.

You cannot attain either goal without painstaking preparation. Conducting a deposition or submitting interrogatories can often be the best way to lay the groundwork for discovery and inspection. Such proceedings enable counsel to find out what physical evidence exists so that he may later notice or move for its discovery and inspection.

You should, therefore, include in the deposition or interrogatories that precede discovery and inspection [9] questions calling for lists and reasonably detailed descriptions of all items likely to be of value or interest to you. As a federal judge suggested, in denying a plaintiff's application for discovery of documents from defendants' files:

---

[9] See discussion at pages 55–57.

It would, perhaps, be helpful for plaintiffs to pursue preliminary examination in order to ascertain the existence of documents and to narrow down the identification of categories.[10]

For reasons that we shall consider in our chapter on interrogatories, that device will often be better suited than a deposition to the purpose of ascertaining and identifying items to be procured by discovery and inspection. We shall also consider there some suggestions on how to frame interrogatories that will give you an enumeration specific enough to enable you to draft proper discovery papers. Let us point out now that an interrogatory calling for a detailed list of, say, correspondence between the parties may serve its purpose even if not answered properly. If your adversary later objects to your notice or motion for discovery as lacking in specificity, you will have a telling argument if you can say that had he answered your interrogatories in the detail requested, your papers in turn would have been more specific.

Preliminary interrogation about items likely to be subject to discovery and inspection may confer additional benefits. Once an opposing party or a witness has described or listed a document, he is committed to its existence. True, an unscrupulous person can falsify his answers to interrogatories or to deposition questions just as readily as he can deliberately overlook papers in complying with a notice or motion for discovery and inspection. However, the individual compiling a list of papers for answers to interrogatories is less apt to "screen" them than he would be if he were collecting the same items for actual delivery to the other side. What is more, your adversary can hardly be heard to claim that a document is privileged or otherwise immune to discovery if all you are trying to do is learn of its existence.[11]

Depositions and interrogatories do not provide the only means of preparing for effective discovery and inspection. Your regular factual research should be directed in part toward making it possible to draw up discovery papers satisfying the two goals we have set forth. You may have, for example, a case involving the writing of letters between your client and the opposing party. Your review of your own client's files will then give you many clues as to what the other side's records will reveal.

Papers (accident reports, for example) filed with a federal or state

---

[10] Edelstein, D.J., in *Automatic Laundry Service, Inc.* v. *Telecoin Corp.*, 16 F.R.D. 26 (S.D. N.Y. 1954).

[11] *Balistrieri* v. *O'Farrell*, 57 F.R.D. 567, 569 (E.D. Wisc. 1972).

agency or with some other non-party such as an insurance carrier may help you in knowing what to ask for in discovery and inspection and how to ask for it. Items that you obtain from such files may have underlying documentation of possible relevance to your action.

2. Working for Comprehensiveness

We have seen that interrogatories, depositions and other efforts preceding discovery and inspection will help the discovering party frame a more precise, specific notice or motion. We shall now consider how such preliminary proceedings will further the objective of completeness.

Pre-trial discovery today is so broad in most jurisdictions that a party may usually get whatever he wants, so long as it has some plausible connection to the case, just by asking for it. The catch here is that to ask for something, one must first know of its existence. A broad, general "catch-all" clause in your notice or motion for discovery may be disallowed by the court.[12] Preliminary questioning can foster the comprehensiveness of discovery and inspection by making possible an exhaustive designation of the material sought.

Assume the most difficult circumstances conceivable. Say that you are suing or being sued by a vast, complicated organization such as a major industrial corporation or a large municipality. Say that your entire case depends on what you can obtain from your adversary's files, but you have not the slightest idea what form the crucial material will take or where in the labyrinth it will be found. Where do you begin?

Circumstances alter cases, but a good first step in the kind of situation just postulated is to study the structure of the organization. Find out what departments and divisions go into its make-up. Ask questions designed to find out what segments of the corporation or other body had responsibility for the subject or subjects of your interest.

Take this hypothetical case as an example:

An experienced attorney sues a toy manufacturer for injuries that a child sustained when the front wheel of a novelly designed

[12] In *Jones Packing Co.* v. *Caldwell*, 510 P.2d 683 (Okl. 1973), the court held improper a clause in an order for discovery and inspection requiring production of "All corporate books, corporate records and minutes of the directors, officers and stockholders of" a corporate party.

scooter collapsed while coasting rapidly downhill. Counsel has alleged, among other things, negligent design and manufacture. He wishes to prove that the manufacturer knew or should have known of the wheel's susceptibility to collapse upon sustaining shocks at relatively high speeds. He has reason to believe that defendant conducted tests in this area. He knows, on the other hand, that if it did not, that may provide him with another basis for charging negligence.

Counsel in this situation might simply serve a notice or motion for discovery and inspection calling for all reports of tests concerning the product in suit. If he does, he will never know whether his categorical designation has missed some crucial item because of imperfect wording, the oversight of the subordinate charged with searching the manufacturer's files or some other cause beyond his knowledge.

Plaintiff's attorney, however, pursues a more sophisticated course. He begins his discovery by serving an exhaustive set of interrogatories. They elicit the section of defendant's design department in which the device originated and the name of each employee who worked on it. They ascertain the branch office through which defendant test-marketed the product and the custodian of that branch's records of customer complaints and returns. The interrogatories also reveal to plaintiff's attorney the name and location of the product manager who made the decision to market the toy nationally. Such information, together with other similar items, enables counsel to specify what he can be reasonably certain constitutes all of the written material concerning the item for whose failure he is suing.

In dealing with a large organization, one's preparation often gains from learning as much as possible about the persons involved, as well as about the organizational structure. If you are going to seek discovery of written instruments, most or all of the papers you are interested in will be external letters and internal memoranda. You are more likely to conduct a successful discovery of communications if you know who is communicating.

Knowing the names of persons in the organization you are opposing and the job that each of them has will tell you a lot about the documents you are after. It may be significant, for example, in an action for breach of a sales contract that the authors of certain correspondence directed copies to the credit department. Corporate correspondence, however, is often addressed to individuals without departmental designation. Thus, unless one knows that a certain individual worked in the credit department, one will not realize that items directed to that individual were intended for that department.

Evidence of all kinds, be it oral or written, means much more to him who understands the organizational background out of which it arose. A letter from Mr. Johnson to Mr. Perrins says, on its face, certain things. Does it not say much more when one learns whether Perrins is Johnson's superior, or *vice versa,* and just what functions each of the two performs in the organization?

If your adversary is an individual or a smaller organization, your problems in preparing for discovery and inspection may be less complex. That does not make them less important. Even if you are examining plaintiff in a personal-injury action, you will wish to devote some time to questioning about the availability of records. Take this example:

> In an automobile collision case where a husband and wife were plaintiffs, defendant's attorney was taking the wife's deposition. He asked if she had written about the accident to any of her relatives. She said that she thought perhaps she had. Counsel elicited the names of several persons, including her mother and a sister, to whom she thought she might have sent such letters. Plaintiff herself had not kept copies of her letters, but the case involved enough to justify defense counsel's tracking down the originals. After an investigator had established the existence of one of the letters, making it impossible for the item to "disappear," counsel subpoenaed the recipient, the mother of the plaintiff's wife, to a deposition. He required her to produce the letter that her daughter had written about the accident. It said in part:
>
>> Actually, I think the whole thing was George's fault for trying to beat the other car to the turn, but the lawyer says that if we let him sue, maybe the insurance company will settle.

Discovery and inspection, we have seen, calls for forethought and planning. We have also seen that such preparation will help you specify what you want and make your demands or requests broad enough to include everything likely to help you.

E. DRAFTING PAPERS THAT DO THE JOB

1. Be Specific

Prudence, we have seen, requires that the parties set down in writing the scope of discovery and inspection. What techniques will make this written specification, be it an informal letter or a formal notice or motion, a more effective instrument in obtaining your desired objective?

Specificity should be your first goal as draftsman. The statute, rules or case law governing your practice may make it a necessity. Generally speaking, courts condemn the catch-all or blunderbuss type of discovery clause.[13] They differ on whether the discovering party must enumerate the individual items he wishes produced or merely set forth categories.[14] Allowing the latter practice may facilitate harassment. Insisting on the former may make it impossible to unearth crucial evidence. The Supreme Court of Illinois voiced a sensible guiding principle in *Monier* v. *Chamberlain*, 35 Ill.2d 351, 356, 221 N.E.2d 410, 414–415 (1966), to wit:

> Basically, the question is whether each document or individual item must be particularly described and identified by the moving party, or whether it is sufficient to request production of such material by groups or categories of similar items. The specificity requirement of the rule is there for two purposes: to provide a reasonable description of the items requested, enabling those from whom discovery is sought to know what is being demanded of them, and to aid the trial court in ascertaining whether the requested material is exempted or privileged from discovery. What will suffice as a reasonable description may well vary from case to case depending on the circumstances of each, but we believe that designation by category ordinarily is sufficient for these purposes . . . No instance in the portions of the order now being reviewed is pointed out to us, nor do we believe there are any, in which the description of the requested material is so inade-

---

[13] In *Balistrieri* v. *O'Farrell*, footnote 11, 57 F.R.D. at page 569, as just one example, Judge Myron Gordon disallowed as excessively broad defendant's request to produce plaintiff's "file pertaining to the defendants." See also the passage quoted at p. 166, from *Automatic Laundry Service, Inc.* v. *Telecoin Corp.*, footnote 10.

[14] See Annotation at 8 A.L.R.2d 1134, 1148 et seq. for authorities on both sides of this issue.

quate as to leave defendant with any real uncertainty regarding what is and what is not included. Requiring minute particularization of each document sought might well unduly lengthen the discovery process by enabling the parties to engage in dilatory practices.

Even though applicable law may allow you to set forth generalized categories, specificity will still usually better serve your purpose. We have discussed in a previous section how proper preparation can help you achieve specificity in your discovery papers. Situations will nevertheless arise where specificity is impossible. You may simply not be able to enumerate or list the documents or exhibits in your adversary's possession and yet you may know for a certainty that he has relevant material. You must, in other words, call for what you want by categories rather than by individual items. How best to deal with that situation provides our next topic.

2. Stick to the Plainly Relevant

What of the lawyer who, for good reasons or bad, finds himself unable to list specific items in his notice or motion for discovery and inspection? A few principles kept in mind should alleviate the disadvantages inherent in his position.

First of all, counsel seeking discovery of categories of documents rather than individual items runs the risk of appearing, in his desire not to omit or overlook anything, to demand too much. As Judge Edelstein said in denying plaintiff's discovery in an antitrust case:

> A number of the plaintiffs' requests, taken alone, might be granted, and the germ of relevancy is discernable generally, but it is all but smothered in elaboration. They have for the most part thrown discretion to the winds. Even where basic relevancy is obvious, they have asked for everything conceivable and added a catch-all to include the inconceivable.[15]

One's inability to name specific items in a notice or motion for discovery, however, need not subject one to such an objection. One may, as one preventive measure, draft categories that show on their face a relationship to one or more issues in the case. In a con-

---

[15] *Automatic Laundry Service, Inc.* v. *Telecoin Corp.*, footnote 10.

tract action, for example, plaintiff's attorney demanded production by defendant of, among other things:

> C. The original and all carbon or other copies of each letter, memorandum or other written communication between defendant's sales and credit departments written between January 1 and May 12, 1974, concerning any alleged breach by plaintiff or the termination or possible termination of the contract attached as Exhibit A to the amended complaint.

Defense counsel would be hard put to allege irrelevance of any paper falling within the scope of such a demand. He would have equal difficulty contending that the demand was ambiguous or unreasonably broad.

The cited example illustrates another point. Plaintiff's attorney called for all copies of each responsive document. He knew that one copy might have pertinent marginal notations added by its recipient and missing from other copies. For example:

> In an action involving alleged constructive fraud, defendant's assistant sales manager had written plaintiff a letter contending that the absence of a written guaranty of the products involved actually benefited rather than prejudiced plaintiff. A copy of the letter had gone to the author's superior, who had scrawled across the top, "Some snow job!" Had plaintiff's counsel not asked for all copies of this communication, he would never have obtained this valuable piece of evidence.

We have considered a discovery demand whose relevance speaks for itself. Let us consider one whose impropriety is obvious:

> A sales agent sued a cigar manufacturer for breach of a contract whereby the agent was to receive a commission on sales of two specified brands of cigars within a stated area. Plaintiffs moved for production of defendant's records of sales of all its brands within the territory in question during the period of the contract. The court had little difficulty perceiving the excessive breadth of plaintiff's demand. It denied his motion.[16]

---

[16] *Blatt* v. *Casa Blanca Cigar Co.*, 51 F.R.D. 312 (M.D. Pa. 1970).

3. Be Unmistakably Understandable

We can pursue our inquiry into how the lawyer unable to name specific documents or other items of evidence may nevertheless prepare a motion or notice of discovery invulnerable to objection. If the category you set forth is one which your adversary can readily comprehend, and if its boundaries are equally perceptible to the court, your motion or request will have a better chance of success. In a federal action, for example, under the anti-fraud provisions of the securities laws, plaintiffs called for disclosure of:

> all documents submitted to the Securities and Exchange Commission (SEC) in connection with the SEC's investigation of the financial collapse of the Penn Central Company.

Distinguishing earlier cases in which discovery by broad categories had been denied, the court directed compliance. It pointed out that:

> . . . it is clear that defendant can identify the documents demanded by plaintiffs. Defendant has already produced these documents to the SEC.[17]

4. Avoid Loopholes and Ambiguities

You want your request or demand for discovery to be comprehensible. To do its job, it should be escape-proof as well. The less the description of a category leaves to the other side's interpretation or construction, the more it will do for you.

To illustrate the point just made, here is an example of what not to do:

> In an action by an employer against a former employee for alleged misappropriation of a secret process, defendant moved for discovery and inspection of, among other things:
>> F. All letters and other communications to persons not in plaintiff's employ forwarding drawings, sketches, diagrams,

---

[17] *Mallinckrodt Chemical Works* v. *Goldman, Sachs & Co.*, 16 F.R. Serv.2d 1517 (S.D. N.Y. 1973).

illustrations or blueprints of the alleged secret process referred to in the complaint herein.

Defendant was contending that the so-called secret process was in fact a matter of public knowledge and that plaintiff itself had helped make it so. Defense counsel did his cause no good by the wording of his demand. The parties differed in their definitions of the allegedly secret process. Defendant's language left plaintiff's counsel free to apply his client's far narrower definition, thereby eliminating much of the material that application of defendant's broad definition would have produced. If defense counsel had spelled out just what he meant by "the alleged secret process," he would have closed this escape hatch.

Take another negative sample:

> Plaintiff in a personal injury action had been injured when the driver of defendant's bus put the vehicle into motion before closing its doors. A company rule forbade this practice. Plaintiff's counsel wished to know how many infractions of the rule the driver involved in his client's accident had committed. His notice for discovery and inspection, therefore, called for:
>
> A. All records of disciplinary action taken by defendant against its employee Carl Pruess as the result of infractions of defendant's Rule 12(e).
>
> As it happened, defendant's practice was to admonish its employees for their first two violations of certain of its rules and then punish them by suspension for the third. A record was kept of both admonitions and suspensions. Two admonitions, including one for the accident in suit, had been given the employee Pruess. Defense counsel, however, took it upon himself to construe "disciplinary action" as meaning actual punishment. He produced nothing in response to plaintiff's demand.

5. Use Definitions

Defining your terms provides one way to deprive your adversary of the opportunity to construe clauses of your notice or motion so as to exclude items he would rather not disclose. If defense counsel in the trade-secret case hypothesized above had set down as an introductory paragraph a definition of the term "trade secret," the results of his discovery would have been more helpful. This technique works especially well when one must make repeated use of a term whose meaning is subject to possible question. Say, for example, that defense counsel in our hypothetical case above wished to define the trade secret as:

> the process, as used in defendant's Bergstown plant, whereby reactivated particles of negatively charged oxides of various metals may be transferred from one surface to another without resort to an augmented source of power.

Now if defendant proposed to set forth only one item concerning the "trade secret," it would serve his purpose just as well to set forth this extensive definition in the text of his demand. If, on the other hand, he had ten or a dozen such items, it would save considerable space, and make his notice or motion far more comprehensible to the court, if, before the enumeration of his demands, he were to state:

> As used in this notice [motion], the term "Bergstown process" shall mean the process whereby reactivated particles of negatively charged. . . .

A party seeking discovery and inspection naturally wishes to avoid creating the impression of harassing or oppressing the other side. If he wishes to call for a given number of categories, the fewer the words he uses to describe those categories the better are his chances of being able successfully to defend himself against a charge of misusing the discovery process.

Definitions of even routine terms can be used to shorten a notice or motion for discovery.

> In a commercial case, plaintiff's attorney wished to demand all papers from defendant's files concerning seven different transactions. He realized, as we all do, that communications intended only for the eyes of those within the organization sometimes reveal far more than letters addressed to outsiders. To make sure of getting everything, he began each of seven paragraphs with:

>> All letters, memoranda, notes, books of account, diary entries, drafts or other written or printed matter of any kind, and all dictating tapes and other recordings as well as secretaries' and stenographers' shorthand notes and all written

communications and written records of oral communications
on the subject of . . .

Had counsel instead used one simple word such as "document,"
instead of this long passage, having defined the word by way of
introduction, his demands would have been far more compact and
thus far less susceptible to objection.

We have discussed a few techniques of drafting an effective notice
or motion for discovery and inspection. We have omitted such obvious
elements as comprehensiveness. It should go without saying that before
drafting papers for discovery and inspection, the thorough practitioner
will review his file and at least consider a demand for material on
every aspect of the case.

Such a practitioner will remember that discovery and inspection,
according to most rules of practice, governs not only material in a
party's possession but also that which is under his control. Federal
Rule 34, for example, allows discovery and inspection of items "in
the possession, custody or control of the party upon whom the request
is served . . ." [18]

Income-tax returns provide a good example of documents that
can sometimes be obtained if this principle is kept in mind. Even
though the opposing party may not have kept a copy of his return,
that paper is under his control in the sense that he may obtain a copy
of it from the authorities. This often subjects tax returns to discovery
and inspection.[19]

F. YOUR OPPONENT'S MOTION OR NOTICE

1. Whether to Oppose

We have been talking about discovery and inspection from the
point of view of the party seeking it. We turn next to some of the
problems that confront the lawyer against whose client a notice or
motion is directed. He must decide first whether to fight the proceeding
or give his adversary what he has demanded. A number of considerations will enter into this decision.

---

[18] See *Buckley* v. *Vidal*, 50 F.R.D. 271, 274 (S.D. N.Y. 1970). See also the
passage quoted at page 106, from In re *Harris*, 27 F. Supp. 480, 481 (S.D. N.Y.
1939).

[19] *Reeves* v. *Pennsylvania R. Co.*, 80 F. Supp. 107 (D. Del. 1948); *Martin* v.
Masini, 90 Ill. App.2d 348, 232 N.E.2d 770 (1967).

The type of procedure being followed for discovery and inspection will be important. We have seen that in some jurisdictions the party wishing discovery and inspection must move for it and make a showing, usually of "good cause" for the discovery. In others, including the federal courts, the discovery party merely serves a notice listing the items he wishes to inspect and copy. In some of the latter jurisdictions, it is the opposing party who must, if he objects, take the initiative of going to court. Other things being equal, a lawyer confronted with an attempt at discovery and inspection will be less inclined to oppose it in the latter type of jurisdiction than in the former.

In most instances more practical considerations will be paramount. The attorney served with discovery papers will ask himself, first of all, whether the harm that turning over a given item is apt to do his case justifies the effort that will be required to oppose discovery. Resisting discovery just to make things difficult for the other side is a luxury few of us can afford.

Secondly, counsel will review his adversary's papers to determine their technical sufficiency. If in his jurisdiction specificity is required, has the standard been met? Are the items called for truly relevant, or do they stand out as obvious efforts at harassment or embarrassment? If the discovering party must proceed by motion, do his papers meet all of the standards set forth in the applicable statute or rule and in the governing case law?

A corollary to the review just mentioned will involve consideration of the weight of the objection counsel is able to interpose. Competent counsel will not in this regard waste time on far-fetched, captious or hypertechnical points. He will know, for example, that if his client lacks actual possession of a document or other object, the court will not likely excuse its production if the client has ready access to it.

Another element that the astute attorney will weigh is somewhat more subtle. He knows that opposing discovery may gain him insights into his adversary's case that he would otherwise be deprived of. If, for example, he challenges clauses in a discovery notice as irrelevant, his adversary will have to defend their relevance. The showing that he makes for this purpose may reveal crucial aspects of the theory of his case.

The point just made justifies considering an example:

> Two ex-partners were involved in litigation arising out of the break-up of their firm. Plaintiff sought an accounting. His lawyer served a notice of discovery that included all records of

the earnings of certain real property held not by the firm but by defendant personally. Defendant moved to strike this part of the notice as calling for material not relevant to the issues. To oppose defendant's motion, plaintiff filed an affidavit spelling out an alleged understanding between the two former partners that certain firm assets would, for tax and other purposes, be held individually in defendant's name. This alleged agreement came as a surprise to defendant's attorney. Had he not moved to oppose plaintiff's discovery, he might not have found out about it until the trial.

Finally, the lawyer upon whom a motion or notice for discovery has been served will consider the effect that opposing his adversary's discovery will have on his own case. We know that many judges, rightly or wrongly, apply the rules of discovery in the light of the adage, "What's sauce for the goose is sauce for the gander." In other words, a party may have serious difficulty obtaining from the other side what he himself has resisted disclosing. Take this example:

A relatively small corporation brought suit against a conglomerate for alleged breach of a merger agreement. Defendant served a notice for discovery and inspection of, among other things, plaintiff's corporate minute books. Plaintiff's attorney knew that yielding to this part of defendant's notice would reveal facts not necessarily prejudicial to his client's position in the litigation at hand but embarrassing to its management for other reasons. Counsel nevertheless decided not to resist discovery of the minute books. He reasoned that if he suceeded in having that item stricken from defendant's notice, he would have a hard time convincing the court that he, plaintiff's attorney, should have discovery of defendant's minute books. He had no hope of making out a case without the latter. Conversely, he knew that his adversary, having demanded production of plaintiff's minute books, would find himself in a difficult position resisting disclosure of corresponding documents from his own client's files.

Strictly speaking, defendant's minute books in this case might be plainly relevant and plaintiff's plainly not. Yet a busy judge may well not bother with such fine distinctions but prefer to apply the rougher standard of what appears to be equal treatment.

These are some of the considerations that will govern the decision whether or not to oppose discovery. We shall turn next to how one goes about interposing such opposition.

2. How to Oppose

a. Facts

Assume now that you have decided to oppose your adversary's effort at discovery and inspection. What do you do, and where do you begin?

A word of caution should come first. Depending on the rules of your jurisdiction, failure to take prompt action against a discovery notice or motion to which you object may result in a waiver of your objections.[20]

Having decided to resist part or all of a notice or motion for discovery, you must first collect your ammunition. This will differ from case to case, but the material to be used in opposition will usually fall into two basic categories, fact and argument.

In most jurisdictions, you will call facts to the court's attention by way of an affidavit. You will advance arguments by way of a brief or memorandum. Losing sight of the basic distinction between these two documents may dilute the strength of your opposition.

Let us take a typical situation. You wish to oppose certain parts of your opponent's notice for discovery first as unreasonably burdensome and secondly as not relevant to the subject-matter of the action. The first ground will probably rest on essentially factual elements, such as the amount of effort that will be required to search out the documents or other material that has been called for. The second ground will rest most likely on argumentative points such as the remoteness of the demanded material to any of the issues raised by the pleadings and rules of substantive law showing the material to lack significance as proof.

Your factual showing will gain in strength if you follow in your opposing affidavit the two simple principles that we mentioned in discussing how to oppose a deposition. First, select an affiant who speaks with first-hand knowledge. Secondly, stick to concrete, specific facts.

An affidavit of this kind will be more effective if made by a client or a client's employee than if signed by counsel. Courts generally do not care if your opponents' move is going to cause you great effort; they care if it threatens to impose an undue burden on your client.

---

[20] *Coffey* v. *Ohrbachs, Inc.*, 22 A.D.2d 317, 254 N.Y.S.2d 596 (1964).

They know that what you say about the latter subject must be second-hand.

Take a case in which you are opposing discovery and inspection, in a products-failure class action, of all letters from consumers complaining of the performance of the product in suit. You wish to point out that producing such items will require searching hundreds of file cabinets in a dozen or more sales branches. You will stand a better chance of success if the person making the affidavit can prove personal knowledge of the problem. He should, of course, set forth that proof, as well as the facts that go to the substance of your objections.

This brings us to the second of the principles that govern a proper affidavit of the kind we are discussing. Whoever makes the opposing affidavit should restrict himself to facts as such. He should leave arguments to counsel in his brief. If burdensomeness is the gravamen of your opposition, the affidavit should prove the burdensomeness, not complain about it. Set forth the estimated number of man-hours that would be required for a file search, if that is involved, and show same features of the task that would make it especially onerous. For example:

> In a medical malpractice case, plaintiff demanded production of all emergency-room records prepared during the 30 days preceding her intestate's admission to defendant hospital. The latter's director of medical records asserted in an opposing affidavit:
>
> > It is a physical impossibility to produce these records as they are not kept by month, but rather filed under the patient's number.
> >
> > It should also be pointed out that there are approximately 5,000 persons that come into our Emergency Room per month and upon whom records are made.

The Court of Appeals of Kentucky held that the order created "a hardship . . . not commensurate with the results that may be attained." It drastically modified the order.[21]

The same principles apply to opposition based on any factual ground. If you object to the expense of transporting voluminous files to the noticed place of discovery and inspection, set forth what that expense will be. Demonstrate, if you can, that it will save money to have examining counsel come to your client's location.[22]

---

[21] *Louisville General Hospital* v. *Hellmann*, 500 S.W.2d 790 (Ky. 1973).

[22] *La Chemise Lacoste* v. *General Mills, Inc.*, 53 F.R.D. 596, 604 (D. Del. 1971), affd. 487 F.2d 312 (3 Cir. 1973).

Assume, as an example of another recurrent situation, that you are opposing discovery and inspection of some engineering drawings on the ground that they represent valuable trade secrets whose disclosure would inflict severe harm on your client's business.[23] You should try to prove, again by a knowledgeable witness rather than by your own second-hand observations, that:

1. The material to be disclosed has real value in that (a) its preparation required the expenditure of money and effort and (b) the material helps the client in his operations;
2. A true "secret" is involved, i.e., no one else knows what the material contains and your client has taken positive steps to prevent leakage to outsiders; and
3. Disclosure would cause genuine harm by, for example, giving your client's competitors a windfall through depriving your client of a hard-earned competitive advantage.

By opposing discovery and inspection, you have chosen to do battle on hostile terrain. You must, therefore, arm yourself with the best weapons at hand. Pertinent facts skillfully and honestly presented will form a part of your arsenal.

b. Argument

We have said that your opposition to discovery and inspection must consist of two elements, fact and argument. We shall now consider the second element, which ranks equal in importance with the first.

In our discussion of how to object effectively to interrogatories,[24] we shall deal with the drafting of a persuasive brief or legal memorandum. Much of what appears in that discussion applies to opposing discovery and inspection. The two situations differ enough to warrant some comments here.

For one thing, opposing discovery and inspection usually presents a more difficult job than does objecting to interrogatories. With

---

[23] Strictly speaking, no privilege exists against discovery of trade secrets or confidential business information. Federal Rule 26(c)(7); *National Utility Service, Inc.* v. *Northwestern Steel & Wire Co.*, 426 F.2d 222, 227 (7 Cir. 1970); *A. H. Robins Co.* v. *Fadely*, 299 F.2d 557 (5 Cir. 1962). *Struthers Scientific & International Corp.* v. *General Foods Corp.*, 51 F.R.D. 149, 154 (D. Del. 1970). Where protection is deemed necessary, it usually takes the form of an order stipulating various safeguards. See, e.g., *Spartanics, Ltd.* v. *Dynetics Engineering Corp.*, 54 F.R.D. 524 (N.D. Ill. 1972); *Bee Chemical Co.* v. *Service Coatings, Inc.*, 116 Ill. App.2d 217, 253 N.E.2d 512 (1969).
[24] Pages 212–220.

interrogatories, you have the matter objected to, the question or questions, that is, visibly before the court. In the case of discovery and inspection, on the other hand, you must deal with an unknown. You are declining to produce papers that the court will not normally see. You must, therefore, overcome the judge's suspicion that even if all your arguments are sound, the papers that you seek to withhold may nevertheless contain something whose disclosure will further the ends of justice.

You can apply any of several tactics to overcome this suspicion. You might, for example:

1. Offer to let the judge himself view the material to whose production you object so that he may see for himself that what you say about it is true. This idea will work only if a relatively small volume of material is involved.

2. Argue that if any of the documents in question contains both objectionable and unobjectionable material, you will accept an order directing production of the material with the objectionable parts excised.

3. Stress, as has already been suggested, the positive harm that will result to your client from the disclosure to which you object. Do not, in other words, expect the judge to be moved by purely technical arguments.

4. Present an argument founded on substantive law.

The fourth of these points calls for some elaboration. In general terms, any substantive legal argument that you can offer will fall into one of these two categories:

A. Production of the material sought would offend an established privilege; or

B. The substantive law governing the case renders the material irrelevant to any issue that can conceivably arise.

Most lawyers recognize immediately the first type of question and prepare themselves to meet it. Many, however, do not make the most of the second kind. Perhaps this happens because questions of discovery arise at a stage of the case where many attorneys have not yet come to grips with the substantive issues of the action and with the law determinative of those issues.

Be that as it may, a solid demonstration that under applicable legal criteria the documents you wish to protect would prove nothing, can tip the scales in your favor when you are opposing discovery and inspection. This federal case from Mississippi [25] illustrates the point:

> The Secretary of Labor sued to enjoin violations of the Fair Labor Standards Act.[26] Defendants sought, among other things, production of complaints filed with the Department of Labor of violations by defendants of any of the wage-and-hour laws. Judge Orma Smith denied production, saying:
>> The charges or complaints, oral or written, if any, received by plaintiff, which may have precipitated this action, are not relevant to any issue in the case. As was said in *Wirtz* v. *Continental Finance & Loan Co. of West End:* "What possible difference does it make who reported to the Secretary that violations had occurred?" There is no requirement in the wage and hour law which requires a complaint as to [*sic*] prerequisite for litigation.[27]

Our discussion of objection to interrogatories will tell you more about organizing and presenting the kind of legal argument most likely to work.[28] We may end this part of our discussion with the admonition that you cannot hope to accomplish so difficult a challenge as defeating discovery and inspection without making full use of all available resources. A convincing argument of law should not be the least of these.

G. CONDUCTING THE DISCOVERY AND INSPECTION

You have served the proper notice or entered the proper order for discovery and inspection. Your papers have survived whatever objections or other resistance your opponent has interposed. The stage is set for the examination itself. What should you keep in mind?

The law today gives you the privilege, almost inconceivable a few decades ago, to scrutinize material in your adversary's possession that might be useful, to you or to him, as evidence. You want to be sure to make the most of this privilege, not to take it for granted.

---

[25] *Shultz* v. *Haxton,* 50 F.R.D. 95 (N.D. Miss. 1970).
[26] 29 U.S.C. §201 et seq.
[27] 50 F.R.D. at page 97. Footnotes omitted from text.
[28] Pages 212–220.

The only way to do that is to take your time and give everything the attention it deserves.

Let us assume for now that you have a substantial body of material to review. If you have not, all the principles that we discuss will apply, but your job will be correspondingly simpler.

As you go through the material that your adversary has submitted, you will look for any indication that he has failed to comply with your notice or order. He may have given you too little or too much.

Meticulousness in your scrutiny of the materials produced will help you detect omissions. If you are, for example, reviewing correspondence, you may see a letter written "in reply to your letter of April 12." If no letter of that date is produced, you will wonder why. If in a commercial action you are suing for damages for defects in certain goods that come to your client in twelve shipments, and if your adversary produced invoices related to only ten, you will have questions to ask.

Excessive production can thwart the goals of discovery and inspection just as effectively as can omissions. Your notice or order has called for the production of certain items. You do not want to spend your valuable time culling those items out of a mass of material in which you have no interest. That should normally be the job of the party producing the material.

As an example:

> In an action to enjoin the enforcement of an order requiring plaintiff to correct an alleged violation of the building code, plaintiff's discovery notice required production of all outside and intra-departmental correspondence concerning infractions of the same sub-section in structures of the same type as plaintiff's (Plaintiff's attorney expected the department to have alleged such violations in only a very few instances and in so doing to have taken a stand inconsistent with that adopted in the proceeding against his client). Counsel for defendant produced several large packing cases of his client's correspondence and told his adversary that he would find what he wanted "in there somewhere." Plaintiff's attorney refused to proceed. He moved for a court order enforcing his notice.

Inspection of the material that has been produced will not always tell you whether the other side has omitted anything. As a wise precaution, then, whenever you conduct a discovery and inspection, be sure to:

Establish as a matter of record what your adversary has produced.

When the time comes for trial, opposing counsel may offer in evidence a document or a physical object that you have not seen before. You may object on the ground that he failed to produce the proposed exhibit for your examination pursuant to your order or notice. He may reply that he did in fact produce it. You should be able to refute his contention.

How best to put yourself in this position depends on the circumstances. If your discovery and inspection involves relatively few documents or objects, make a detailed list of them. Send it to your adversary and ask him to let you know if he finds your list incorrect or incomplete in any way.

If your case is a documentary one, and if more papers are produced than you can conveniently list, consider making copies of all the items produced. You can put your set of copies in a special binder or other container and thereby have proof of what was and was not produced.

In cases involving massive documentary material, lawyers sometimes bring their own copying machines to a discovery and inspection. This may provide, in an action whose size justifies the expense, a means of thwarting your adversary's attempt to frustrate discovery by producing a few worthwhile items buried in a mass of meaningless paper.

Whether or not it is feasible to make a copy of every paper produced, you should be able to mark the originals (i.e., the documents actually produced) in a way that will enable you to know for sure whether any item that turns up later, as proffered evidence or otherwise, was part of the production.

One way to do this is to number all the pages produced in a distinctive way. You can use a pen with a particular color ink, or you can employ the kind of rubber-stamp numbering machine that you will find at any stationer's. As a precaution, you or the person to whom you delegate the numbering might add his initials or some other special mark to each number.

In the case of multi-page documents, incidentally, you will find it best to number each page, not just the first. Then if a document turns out to be incomplete, you will at least know whether the missing page disappeared after your inspection.

Getting permission to mark your opponent's papers should present no problem. He will be as anxious as you to establish for the record what he has shown you. If he is not, you may have all the more reason to make a conclusive record yourself, by whatever means is feasible.

We have talked mainly so far about the production for discovery and inspection of documentary evidence. The documentary case is the one that usually presents the most difficult discovery problems. If your case leads to discovery and inspection of objects other than papers, the principles we have been discussing will still apply, though in somewhat modified form.

You cannot make a photostatic or like copy of a nondocumentary object. You can, however, take a picture of it, or better yet, enough pictures of it to remove any likelihood of later confusion concerning its identity. In addition to a photographer (or your own camera), you might take along on your discovery and inspection expedition a supply of ordinary tags, stickers or both. They may enable you to mark or label physical objects to prove later that they were the ones produced for your examination.

To return for a moment to the documentary case, you, as the party conducting the discovery, will normally bear the expense of copying whatever papers you select. You will accomplish the copying either by borrowing the papers in question and returning them after reproduction or indicating to your adversary the items you have chosen and letting him make the copies. We have also mentioned the possibility of taking along your own copying machine. Whichever way you choose, conclusive identification of the documents you have selected will preclude the embarrassment and possible prejudice of the disappearance of an item at one stage or another of the procedure.

H. DESTRUCTIVE AND OTHER TESTS

1. Some Threshold Problems

When you go after discovery of papers, you probably wish only to look at what your adversary produces and make copies of it. In the case of a physical object, you may wish also to use it, test it or do something else with it. Anything of that sort creates special problems.

Typical is the situation where your adversary has possession of an object whose failure or alleged inadequacy gave rise to the litigation.

You feel the need not just to look at the object and photograph it, but to subject it to tests. What should you do?

First of all, you must find out:

1. What rights you have; and
2. What you need do to assert them.

The statute or rules governing pre-trial discovery in your jurisdiction may have a special provision governing the testing of physical objects or materials. You may require a court order, or a simple request to your adversary may suffice.

In federal practice, for example, Rule 34 permits a party merely to serve a written request that another party "produce and permit the party making the request . . . to inspect and copy, test, or sample any tangible things which constitute or contain matters within the scope of Rule 26(b). . . ." According to the same provision, the party upon whom the request is served has 30 days in which to respond. If the response is in the negative, the requesting party may move under Rule 37(a) for an enforcement order.

If, of course, you are the one who has possession of an object whose condition is material to the action, you may conclude simply to test it, even destructively, without a court order. You should remember, however, that by so doing you risk having to turn over the results of your work to your adversary.[29] You will normally be better advised to proceed with caution and deliberation. Let us review some of the factors you will weigh.

2. Crucial Questions to Ask

Having determined what your rights are and how to implement them, you must ask the basic question whether the testing you are contemplating will really work to your client's advantage. You might break this question down into components such as:

Question 1: *Is the test I am considering likely to do more harm than good by destroying or materially altering evidence which, in its present condition, provides vivid proof of the point I am urging?* You may, for example, be seeking discovery of a section of metal cable that broke and caused your client serious injuries.

---

[29] *Ex parte Turner,* 57 F.R.D. 109 (S.D. Tex. 1972), although involving destructive tests by a non-party, illustrates the point.

The frayed ends of the cable may, in practical terms, provide far more dramatic evidence of the defective condition on which you rely than would a piece of paper showing the results of metallurgical tests that required destruction of the cable.

Question 2: *Is it feasible to consider deferring the testing until the trial, and conducting it as a courtroom experiment?* You, as plaintiff's attorney, may wish to show that the extreme flammability of a drapery material made by defendant caused or aggravated a fire in your client's building. You cannot test the one surviving piece of material without burning it up. You are sure enough of the results of such a test to decide to wait until the trial and offer to demonstrate the flammability before the jury.

Question 3: *Will the disadvantages of my proposed testing outweigh whatever I may gain from it?* In granting you leave to conduct destructive tests, the court may require you to do them in your adversary's presence. It may direct you to give him a copy of whatever report results from the tests. You may conclude that this would reduce the advantage that you enjoy over your adversary in the realm of technical preparation and that this drawback outweighs the benefit to be derived from the tests.

Question 4: *Am I confident enough of the results of the tests to stake my case on them?* Whatever the terms of any order authorizing the tests, you must usually take it for granted that sooner or later, the results of the tests will be disclosed to the trier of the facts.

Question 5: *Even if my proposed tests are permissible under the rules of discovery, will the court receive them in evidence on the trial?* You can answer this question only by checking your local rules of evidence. Keep in mind the warning of a federal appellate court that:

> Test results should not even be admissible as evidence, unless made by a qualified, independent expert or unless the opposing party has the opportunity to participate in the test . . .[30]

These are some of the considerations that a lawyer must weigh before he decides whether to engage in the testing of an item made available for his discovery and inspection. If he decides in the affirmative, his next steps must be taken with care.

---

[30] *Fortunato* v. *Ford Motor Co.*, 464 F.2d 962, 966 (2 Cir. 1972), *cert. denied*, 409 U.S. 1038, 93 S.Ct. 517, — L.Ed.2d — (1972).

3. Proceeding with the Testing

You have decided in favor of proceeding with destructive tests or something of the kind. Your next step will be to disclose to the court and your adversary, as your procedure requires, precisely and completely just what you propose to do.

The place to make such disclosure is in the notice or motion papers with which you initiate the discovery and inspection. If, for example, you seek leave to inspect a parcel of real property and wish to take samples of the soil in the process, your motion for leave to make the inspection should so state.[31] The order that you later draft for the judge's signature should be framed with equal precision.[32]

If you are destroying or altering material evidence, you must enable yourself to prove that you did so with the full knowledge and the explicit consent of the court and opposing counsel. The adversary who casually says "O.K." to your remark that you may "run a few tests" on the object that he is turning over to you for discovery may not remember his words when the crucial evidence turns up missing on the trial, or when more systematic counsel replaces him. Take no chances; make candid disclosure of any possibility that your intended test will destroy the object to be discovered.

Remember that under some circumstances the court will be interested in preserving not only the object that you wish to test, but also the structure or apparatus from which you must remove it. Such would be the case, for example, if you represented the maker or supplier of building materials and wished to remove for testing an allegedly defective component of the structure out of which the action arose. The court might well impose measures to insure preservation of the building and restoration to its original condition.[33]

You will next reach understanding on the details of all other aspects of the proposed tests. The expense involved, for example, may be substantial. If your adversary is to share in the results of your tests, you may think it a good idea to ask that he likewise share the cost.

When the time comes to conduct the tests for which you have ap-

---

[31] *Salmon* v. *Lewis,* 29 Conn. Sup. 363, 288 A.2d 686 (1971).

[32] See the exhaustive order signed by Chief Judge Solomon in *Martin* v. *Reynolds Metals Corp.,* 297 F.2d 49, 53, (9th Cir. 1961). It provided for postmortem examinations of allegedly poisoned cattle and a variety of other tests and inspections.

[33] *City of Kingsport* v. *SCM Corp.,* 352 F. Supp. 287, 288 (E.D. Tenn. 1972).

plied, you must proceed precisely as specified in the order, notice, stipulation, or other instrument under which you are operating. If a court order states that tests will be conducted by a certain party at a particular time or place, and if it proves impossible to follow the directive literally, you will not be wasting your time by arranging an amendment, if only by means of an exchange of letters with your opponent. If something goes wrong, such as the unanticipated destruction of the material, you do not want to have to explain that no causal connection existed between your violation, however technical, of the applicable order and the accident.

As a further precaution, counsel supervising the testing or other use of items in discovery often make an exhaustive record of everything that ensues, from the date, time and place of delivery to them of the object or material in question to the return of the item to its owner after completion of the job. Photographs, where possible, help in this regard. Meticulous notes will sometimes suffice. When one is concerned with the physical integrity of something on which a substantial case may turn, he cannot be too careful. What is more, when you come to offer in evidence the results of the tests you have arranged to conduct, your precise records may come in handy.

4. The Report

We must, in conclusion, consider a few points concerning the way in which the results of the testing are reported to you. It will often help, first of all, to have the report put in the form of a letter to you. Such a precaution can do no harm. It may later help you in a claim of attorney-client privilege or work-product.

Do not, under any circumstances, acquiesce in the tactic of a few professional experts, who propose to prepare two reports, one for you to show the other side, and another, usually more candid, for your own "confidential" use. Opposing counsel will likely bring out on cross-examination the fact of two reports. This apparent effort at deception cannot help damaging your case. If the report that you receive seems to you incomplete or inadequate, direct a letter to its author and explain in frank terms that you would like his report supplemented. If the time comes to disclose the report, you will, of course, include whatever supplement your request has produced.

The pages above have surveyed the problems and opportunities likely to arise when, as usually happens, one party conducts discovery and inspection against another. Occasionally, however, the process involves outsiders.

I. DISCOVERY AND INSPECTION AGAINST NON-PARTIES

Most of what we have discussed so far has had to do with obtaining evidence from another party to the action. You may sometimes wish to obtain documents or other material from a non-litigant. Many of the same considerations apply to that problem, but some differences obtain.

First of all, the usual notice to other counsel, although essential, will not suffice to procure the production of evidence by a non-party.[34] Personal jurisdiction must be obtained. To effect the production of material for use in the deposition of a nonparty, you will need a *subpoena duces tecum* served personally on the person from whom you wish to obtain discovery.[35] Otherwise it may be necessary, in federal practice for example, to institute a separate action against the non-party.[36] Once that is done, counsel seeking discovery and inspection will proceed as he would against a party to the original action.[37]

Some states permit discovery and inspection against non-parties without the commencement of a separate action.[38] Here again, personal jurisdiction must be obtained. The procedure otherwise does not differ substantially from that provided with respect to parties.

---

[34] Federal Rule 34(a), for example, provides for the service of a request "on any other party."

[35] See Federal Rule 45(d). *Continental Coatings Corp.* v. *Metco, Inc.*, 50 F.R.D. 382 (N.D. Ill. 1970).

[36] See, e.g., Federal Rule 34(c).

[37] 4A MOORE'S FEDERAL PRACTICE ¶34.22.

[38] See, e.g., New York Civil Practice Law and Rules, Rule 3120(b).

Chapter VI

GETTING RESULTS
WITH INTERROGATORIES

A. WHEN TO USE, AND NOT USE INTERROGATORIES

1. The Function and Scope of Interrogatories

The Federal Rules and comparable provisions in most states provide for interrogatories as an alternative or supplement to the deposition. Interrogatories are no more than written questions requiring written, sworn answers. In choosing this method of discovery, a lawyer must weigh carefully its assets and liabilities as they apply to the circumstances of his case. In most jurisdictions interrogatories have the same breadth of subject-matter as depositions.[1]

Can a litigant use interrogatories as a short-cut to discovery and inspection by asking the interrogated party to attach, *e.g.*, copies of papers to his answers to interrogatories? In jurisdictions where one must make an affirmative showing of "good cause" before obtaining discovery and inspection, it will usually be deemed improper to use interrogatories to request production of documentary material.[2] Such jurisdictions are diminishing in number, however, and the distinction between a notice to produce and interrogatories as a means of calling for production of physical evidence seems inconsequential.[3] At least one state expressly permits interrogatories calling for the production of relevant "documents or photographs. . . . unless opportunity for . . . examination and copying be afforded." [4]

Interrogatories possess some of the advantages that we saw in our

---

[1] Federal Rule 33(b) expressly so provides in the case of federal actions.
[2] *Norman Plumbing Supply Co.* v. *Gilles*, 512 P.2d 1177, 1179–1180 (Okl. 1973).
[3] See discussion at 4A MOORE'S FEDERAL PRACTICE ¶33.22.
[4] N.Y. CPLR §3131.

general appraisal of discovery procedures and some of the same strong points that a deposition features. Your opponent's answers to your interrogatories are generally admissible in evidence on your behalf.[5] Thus they provide a means of preserving evidence until the trial. Interrogatories serve also to record an adverse party's sworn version of relevant matter, just as do answers given at a deposition. In neither case, however, is the party "committed" in the sense of being barred from introducing contradictory evidence.[6]

2. In Favor of Interrogatories

a. They Save Money and Time

Consider the advantages that interrogatories have over the oral deposition.[7] First comes the obvious one of cost. As lawyers' time charges and court reporters' fees go up, the deposition grows more expensive. Interrogatories involve no cash outlay beyond postage.

Secondly, interrogatories are relatively swift and sure. Particularly in cases with numerous parties, depositions are almost routinely scheduled, adjourned and rescheduled, sometimes for months. The lawyer seeking to take the deposition often has limited practical control over the extent of these delays, which can sometimes be prejudicial. Counsel can, on the other hand, prepare and serve interrogatories as promptly as his own schedule permits. He can be reasonably strict about granting extensions of time.

Interrogatories can save time in other ways. Hours can be wasted at a deposition while the enquiring attorney waits for a witness to look up obscure data or rummage through voluminous files. An adjourned session is often necessary to permit the necessary search to be made for such material. All of this can be avoided by submitting

---

[5] Federal Rule 33(b); *Household Finance Corp.* v. *Ensley*, 127 Ga. App. 876, 195 S.E.2d 236 (1973). Interrogatory answers are admissible only against the answering party. *Rosenthal* v. *Poland*, 337 F. Supp. 1161, 1170 (S.D. N.Y. 1972). A party may not offer his own answers to interrogatories in evidence. *Crabtree* v. *Measday*, 85 N.M. 20, 508 P.2d 1317, 1322 (1973), cert. den., 85 N.M. 5, 508 P.2d 1302 (1973); *Sympson* v. *Mor-Win Products, Inc.*, 501 S.W.2d 362, 364 (Tex. Civ. App. 1973).

[6] See discussion, at pages 234–239, contrasting formal admissions with answers to interrogatories. See, however, *Saum* v. *Venick*, 33 Ohio App.2d 11, 293 N.E.2d 313 (1972), where it was held improper to allow a party to introduce evidence contradicting his answers to interrogatories.

[7] Sunderland, *Discovery Before Trial*, 42 YALE LAW JOURNAL 863, 874–877 (1933), contains some observations still pertinent today.

interrogatories that let the party or witness do research for his answers on his own time.

In jurisdictions which permit inquiry into a party's contentions,[8] interrogatories may prove a valuable substitute for the now largely outdated bill of particulars. If, for example, in a suit for misappropriation of trade-secrets, you wish to make your adversary specify which of a complex variety of processes he claims constitute the secret, interrogatories will likely serve you more efficiently than one or more depositions and will be more likely to elicit authoritative answers.[9] As another example, a defendant in a personal-injury or wrongful death case may use interrogatories to make plaintiff particularize his general allegations of negligence.[10] Plaintiff, in turn, may succeed in requiring defendant to specify what it contends "was the cause of" the accident.[11]

b. They Enhance Precision

The example just cited brings out another advantage to interrogatories. They usually get definitive answers. A party or witness can claim, after the fact, to have misspoken himself or not to have understood a question at a deposition. That is not apt to happen after he has signed written answers to written questions.

c. They Find the One Who Knows

Finally, interrogatories should eliminate the vexing problem of finding the proper spokesman. A lawyer opposing a corporation or other large organization often takes the depositions of several of its officers or employees before he gets what he is after, either because the corporation (perhaps deliberately) sends somone uninformed to testify in the first instance or because the information desired must come from multiple sources.

A federal case shows the "run-around" to which counsel can subject himself by trying to elicit information from a large organization by the deposition technique. Reversing a judgment for defendants in a personal-injury action because of their failure to produce a knowledgeable spokesman for pre-trial testimony, the U.S. Court of Appeals for the Fourth Circuit said, *per curiam:*

---

[8] See, e.g., Federal Rule 33(b).

[9] *Struthers Scientific & International Corp.* v. *General Foods Corp.*, 51 F.R.D. 149 (D. Del. 1970), provides an example of this use of interrogatories.

[10] *Rogers* v. *Tri-State Materials Corp.*, 51 F.R.D. 234 (N.D. W. Va. 1970).

[11] *Handlos* v. *Litton Industries, Inc.*, 51 F.R.D. 23, 24 (E.D. Wisc. 1970).

Dealing with a large corporation, it is difficult for counsel to do more than summon the chief officer, depending upon him to select the appropriate subordinate.

The obstacle arising from this difficulty entered into the deposition hearing, Ford testifying then that the head of the claims operation was Nicholas Black. It reappeared at the hearing on the day of trial. Maxim was then pointed out to the Court as the one familiar with the file. The Court asked for Black, but was casually told that he presumably was in the Washington office. Thus Raynor was first named as the key man, then Black and finally Maxim. At no time, did the defendants or their insurer offer to bring to the deposition or to court the person with the requisite knowledge. When the Court entered its order on January 8, 1963 for the appearance of Ford, the defendants could readily have then advised that he was not familiar with the records. No such suggestion was forthcoming. The District Judge aptly termed it all as "bandying." [12]

Answers to interrogatories, in contrast, speak for the organization. A corporate party on whom interrogatories are served must answer them through a knowledgeable spokesman, who must, at least in a federal case, "furnish such information as is available to the party." [13] It may not avoid that duty by, for example, designating someone entitled to invoke the privilege against self-incrimination. [14] In *Hickman* v. *Taylor*, the Supreme Court of the United States said:

> A party clearly cannot refuse to answer interrogatories on the ground that the information sought is solely within the knowledge of his attorney. [15]

To be sure, a corporate party may default on its obligations respecting interrogatories, just as it may send an unknowledgeable representative to speak for it at a deposition. A fruitless set of interrogatories, however, represents a far less expensive misadventure than an unproductive deposition.

---

[12] *Haney* v. *Woodward & Lothrop, Inc.,* 330 F.2d 940, 944 (4 Cir. 1964).

[13] Federal Rule 33(a); *Holt* v. *Southern Railway Co.,* 51 F.R.D. 296, 299–300 (E.D. Tenn. 1969), and cases cited.

[14] *United States* v. *Kordel,* 397 U.S. 1, 8, 90 S. Ct. 763, 767, 25 L.Ed.2d 1 (1970); *General Dynamics Corp.* v. *Selb Mfg. Co.,* 481 F.2d 1204, 1210 (8th Cir. 1973), *cert. denied,* — U.S. —.

[15] 329 U.S. 495, 504, 67 S. Ct. 385, 390, 91 L.Ed. 451, 459 (1947). See also *Ballard* v. *Allegheny Airlines, Inc.,* 54 F.R.D. 67, 69 (E.D. Pa. 1972).

3. Against Interrogatories

a. Beware the Prepared Answer

The drawbacks of interrogatories relate closely to some of their advantages. To begin, never forget that by posing written interrogatories, you will surely be getting a lawyer's answers.[16] The live witness at a deposition may be well-rehearsed, but examining counsel has at least the satisfaction of knowing that he is getting words from the witness's own mouth. With answers to interrogatories, he must count on material that opposing counsel has screened and phrased in the most helpful or least harmful terms possible. If damaging admissions must be made, you can be sure that your adversary will have diluted and qualified your evidence far more than the most adroit witness could have achieved.

A good point to remember in this regard, whether you are drafting or answering interrogatories: The answering party will rarely be restricted to a "yes" or "no" answer.[17]

b. Finality, Not Always a Help

Examining counsel is "stuck" with answers to interrogatories much more than he is with answers at a deposition. An attorney who thinks that a deposition witness is being evasive or otherwise unresponsive may repeat or rephrase the question, return to it later or insist in other ways. The recipient of an unsatisfactory answer to an interrogatory has a harder job. He probably will have no alternative to going to court to compel a proper answer. This will prove a far more bothersome procedure than the self-help techniques available, at least as a first resort, at a deposition.

c. The Lack of Adaptability

Another weakness of interrogatories arises from their inflexibility. No matter how excellent his outline, the lawyer taking a deposition can let a surprise answer to one question suggest questions previously

---

[16] Answers composed by the lawyer, that is, for his client's signature and verification. An attorney may not usually himself sign or swear to the answers to interrogatories as if they were a kind of pleading. See, e.g., *Gregory* v. *King Plumbing, Inc.*, 127 Ga. App. 512, 194 S.E.2d 271 (1972). *Contra: Fernandes* v. *United Fruit Co.*, 50 F.R.D. 82, 85–86 (D. Md. 1970).

[17] *Ballard* v. *Allegheny Airlines, Inc.*, footnote 15, 54 F.R.D. at pages 68–69.

not thought of. The draftsman of interrogatories lacks this freedom. If he wishes to make a question dependent on the answer to the one before it, he must, to be safe, provide for all possible answers to the earlier question. This will make his interrogatories cumbersome, longer and more complex than he would like to have them. It may also leave gaps through which the answering party can wriggle out, gaps that could easily be closed at an oral deposition.

d. Forcing Your Opponent to Prepare

Interrogatories have a drawback that does not occur to some practitioners. By making your adversary respond to exhaustive interrogation, you may be forcing him to engage in preparation that he otherwise might forego or overlook. This point applies particularly to more complex kinds of litigation. Let us take an example:

> An experienced attorney was defending an action for treble damages for price discrimination in alleged violation of the Robinson-Patman Act. He suspected that his opponent, new to this kind of litigation, did not appreciate the intricacies of computing the proper measure of damages. Defense counsel decided, therefore, not to submit the detailed interrogatories that might strike one as imperative in that situation. Instead, he established by a few questions on deposition that plaintiff had not made the necessary computations. He let the matter go at that. On the trial, plaintiff failed completely to make out a case in damages. The court granted a nonsuit.

Defense counsel in the example just cited took a chance. Had plaintiff, some time between the taking of his deposition and the trial, awakened to the deficiency in his case, defense counsel might have been surprised by competent proof of damages during the trial. As happens so often in litigation, one must risk a loss to achieve a worthwhile gain.

The 1970 revision of Federal Rule 33 added a subparagraph that reduces the risk of forcing one's adversary to prepare his case by serving interrogatories on him. The addition provides:

> Option to Produce Business Records. Where the answer to an interrogatory may be derived or ascertained from the business records of the party upon whom the interrogatory has been served or from an examination, audit or inspection of such business rec-

> ords, or from a compilation, abstract or summary based thereon,
> and the burden of deriving or ascertaining the answer is substan-
> tially the same for the party serving the interrogatory as for the
> party served, it is a sufficient answer to such interrogatory to
> specify the records from which the answer may be derived or
> ascertained and to afford to the party serving the interrogatory
> reasonable opportunity to examine, audit or inspect such records
> and to make copies, compilations, abstracts or summaries.

Having extensive interrogatories answered by resort to this provision
may be initially irritating, but it may constitute a blessing in disguise.
Your opponent's saving himself the trouble of combing through his
client's records may mean more work for you, but it may also put you
that much ahead of him in trial preparation.

Remember, in any event, that if your adversary takes advantage
of the provision quoted above, he must specify the records from which
answers to your questions may be gleaned. A broad statement that
answers are obtainable from documents which will be made available
does not suffice.[18]

e. Limited Scope or Availability

In some states interrogatories are available only against "adverse"
parties.[19] That was true in federal practice until a 1970 amendment
to Federal Rule 33(a) allowed the service of interrogatories on
"any other party."

A few states limit the extent of interrogatories. A Massachusetts
statute, for example, provides in part:

> No party shall file as of right more than thirty interrogatories,
> including interrogatories subsidiary or incidental to, or dependent
> upon, other interrogatories, and however the same may be
> grouped, combined or arranged; but for adequate cause shown,
> the court may allow additional interrogatories to be filed.[20]

In South Carolina, one may ask only six "standard interrogatories"
whose text is set forth in the applicable rule.[21] A New York statute
forbids interrogatories in actions, among others for "personal injury,
resulting from negligence." [22]

---

[18] *Budget Rent-a-Car of Missouri, Inc.* v. *Hertz Corp.,* 55 F.R.D. 354, 357 (W.D.
Mo. 1972).
[19] See, e.g., 8 Ann. Laws Mass. 231, §61.
[20] Ibid.
[21] Rule 90, Rules of Practice for the Circuit Courts of South Carolina.
[22] N.Y. CPLR 3130.

Among other considerations, then, the relative desirability of interrogatories as opposed to other discovery devices may depend on the kind of action in which you are involved.

4. Summing Up: Some Guiding Principles

With these and perhaps other elements to deal with, how is one to choose between the deposition and interrogatories? No hard and fast formula can be devised, but our observations above would seem to justify these general rules:

1. If you are seeking information of a voluminous documentary, statistical or like character, interrogatories may work to your advantage. This is true particularly where the material sought is routine or not likely to be challenged or controverted.

2. If, on the other hand, you wish to question a party or witness about live events in which he participated, you will probably be wise to use an oral deposition.

3. If you have questions to direct to an organization, corporate or otherwise, and you think the answers will require the knowledge of several of its members or employees, or if you are not sure which of its representatives can supply the answers, interrogatories may solve your problem.

4. In many cases, a combination of interrogatories, depositions and discovery and inspection will be necessary to achieve the best possible trial preparation.

Remember that in most jurisdictions, interrogatories and the deposition do not exclude each other.[23] The best choice will often be to combine the two devices, using each where its particular advantages apply. One might for example, in a commercial action involving many documented transactions, use interrogatories to identify the participants and to obtain a list of documents and question the participants at oral depositions. As a federal judge has said:

. . . information garnered from interrogatories may lay the foundation for questions asked at the oral examination and may

---

[23] Federal Rule 26(a) permits discovery "by one or more of the following methods: depositions . . . written interrogatories. . . ." See *Rogers* v. *Tri-State Materials Corp.*, 51 F.R.D. 234, 241 (N.D. W.Va. 1970); *Stonybrook Tenants Assoc.* v. *Alpert*, 29 F.R.D. 165, 167 (D. Conn. 1961). See also Calif. Code of Civil Procedure §2030(b).

narrow the issues so as to expedite the handling of the oral deposition.[24]

Likewise, interrogatories can, as we have seen, be a useful preliminary for discovery and inspection proceedings.[25]

We have examined the considerations that will enter into your decision whether or not to resort to interrogatories. Next comes a review of the ways in which the practicing lawyer can make best use of that device.

B. DRAFTING INTERROGATORIES

1. Avoid Second-Hand Questions

Once you have decided to use interrogatories, you face the job of drafting them. To accomplish your purpose, your questions must achieve two goals. They must survive any objections interposed by the opposition. They must then elicit the information you want.

Authorities may differ on what is the best technique to use in drafting interrogatories. They will surely agree on what is the worst, namely, the use of stereotyped or "canned" questions. Mass-production litigators have sometimes been guilty of this practice. Some have been known to compound the error by issuing their questions in printed or mimeographed form, as if to advertise their slipshod approach to discovery. We shall not pass judgment on those whose professional standards let them resort to such a device. We will say that any time saved by using such standardized interrogatories represents the plainest form of false economy.

Adapting interrogatories from one case to the next can come dangerously close to the use of standardized questions. If you follow this practice, as everyone does at least occasionally, you must recognize it as a calculated risk. Under the pressure of limited time, which is usually what compels resort to this device, the eye glides easily over inconsistencies or contradictions that will stand out as though underlined in red to opposing counsel and the judge. For example:

Defense counsel in a federal Securities Act case submitted interrogatories to plaintiffs about the details of their purchases

---

[24] *Franchise Programs, Inc.* v. *Mr. Aqua Spray, Inc.*, 41 F.R.D. 172, 174 (S.D. N.Y. 1966).

[25] See discussion at pages 55–56.

of the stock in question. He adapted interrogatories that he had used in an earlier, similar action. The earlier case, however, had involved warrants instead of shares of stock. This forced the draftsman, in addition to making other changes, to go through the older interrogatories and change "warrants" to "shares" in almost every one of over 35 questions. In his haste, he did not check his work and overlooked two of the necessary changes. The two anomalous references to "warrants" made it easy for opposing counsel to argue, in objecting to the extensive interrogatories, that his client was being harassed by warmed-over questions from another case.

Second-hand or remodeled interrogatories have another liability. Every lawsuit is unique. Transplanting a series of questions from one case to another may lead either to overlooking items in the latter case that were missing from the former or to the opposite error of using in the second case questions that could easily be deleted. If, then, you re-use interrogatories from one case to another, do not be content with checking them carefully for consistency in wording and subject matter. Look at them in their entirety to make sure they suit their new environment. Does, for example, the new case have issues not present in the former one and thus not covered by the interrogatories you are adapting? Have you taken advantage of every opportunity to shorten your new interrogatories by striking questions not necessary in their new context?

It would be foolish, of course, not to take advantage of your past work in drafting interrogatories. You should, for example, in personal-injury cases have a standard interrogatory asking for the identity of persons having knowledge of the accident, information to which you are in some jurisdictions entitled as a matter of right.[26] Just remember that part of the time saved by using standard or adapted questions should be devoted to an exhaustive study of whether in the transition anything of value has been lost or any excess baggage retained.

2. The Art of Framing Questions: Conciseness

Let us look at the problem of drafting interrogatories from a positive point of view. Two features certain to help you get what you want and overcome objections to your questions are brevity and pertinence. They go hand in hand.

---

[26] Federal Rule 26(b)(1); *Edgar* v. *Finley,* 312 F.2d 533 (8 Cir. 1963). See also cases cited at footnote 6, Chapter I.

In drafting interrogatories, one who strives for comprehensiveness through the use of lengthy and involved clauses will probably do his client more harm than good. An answer to a complex interrogatory will not likely be of much help, for evidentiary purposes, particularly in a jury case. Secondly, a busy judge ruling on objections to interrogatories may show little patience with questions whose meaning lies hidden in a tangled thicket of verbiage. Thirdly, the answering attorney who is determined to avoid a crucial question, or to dilute the damaging effect of any admission he must make, is not likely to be stopped by laboriously precise phraseology. If he is scrupulous, he will answer your question to the extent that he must. If he is not scrupulous, your draftsmanship will not likely corner him. In fact, long complex questions facilitate a favorite evasive device of unprincipled counsel, the deliberate "misunderstanding" of questions that reach into sensitive areas. Such questions similarly make it more difficult to prove the bad faith behind such tactics.

How, then, can you attain brevity without sacrificing scope and a reasonable degree of exactness? The answer lies in the effective use of language, an art to be practiced in drafting interrogatories, just as in any other form of composition. Other authorities have set forth excellent principles in this field,[27] so we need not dwell on them here. We should, however, list a few of the most common abuses that go to defeat the goal of brevity in drafting interrogatories.

To begin, simplicity and directness in language will do more than help you achieve brevity. It will also serve to clarify your thinking. You can improve your chances of defeating a motion to strike your interrogatories by phrasing them in the most precise terms consistent with your needs. Courts frequently show impatience with interrogatories phrased in broad, sweeping terms.[28] Try always, therefore, to:

1. Favor the shorter word over the longer;
2. Avoid circumlocutions, and;
3. Free your questions of structural complexities.

Economy of questions may go as far as economy of words in achieving conciseness in interrogatories. The sheer number of responses

---

[27] See, *e.g.*, Rossman (Ed.), ADVOCACY AND THE KING'S ENGLISH (Indianapolis and New York, Bobbs-Merrill Co., 1960); Strunk & White, THE ELEMENTS OF STYLE (N.Y., The Macmillan Co., 1959); Flesch, THE ART OF PLAIN TALK (N.Y., Collier Books, 1946).

[28] See, e.g., *Avco Security Corp.* v. *Post*, 42 A.D.2d 395, 399, 348 N.Y.S.2d 409 (4th Dept. 1973).

required may dispose a judge to sustain objections to your interrogatories or to deny you enforcement.[29] Rather than sort out the proper from the improper questions, the court may conserve its own time by invalidating the entire set of interrogatories.

Use the scalpel, therefore, sensibly but firmly. After you have prepared a comprehensive set of interrogatories, see how many you can weed out without prejudicing your case. Some questions will pertain to areas not seriously in controversy. Others may bear on matters that pique your or your client's curiosity, but will not contribute anything to your case. If you check back to the pleadings, you may find that some of your questions have already been answered, by denials as well as by admissions.

Consolidation often provides a means of shortening substantially the length of interrogatories. A little thought can often combine a number of questions into just one or two. Suppose, for example, that you wish to learn the names of all persons who served as directors of a corporation you are suing. Suppose furthermore that you are interested in the ten years beginning in 1962. You might frame an interrogatory like this:

1. List all persons who served as members of defendant's board of directors during the year 1962.

You might follow this question with nine more like it, one for each of the succeeding years. This would give you a total of ten questions on the subject of membership on defendant's board of directors. Instead, you might pose one question such as:

1. List all persons who served as members of defendant's board of directors during each of the years 1962 through 1971.

You have thus asked for the same information in one-tenth the number of questions. Before you reject this example as absurdly obvious, take at random any set of interrogatories from your files. You may be surprised how many questions could have been eliminated by the technique just illustrated.

Definitions offer another way to cut down the length of interrogatories. If a series of questions must be asked about an item impossible to describe or denote in brief terms, e.g., a tract of land, a secret

[29] *Spector Freight Systems, Inc.* v. *Home Indemnity Co.*, 58 F.R.D. 162 (N.D. Ill. 1973); *H. O. Dyer, Inc.* v. *Steele*, 489 S.W.2d 686, 689 (Tex. Civ. App. 1973); *Hutter* v. *Frederickson*, 58 F.R.D. 52 (E.D. Wisc. 1972).

process or a document, you may find it prudent to define it thoroughly once and refer to it thereafter by some abbreviated designation.

There are several ways to do this. You might begin your interrogatories with a section headed *Definitions,* including a passage such as:

> As used in these interrogatories, "the Church tract" shall mean the certain tract of land lying [description in metes and bounds].

This device will spare you a lengthy description each time you wish to refer to the land in question.

If you have but one or two terms that lend themselves to definition in the interests of brevity, a simpler technique might be to define each of them thus:

> 7. List the names of all of plaintiff's employees who approved the license agreement of February 7, 1974, between plaintiff and the estate of Lyman Shephard, hereinafter referred to as "the 1974 agreement," before its execution.

A third technique, perhaps the best of all for reasons to be discussed, involves reference to the pleadings. One of your first interrogatories, for example, might read:

> 3. List each publication, including trade journals, in which plaintiff or any of its employees has made reference, direct or indirect, to the process referred to in Paragraph 4 of the amended complaint, designated elsewhere throughout these interrogatories as "the Paragraph 4 process."

This third technique, we shall see, has an additional advantage by way of manifesting the relevance of your interrogatories. We turn to that subject shortly.

A recurring source of excessive length in interrogatories arises from the tendency of lawyers to use them as weapons rather than as tools. Interrogatories present a favorite weapon with which to plague one's adversary, to "soften him up" and make him more amenable to settlement. After having labored to answer an endless series of intricate questions of sweeping breadth, who is not tempted to retaliate in kind?

Illinois Supreme Court Rule 213(b) carries this admonition, which all of us would do well to bear in mind:

It is the duty of an attorney directing interrogatories to restrict them to the subject matter of the particular case, to avoid undue detail, and to avoid the imposition of any unnecessary burden or expense on the answering party.

Here is where the true professional distinguishes himself from the crowd of ordinary lawyers. Comforting as it may be to picture your adversary struggling as you did, you can surely put your limited trial-preparation time to better use than drafting questions that serve no purpose but harassment. Force yourself to rise above the urge to get even. Use interrogatories for their intended purpose and you will benefit your client's cause by using your time to better advantage and very likely improve your standing in the judge's eyes to boot. Here, by the way, as in other areas, it is your conscience, not your client's, that should govern.

3. The Art of Framing Questions: Pertinence

We pointed out at the beginning of this chapter that interrogatories, to achieve their goal of surviving objections and eliciting information, should possess two salient attributes, conciseness and pertinence. We shall deal now with the second of these two attributes.

In drafting interrogatories, you are going to try to compose questions that will convince both your adversary and any reviewing judge that they are legitimate, that is, that they inquire into subject-matter into which you are entitled to delve. You will have little chance of succeeding in this respect if you yourself lack faith in what you are doing.

Regardless, therefore, of how you draft your interrogatories, you should review each one in the light of the question, "How will the answer to this interrogatory help me uncover evidence germane to my own or my adversary's case?" If you cannot come up with a cogent answer to this question, as distinguished from a captious excuse, you had better give serious thought to abandoning that interrogatory. If your adversary objects to any of your interrogatories, and if the judge finds just one that plainly has no place, he may begin to suspect your motives throughout. Your overreaching, therefore, may effectively shift to you the burden of defending the interrogatories instead of leaving with your adversary the burden of attacking them.

Before you begin drafting questions, you should make sure that each topic of interrogation comes within the scope of applicable substantive law. Presiding Justice Goldman of New York's Appellate Division for the Fourth Department, speaking for a unanimous court, put it this way:

> In order to determine whether the information sought by appellant's interrogatories is necessary and material, it is essential to refer to the law concerning consumer credit transaction where in situations like the case at bar there is usually a tripartite transaction involving a lending or credit company, the vendor . . . and the vendee maker of a negotiable instrument. The lending institution must sustain its status as a holder in due course if it is to succeed. . . . Any material relevant to [respondent's] holder in due course status should be discoverable.[30]

Do not, it follows, plan to pose interrogatories into areas to which you have reason to believe the court will not extend its jurisdiction or into matters having no bearing on the statutory standard governing your case.[31]

Once you have limited your interrogatories to areas that you know are proper, how can you draft questions that will convey their legitimacy to whoever reads them? In defending interrogatories against objections, you will probably have the chance to advance legal and factual arguments, but opposing counsel and the judge will surely read the questions themselves before considering any arguments supporting them. Interrogatories that demonstrate their own relevance have a head start in the defense of their propriety.

We have seen that although courts no longer unanimously limit the scope of discovery to the dimensions of the pleadings, they still resort to the complaint, answer, etc. in determining the propriety of discovery moves.[32] Why not, therefore, tie each of your interrogatories to a specific allegation of a pleading, preferably your adversary's?

If, for example, you represent a manufacturer and are defending an action to rescind the purchase of several thousand household appliances on the grounds of fraud and breach of warranty, and if your adversary, a jobber, has alleged that he sustained damages by

---

[30] *Avco Security Corp.* v. *Post*, footnote 28, 42 A.D.2d at page 398, 348 N.Y.S.2d at page 412.

[31] *Brookchester Tenants' Rights Corp.* v. *Brunetti Apartments*, 123 N.J. Super 341, 303 A.2d 85 (1973).

[32] See discussion at pages 23–29.

reason of the inordinately large number of returns by his retailer customers, you might ask for details of his claimed losses in terms like these:

> 8. Give the details of every transaction involving the return of any "Softglo" lamps manufactured by defendant, or involving a demand for a refund of the purchase price of any such lamp, at any time from January 1, 1972, up to the date of the commencement of this action.

You might think that the legitimacy of such an interrogatory would be relatively easy to defend. Would not the defense be even easier, however, if you were to ask:

> 8. Set forth the details of each of the returns and demands for refunds referred to in Paragraph 5 of the complaint for the period of time beginning with the first of the purchases alleged in Paragraph 3 of the complaint and continuing through September 25, 1973.

The latter alternative, eliciting exactly the same information as the first, actually advertises its pertinence.

Let us say, as another example, that in a personal-injury action in which you represent defendant, you wish to find out about plaintiff's income-tax returns. Instead of simply asking whether he filed such papers during each of a number of listed years, you might ask:

> 14. State whether you filed a federal income tax return for the year for which a loss of income is alleged in Paragraph 8 of the complaint to have been sustained and for each of the four years preceding that year.

We suggested in a previous chapter that in an action involving extensive documentary evidence, interrogatories might provide a more efficient way than deposition questioning of eliciting an inventory of the relevant material in another party's possession. In pursuing this objective, you will wish to have your questions display their relevance. You might draft something such as:

> 9. Set forth a list showing the date, author, addressee or addressees, designated recipients of copies and title or caption

of every writing (as defined in Paragraph C of the Definitions appended to these interrogatories) referring to or concerning:

> a) The contract of sale referred to in Paragraph 3 of the amended complaint;
>
> b) The amendment alleged in Paragraph 4 of the amended complaint; and
>
> c) The conference or meeting in St. Paul, Minnesota, held on or about March 19, 1972, according to the testimony of plaintiff's vice president Paul Meurice at pages 90 through 103 of the transcript of his deposition, held on September 12, 1973.

The illustrations above employ references to the opposing party's rather than one's own pleading. That is not an essential feature of the technique we are discussing, but it is certainly preferable. If your adversary challenges your interrogatories, he may try to counteract the effect of references in them to your own pleading by pointing out flaws or superfluities in your allegations. He can hardly do so if you have tied your interrogatories to his pleading.

Organizing interrogatories provides another way of letting them manifest their own relevance. If the complaint, for example, is divided into several causes of action, you might break your interrogatories down accordingly, using appropriate sub-headings. You might likewise arrange questions according to the affirmative defenses and counterclaims pleaded by defendant.

Your opponent may have introduced subject-matter or an issue into the case other than by his pleading. His own discovery, or perhaps a motion he has made, has brought up a topic into which you think you have the right to inquire. Consider this example:

> Plaintiff's attorney in a stockholder's derivative suit is attending the deposition of his client. Defense counsel asks about plaintiff's conversations, before he commenced suit, with certain of the corporation's ex-employees concerning alleged financial improprieties for whose disclosure they had been discharged. Plaintiff's attorney doubts the relevance of the questions, but lets them be answered. Later he drafts interrogatories. He wishes to confirm or supplement what his client learned about the corporation's affairs from his conversations with the ex-employees in question. He frames his question thus:
>
> 11. With respect to each of the four former employees of defendant named by defendants' attorney at page 29,

lines 14–20, of the transcript of plaintiff's deposition, set forth:

a. The date on which such employee was discharged or his resignation requested;

b. The circumstances that caused defendant to discharge such employee or to request his resignation; and

c. A list of all memoranda, letters, reports and other written instruments dealing with or referring to the discharge or request for resignation or the grounds therefor.

Questions such as these might enable plaintiff's attorney to broaden the complaint with potent allegations of corporate wrongdoing. Defendant's attorney would hesitate to object to them as falling outside the scope of the pleadings.

Interrogatories, as we have seen, do not always provide an equivalent substitute for a deposition. They do provide a convenient, economical way of eliciting information that should help your preparation of a case for trial. They will serve their purpose better if you can avoid excessive length in composing them and let their content speak for their relevance to the subject-matter of the action.

C. OBJECTING TO OR DEFENDING INTERROGATORIES

1. Whether to Object

We have been looking at interrogatories from the draftsman's point of view. We consider them now from the standpoint of the recipient. His first problem will be whether to object to any of the questions.

To begin, counsel will face the obvious question whether the interrogatories are in fact objectionable. He will ask himself whether any objections that he makes are likely to stand up. Secondly, the attorney will ask whether answering the interrogatories, even if they are technically objectionable, will effect real prejudice to his client's case. No sensible lawyer will waste time objecting to interrogatories when answering them will do no harm.

The two questions just mentioned are basic. They will serve as the prime determinants in the decision whether to object to interrogatories. Because these two elements vary so much from case to case, we cannot generalize much on them here. We can, however, point out a number of secondary factors that should in many cases tip the scales for or against objecting to interrogatories.

Many lawyers fall into a trap when raising objections to interrogatories. To strengthen his objection, an attorney will construe the offending question so as to put it in the worst possible light. He will resolve every ambiguity in a way that supports his objection and thereby broadens the question. His construction may come back to haunt him in the event the court overrules the objection and he must answer the interrogatory.

Take this example:

An employee sues his former employer for wrongful termination of the employment in breach of plaintiff's pension rights. He alleges, among other things, that defendant had established a practice of awarding pensions to terminated employees with long periods of service, such as plaintiff had, regardless of whether they had reached the age to qualify under the pension plan. Plaintiff poses the following interrogatory:

5. Give the name and last-known address of each employee of defendant to whom defendant has paid a pension notwithstanding the employee's failure, by reason of the termination of his employment, to qualify under the terms of defendant's pension plan.

Defense counsel's first inclination is to object to this question as unreasonably burdensome and remote to the issues. He begins fashioning an argument based on the reams of personnel records through which defendant must comb to answer the question. He thinks of the thousands of employees who have retired since his client inaugurated a pension program thirty years earlier and of the exceptions to its provisions that have been granted on a variety of grounds. He counts the number of locations where the records in question are stored and the number of man-hours that will be needed to study those records. Then it dawns on counsel that the interrogatory contains ambiguities. He realizes that in formulating his objections he is resolving those ambiguities against himself by interpreting the question as broadly rather than as narrowly as possible. He sees that if the judge overrules the objection, he, defendant's attorney, will be effectively bound by the construction he himself has urged. He will then have to make the laborious search that he is now decrying.

Counsel decides, therefore, to answer the question but to construe it as narrowly as is honestly possible. He determines, for example, that he will deem the term "defendant's pension plan" to mean the plan to which the complaint refers and under which plaintiff is suing. That particular plan went into effect just three years before the action commenced, long after the corporation first inaugurated a retirement program. He decides also to limit his answer to exceptions made on the ground applicable to plaintiff's situation, that is, failure to attain the qualifying age. By answering the interrogatory in the light of these and other legitimate interpretations, defendant's attorney substantially lightens his own job and avoids the risk of having to fulfill his own prophesy of a crushingly laborious compilation and analysis of records.

As another of the secondary considerations entering into his decision whether to object to or answer a questionable interrogatory, the astute attorney will bear in mind that an objection will sometimes reveal more damaging evidence than will an answer to the question. For example:

> In an antitrust treble damage action, plaintiff, an auto-parts jobber, was served with interrogatories asking for, among other things, his ten largest customers for certain products. His attorney prepared to object on the ground that the information constituted a jealously guarded business secret. He drafted an affidavit outlining the tactics to which his client and its competitors resorted in order to learn the identity of each other's principal customers and the relative volume of sales to those customers. He realized that in order to make his argument effective, he had to disclose some of the surreptitious tactics used by plaintiff to gain information of this kind. After consulting his client, counsel decided that giving the list in question without objection represented the lesser evil.

As a third factor, counsel debating objections to interrogatories will bear in mind that the arguments that he uses to attack his opponent's questions may later be turned against him. Take this case:

> A manufacturer was suing a supplier for breach of a contract to make and deliver certain fixtures. The principal issue was the amount of plaintiff's damages. Plaintiff served interrogatories calling for factory data going back ten years before the complaint was served. Defense counsel objected on the ground that such information was too remote in time to be relevant to the subject-matter of the action. The court agreed and limited plaintiff's interrogatories to but four years before the filing of the complaint. Later, however, defense counsel learned that an

examination of plaintiff's books would show that its sales dropped sharply for a year or two after each national decline in housing starts. The attorney saw that such data might explain the loss in sales and earnings that plaintiff now attributed to the alleged breach. When he asked, by interrogatories, for data going back far enough to illustrate the phenomenon that he wished to prove, he was met by the very "remoteness" argument that he himself had fashioned. Objections to his interrogatories were sustained.

These are some of the elements to consider in deciding whether to object to interrogatories. Next will come a review of the most effective way to present whatever objections one has decided to make.

2. How to Object

a. Acting in Time

Once having made up his mind to object to interrogatories, the attorney will proceed to construct and support his objections. This procedure challenges his skill in a number of ways.

We take for granted that counsel makes his objections in the prescribed form and within the time limit applicable. He must in some jurisdictions take the initiative in objecting to interrogatories rather than waiting to interpose objections upon the institution of enforcement proceedings by the interrogating party.[33] If he follows the latter course, his objections may appear to the court to be afterthoughts.

In some jurisdictions, one's time to object to interrogatories expires before his time to answer them. Whether that is so or not, failure to make timely objections often amounts to waiving them.

b. Phrasing and Supporting Objections

Counsel with experience will avoid one basic mistake in objecting to interrogatories. He will not simply list the questions to which he objects, leaving the court to figure out what is wrong with them. Broad, general objections to interrogatories as a group do not work.[34]

---

[33] *Harris* v. *Nelson*, 394 U.S. 286, 297, 89 S. Ct. 1082, 1089, 22 L.E.2d 281 (1967); *Sneider* v. *English*, 129 Ga. App. 638, 200 S.E.2d 469 (1973). The 1970 amendment to Federal Rule 33(a) modified this requirement as to federal practice. The objecting party in a federal case should still take the initiative by serving objections.

[34] See *Wurlitzer Co.* v. *U.S.E.E.O.C.*, 50 F.R.D. 421, 424 (N.D. Miss. 1970).

Counsel who knows what he is doing will state, clearly and concisely, the grounds of his objection to each challenged interrogatory. A typical objection might read thus:

> Plaintiff objects to Interrogatory No. 9 as calling for information neither relevant to the subject matter of the action nor reasonably calculated to lead to the discovery of admissible evidence in that it calls for information applicable to transactions not mentioned in the complaint and involving products other than those enumerated in the contract between the parties.

The prudent lawyer will do more than state his objections with care. He will support them. His support will consist of facts, argument or both. He will take care to make the most of each form of support and not to blur the distinction between the two.

c. The Supporting Affidavit

The grounds on which you object to interrogatories may involve purely questions of law. You may wish to show that none of the questions confronting you can conceivably elicit evidence germane to any material substantive issue.[35] More commonly you will seek to make a point requiring reference to something beyond the scope of the interrogatories themselves and the pleadings and other papers already on file. If, for example, you contend that answering interrogatories will impose unreasonable burdens on your client or will require the disclosure of business secrets,[36] you must present the court with facts backing up your contention.

Factual support for objections to interrogatories will usually consist of an affidavit. We may list several points worth keeping in mind in drafting such a paper.

We have said before that an affidavit will create a better impression if made by the client or a qualified witness than if it is made by counsel. The attorney's knowledge will usually be second-hand. No matter how thoroughly counsel has briefed himself on the facts to which he is swearing, his assertions on information and belief raise the question why he, instead of someone with direct knowledge, is speaking.

An affidavit, again to repeat, should stick to facts. It should not cite cases or present other forms of legal argument. It should give

---

[35] See, e.g., *Lantz International Corp.* v. *Industria Termotecnica Campana*, 358 F. Supp. 510, 516 (E.D. Pa. 1973).

[36] See footnote 23, Chapter V.

concrete details rather than conclusions. Instead, for example, of merely calling an interrogatory "burdensome" and "oppressive," the person making the affidavit should spell out wherein the burdensomeness and oppression lie. He should set forth, in specific terms, the amount of work that would be required to answer the question. If possible, he should state the number of file cabinets that would have to be searched, the number of employees that would have to be interviewed, etc.

An argument, incidentally, based on the allegedly burdensome or oppressive character of your opponent's questions will have a greater chance of success if you can also show that the information sought is equally available to the interrogating party.[37]

In the same way, if one is attacking an interrogatory as calling for confidential business information, the affidavit should tell enough, in factual terms, about the industry or area of commerce involved to demonstrate the harmful effects that would result from disclosure of the information demanded.

You should try, where possible, to set forth facts that enable you to avail yourself of policy grounds to oppose or limit your opponent's interrogatories. In one case discovery against a school district was sharply curtailed because full compliance with plaintiffs' exhaustive interrogatories would have strained defendants' limited budget and thereby have had the effect of curtailing educational opportunities.[38]

As we saw when we considered the problem of opposing a deposition,[39] an argument resting on hardship or infringement of rights will carry more weight if it applies to an outsider's hardship or rights. Your client, as a litigant, must expect certain inconveniences and deprivations as part of the price of justice. The judge, however, will be less willing to impose on non-parties.[40]

In all likelihood it will be counsel who drafts the affidavit supporting objections to interrogatories, no matter who signs it. That is entirely proper and to be expected. It can, however, lead to some costly blunders.

First of all, an affidavit drafted for a layman should use laymen's language. If you use legalistic terms like "hereinabove," "hereinafter," "aforesaid," "whereas" and so forth, forego them for purposes of a

---

[37] *Spector Freight Systems, Inc.* v. *Home Indemnity Co.*, 58 F.R.D. 162 (N.D. Ill. 1973); *King* v. *Georgia Power Co.*, 50 F.R.D. 134, 136 (N.D. Ga. 1970).

[38] *Gonzalez* v. *School District of Phila.*, 8 Pa. Cmnwlth 130, 141, 301 A.2d 99, 105 (1973).

[39] Pages 136–141.

[40] See *Reed* v. *Smith, Barney & Co.*, 50 F.R.D. 128, 130 (S.D. N.Y. 1970).

document embodying your client's, not your own, statements. In the same way, content yourself with stating facts. Once you begin making legal arguments, citing cases or the like, the judge will see your client's signature as a fiction.

A second mistake easy to make when composing an affidavit to be signed by a layman involves carelessness with the facts. What the affiant is swearing to should consist of his own actual knowledge, unless he explicitly states it on information and belief. Putting words into a mouth that cannot utter them truthfully involves more than a breach of legal ethics. It asks for trouble.

Finally, treat any affidavit or similar paper that you prepare for a client or witness, whether it be to support objections to interrogatories or for some other purpose, with the same care that you would use in preparing direct testimony. Make sure, in short, not only that what you put down is the truth from the affiant's standpoint but also that it satisfies the rules of evidence.

The affidavit supporting objections to interrogatories will begin, therefore, by qualifying the affiant. He will explain his relationship to the party for whom his affidavit is to be filed. He will show in factual terms his familiarity with the subject-matter of the objections. Here, for example, is how one might begin an affidavit by an employee of defendant in a substantial commercial action. Counsel intends the affidavit to show that the information sought by plaintiff's interrogatories would be unreasonably burdensome to collect and that its disclosure, in view of its confidential character, would harm defendant's business. The affidavit begins:

1. I am employed by defendant as its corporate secretary. I have had that position for eight years. Before that I was defendant's general sales manager for four years. I have worked for defendant for twenty-two years.

2. As part of my present job, I have charge of the records maintained at the company's headquarters in Graceville and at its several branch offices. I determine how long records are to be kept, what reports are to be made by employees at various levels and similar questions concerning the contents of our files. My experience in my previous position likewise familiarized me with the nature of our records. As general sales manager, I made regular reports myself and regularly reviewed reports made by many of my fellow employees.

3. I am also familiar with competitive conditions in our industry.

I attend the monthly meetings of our Executive Committee, at which competitive and other business conditions come up for discussion. I have the job of reviewing and condensing the monthly written report that each General Manager must file. As general sales manager, I was likewise required to know about competitive and related conditions.

These three paragraphs lay a factual foundation for averments concerning what is to be found in defendant's files and how the disclosure of commercial secrets will prejudice the corporation competitively. They should strengthen those averments accordingly.

If you are representing an individual or a smaller business, a single affidavit should suffice to establish the facts on which you base your objections to interrogatories. Do not, on the other hand, hesitate to use multiple affidavits if the nature of the case and of your client's organization qualifies one person to speak in one area and someone else in another. You should bolster your argument with as many relevant facts as you can. Getting each of those facts from the most knowledgeable source available can only benefit your case.

d. The Supporting Memorandum

In addition to setting forth the factual basis of your objections to interrogatories, you will wish to submit a written argument in the form of a brief or memorandum. You are, after all, asking a busy judge to take the time to consider your plea for relief from a proceeding launched by your adversary. As an officer of the court, you should be willing in return to set down in organized fashion the reasons why he should come to your rescue. Your effort in this regard will help your case as well as make the judge's job easier.

We have already pointed out that your objections to interrogatories may involve questions of substantive law. The memorandum, obviously, is the place for arguments on those questions.

A brief or legal memorandum supporting objections to interrogatories may differ from the written argument usually submitted in support, say, of a motion. You will likely be relying less on precedent than on logic. The interrogatories to which you are objecting will probably be unique. No case law is apt to be squarely in point. Your argument will consist for the most part of reasoning that demonstrates the impropriety of the particular questions before you under the particular circumstances of your case.

For example, in support of an argument that interrogatories are unreasonably burdensome, you will try to emphasize the remoteness of the questions to any issues in the case. Interrogatories, you will remember, are less apt to be stricken as burdensome if they go to the heart of the matter in dispute.[41]

You will nevertheless generally cite at least a few cases for the general propositions, usually undisputed, on which you are relying in your objections. A case might show, for example, that interrogatories may not inquire into privileged matters or that they may be vacated if they bear no reasonable relation to the subject-matter of the action.

In selecting whatever precedent you use, you should bear in mind that authority arising out of one area of discovery will probably be held applicable to any other field. A decision, for instance, that defendant in an automobile accident case may or may not be asked at his deposition whether he has liability insurance will surely be deemed applicable to a question on the same subject posed through interrogatories. You must, having selected precedents of general applicability, take it from there and show that the question or questions that you oppose fall within the prohibited category. This calls for the practice of the very essence of the lawyer's craft. You will marshal every bit of available material, including the interrogatories themselves, the facts that you have set forth in the affidavit supporting the objections, allegations in your own and your adversary's pleadings, deposition testimony and whatever else of pertinence you can muster. You will fashion this diverse material into logical argument intended to convince the court that the prejudice to your client that will result from allowing the disputed question outweighs the interests of full and free disclosure.

Take an example:

> In a personal-injury action, defendant served interrogatories asking extensive questions about plaintiff's employment record, earnings, and like matters. Plaintiff's attorney objected. He raised these arguments in support of his objections:
>
> A. Defendant obtained at its deposition of plaintiff full details of plaintiff's lost earnings.
>
> B. Plaintiff does not allege permanent incapacity or make any other allegation as to which defendant's interrogatories would disclose evidence or leads to evidence.
>
> C. The matters as to which the interrogatories inquire

---

[41] *King* v. *Georgia Power Co.*, footnote 37.

have no bearing on any of the affirmative defenses raised by
the answer.

D. Answering the interrogatories in question would subject plaintiff to embarrassment and potential harassment and
would confer no legitimate benefit on defendant.

This raises the question of how to organize your legal argument. If,
as in the situation just hypothesized, the interrogatories to which you
object all deal with the same subject, your problem in this area is
simple. You may, on the other hand, be objecting to different categories of interrogatories on a variety of grounds. Should you arrange
your argument interrogatory-by-interrogatory, or should you group
together those that have points in common? The right answer will vary
from case to case, but generally the latter approach will prove the
sounder one.

Here, for example, is how one might outline a memorandum of law
urging objections to interrogatories:

I. Interrogatories 3, 8, 12 and 14 relate solely to the
work-product of plaintiffs' attorneys.

II. Nos. 4, 7 and 12 of defendant's interrogatories demand
the content of privileged communications between one or more
of plaintiffs and their attorneys.

III. Interrogatories 3, 7 and 9 deal with matters lacking the
remotest relation to any of the issues raised in the pleadings.

IV. Answering any of the interrogatories objected to will subject plaintiffs to substantial prejudice, to harassment and to a
burden unnecessary to the defense or prosecution of the action.

Such a system of organization avoids the repetition that would
result if the challenged interrogatories were taken up seriatim. Why,
for example, repeat the work-product argument for each of the
four objections interposed on that ground? The applicability of some
of the objections to more than one interrogatory, not an unusual
phenomenon, helps the approach now recommended achieve further
economy of space. Suppose counsel in the above instance had organized his argument interrogatory-by-interrogatory. When he reached
No. 12, he would be advancing two arguments, both of them for
the second time.

As with any legal argument, the brief of memorandum supporting
objections to interrogatories should have a visible system of organization. A table of contents showing the various headings and sub-head-

ings of your arguments will both guide the court in following what you have to say and provide it with a succinct summary of your argument. For this reason, the outline constituting your table of contents should, wherever possible, proceed syllogistically, providing a sort of miniature argument in itself. Here, as an example, is how counsel might organize the objections to be made under Point I of the argument outlined above:

I. *Interrogatories 3, 8, 12 and 14 relate solely to the work-product of plaintiffs' attorneys.*
A. Interrogatories 3, 8 and 14 deal with the period beginning March 12, 1973.
B. The affidavit supporting plaintiffs' objections shows that they retained counsel in the matter in suit before March 1, 1973.
C. By their terms, therefore, Interrogatories 3, 8 and 14 call only for material prepared by plaintiffs' attorneys acting in their professional capacity and in preparation for litigation.
D. Facts established at plaintiff Wilson's deposition show that any information responsive to Interrogatory No. 12 would have to come from a report made by one of plaintiffs' attorneys acting as such.

You will help the court follow and understand your legal argument if you begin your brief or argument with an "Introduction" or "Statement of Facts." This section should let the reader know what the action is about and how the dispute presently before the court arose. You will make a better impression on most judges if you phrase this part of your argument in the most objective terms possible.

The beginning of a memorandum filed in support of objections to interrogatories might consist of something like this:

Introduction

Defendant submits this memorandum to support her objections to Nos. 4, and 8 through 12 of the interrogatories served by plaintiff on May 17, 1973. The text of each question to which defendant objects follows the appropriate objection.

Defendant's attorney filed the objections on June 10. A notice of hearing and an affidavit by defendant accompanied the objections.

This is a suit for an accounting of the earnings and assets of a dissolved partnership. Plaintiff, defendant and one Robertson, now deceased, comprised the members of the firm. A copy of the complaint, filed December 1, 1972, appears as Exhibit A to defendant's affidavit. A copy of the answer, which contains two counterclaims alleging defamation of character, appears as Exhibit B.

The interrogatories to which defendant objects bear on the dissolved firm's dealings with one Ambrose Watkins. Defendant contends, among other things, that plaintiff has and always had full knowledge of those dealings and that in any event the transactions with Watkins fell outside the period of time referred to in the complaint and have for other reasons no bearing on any of the issues at bar.

Plaintiff has submitted an affidavit of counsel in opposition to the objections. The present brief refers several times to defendant's deposition of plaintiff, taken April 12 and 13, 1973. The original transcript, signed by plaintiff on May 8, is on file in the clerk's office.

The principles governing the presentation of an argument supporting objections to interrogatories differ only slightly if at all from the rules that you will follow in presenting your side of any controverted position. The paragraphs above point out some of the special problems that arise and some of the techniques that can be used in urging such objections.

3. Defending Interrogatories Against Objections

Assume now that you are in the position opposite to that on which the previous discussion is based. Opposing counsel has made objection to several of the interrogatories you have served. How can you best defend your questions?

By the time you receive objections to your interrogatories, most of your work defending them should already have been done. The interrogatories themselves, that is to say, having been honestly and skillfully drafted and organized and bearing their own proof of pertinence, will provide the best possible answer to any objections. You will nevertheless wish to take some defensive measures.

If, of course, the affidavit or other factual presentation supporting the objections distorts the facts or omits matters that you consider crucial, you must file your own statement of facts, whether by affidavit or otherwise. In doing so, you will follow generally the same rules as those set forth in the discussion above of how to object to interrogatories. In other words, you will preferably choose someone other than counsel to make the affidavit, you will check the factual statement with your client for the accuracy of every detail, and you will draft the paper as a statement of facts, not as argument or as the recital of conclusions.

In defending his interrogatories against objections, the sensible lawyer does not content himself with showing that his questions fall within the limits of permissible discovery. He seeks to show that sustaining the objections will prejudice the merits of his case. He has in mind the principle enunciated in these terms by the Supreme Court of Oklahoma:

> . . . a party who seeks reversal of the trial court's judgment due to error in sustaining objections to interrogatories has the burden to show the trial court erred in sustaining objections to the interrogatories and that such error prejudiced his case.[42]

In preparing the written argument by which you will oppose your adversary's objections to your interrogatories, do not neglect to comb the record for helpful items. If your case is a lengthy or complex one, your adversary may well have taken a position inconsistent with what he must urge in objecting to your questions. A deposition taken by the other side can be especially fruitful in this regard, since the questions asked at such a proceeding are often spontaneous rather than thoughtfully planned. Here, for example, is an argument made in defense of interrogatories in a mortgage-foreclosure suit:

> Plaintiff submits that defense counsel, in urging his objection to plaintiff's interrogatory 4, has a short memory. That interrogatory, the Court will recall, asks about occupancy of the property before defendant took possession. Defendant, at page 9 of his memorandum, calls that matter "totally remote," yet page 32 of the same attorney's deposition of plaintiff shows the following:
> **Q.** Were you aware who had possession of the property before Mr. Becker moved in?
> **A.** No, I lived out of state then, and had a manager to take care of the property.

Careful reading of the pleadings and all motion and other preliminary proceedings may produce similar arguments.

---

[42] *Norman Plumbing Supply Co.* v. *Gilles,* 512 P.2d 1177, 1178 (Okl. 1973).

The arguments offered in defending interrogatories will vary widely from case to case. You can be sure nevertheless that a few points will have recurring applicability. They include:

1. Courts favor the broadest possible construction of discovery statutes and rules.

2. In most jurisdictions, material need not be admissible evidence to be subject to discovery. Usually, if something promises to supply "leads" to evidence, courts will direct its disclosure.

3. Practically speaking, if not by explicit rule, the party objecting to discovery in any form bears the burden of proof.

4. Material to be discovered need not relate to the case of the party asking the interrogatories. One is entitled also to seek out facts pertinent to what the other side, too, must prove.

Apart from these ever-present considerations, the arguments that you make to oppose objections to your interrogatories will depend upon the individual facts and other features of your own case. They will likewise make use of the same talents and resources upon which you must draw in other phases of your practice.

D. ANSWERING INTERROGATORIES

1. Your Goals

Whether objected to or not, most interrogatories must sooner or later be answered. We have mentioned that interrogatories have the disadvantage to the discovering party of being answerable by counsel rather than spontaneously by a party or witness. As attorney for the party served with interrogatories, you should make the most of the advantage thus accorded you.

In answering interrogatories, you will have three paramount goals in mind. You will wish:

1. To provide accurate, complete answers to which your client can swear in good conscience;

2. To give your adversary no more information than you have to; and

3. To disclose what you must in the form least likely to harm your case.

We shall consider these three objectives in the order listed. Some techniques, of course, will apply to more than one of them.

2. Getting the Facts Straight

Accuracy means more than satisfying the lawyer's own conscience by coming up with a factual source for each answer. It means getting to the truth as your client knows it. If, in compiling answers to interrogatories, you have the slightest doubt of the thoroughness of your client's research, or if you have any reason to believe that he lacks absolute candor, you must verify what he has told you. It may provide momentary security to take at face value whatever you are told by a knowledgeable informant, but it is you who will be held ultimately responsible for the success or failure of the litigation. Thus it is you who must be satisfied that the material being made a part of the record is factually correct.

We have spoken of the problem of a client's candor with his own counsel. If by the time you are answering interrogatories, you have not confronted that problem and solved it, you probably face your last chance to do so. A lawyer may deal with an implausible or incredible recital of supposed facts by shrugging his shoulders and saying, "Well, that's what the client told me." If he does, he abdicates his function.

Pragmatic as well as ethical considerations argue for accuracy and candor in answers to interrogatories. An alert adversary will always be ready to remind the court of any omissions or deficiencies in your sworn answers to his questions. As a federal appellate court has said:

> Misleading and evasive answers to interrogatories justify the court's viewing with suspicion the contentions of the party so answering.[43]

Meaningless answers such as "Not applicable" or "Don't recall" can provoke more serious sanctions.[44]

Sometimes, to be sure, you cannot be positive of the accuracy or completeness of your answers to interrogatories. You may represent a large corporation or other organization and be answering an interrogatory that, taken literally, would require interviewing hundreds or

---

[43] *Ruiz* v. *Hamburg-American Line*, 478 F.2d 29, 33 (9th Cir. 1973).

[44] See, e.g., *Philadelphia Housing Authority* v. *American Radiator & Standard Sanitary Corp.*, 50 F.R.D. 13, 18–19 (E.D. Pa. 1970), *aff'd., sub nom. Mangano* v. *American Radiator & Standard Sanitary Corp.*, 438 F.2d 1187 (3 Cir. 1971).

thousands of employees or checking innumerable repositories of records. If that situation arises, your answer should show its limited applicability.

As an example:

> A manufacturer is being sued for failure to warn the public of an alleged danger in one of its products. Plaintiff's attorney is trying to prove notice of the danger. He asks by interrogatory for every instance known to the corporation of a consumer's report or complaint of the dangerous attribute. Defense counsel's investigation shows that most such reports or complaints go routinely to his client's claims department but that to be sure of tracking down all such complaints over a period of several years, someone would have to comb through voluminous records at all of the company's fourteen sales branches. Defendant's attorney prefaces his answer to the interrogatory in question with:
> According to records maintained by defendant's claims department. . . .

You should nevertheless make your answer complete within itself. Unless you are making proper use of a procedure such as that provided by Federal Rule 33(c), which permits a party to designate and make available applicable records in lieu of answering interrogatories, you place an unfair burden on your adversary by merely telling him where the answer to his question will be found.[45]

3. Sources of Information

This brings up the question of what sources you must consult to compile answers to interrogatories. As an experienced lawyer, you should know that interrogatories, like other discovery devices, call for the party's or witness's own knowledge only. For that reason, the client, not you, should sign the answers.[46] Remember in this regard that the court may treat unsigned or unsworn answers to interrogatories as a nullity.[47]

Neither you nor the client need engage in outside research. The

---

[45] *Budget Rent-a-Car of Missouri, Inc.* v. *Hertz Corp.*, footnote 18, 55 F.R.D. 354, at page 357.

[46] See cases cited at footnote 16.

[47] *Cabales* v. *United States*, 51 F.R.D. 498, 499 (S.D. N.Y. 1970), *affd.*, 447 F.2d 1358 (2 Cir. 1971).

knowledge of former employees, for example, is ordinarily not required.[48]

On the other hand, your answers to interrogatories should represent, as far as possible, the knowledge of the entire entity that you represent. It would be unfair, for example, to answer interrogatories directed to a corporation by giving merely the knowledge of one of its officers or employees. In the case of a corporate party, moreover, you are probably required, in answering interrogatories, to divulge information in the possession of its subsidiaries.[49]

If your search for responsive information comes to naught, you may usually so answer. As a federal judge in Pennsylvania has said:

> If the answers [to interrogatories] are not available after reasonable inquiries to defendant's employees who have knowledge of the alleged incident, the answer may so state.[50]

Just as was suggested above in the case of positive answers to interrogatories, it will sometimes be wise to let an answer denying knowledge give some idea of the scope of your inquiry. An answer might, for example, begin:

> Inquiry among all of this defendant's employees on duty at its March Street Terminal on the date of the accident reveals no information. . . .

If you understand the function of interrogatories and view that function in the light of the policy underlying discovery, you will have no serious difficulty determining what sources you must consult in preparing answers in a given case.

4. The Draftsman

As one step in achieving the goal of accuracy, as well as for other purposes, the lawyer himself should compose the answers to interrogatories. Delivering interrogatories to a client and letting him draft the answers as though some routine questionnaire were involved repre-

---

[48] Compare *United States* v. *Ciba Corp.*, 16 F.R. Serv.2d 95 (D. N.J. 1971), and *Heng Hsin Co.* v. *Stern, Morgenthau & Co.*, 20 F.R. Serv. 33.42, Case 2 (S.D. N.Y. 1954).

[49] *Sol S. Turnoff Drug Distributors, Inc.* v. *N. V. Nederlandsche Combinatie*, 16 F.R. Serv.2d 113 (E.D. Pa. 1972), and cases cited.

[50] *Ballard* v. *Allegheny Airlines, Inc.*, 54 F.R.D. 67, 69 (E.D. Pa. 1972).

sents another easy way out of a challenge that must be met head-on if the attorney wishes to do his duty.

Reasons why the lawyer should draft answers to interrogatories come too readily to mind to require much discussion. The lawyer is trained and experienced in reading questions and in seeing how much it takes to answer them. He alone understands the action as a whole and can therefore appreciate the ramifications of different versions of the same basic facts. Finally, the lawyer, to retain ultimate responsibility for the management and outcome of the litigation, must exercise control over all of the utterances emanating from his side.

5. The Helpful Construction of Questions

Accuracy stands as your first goal in answering interrogatories. Secondly, you will naturally wish to give your adversary as little information as you properly can. Here again your skill as a lawyer comes into play.

The most expertly drafted interrogatories leave room for interpretation or construction. The lawyer upon whom the questions have been served will strive to place upon them whatever fair interpretation works out best for his side of the case. That will usually be the interpretation calling for the narrowest disclosure.

Let us consider an example:

> A farmer sued the manufacturer of a fertilizer alleged to have ruined one of plaintiff's crops. Plaintiff's attorney posed this interrogatory:
>
> > 6. List each instance in which any person has brought an action or made a claim against defendant arising out of the destruction of or damage to a crop as the result of using defendant's product.
>
> Defense counsel had to interpret "defendant's product." His client made several different agricultural chemicals. The complaint mentioned only one of them. Defense counsel decided that he could reasonably construe the interrogatory as applicable only to the product mentioned in the complaint. This enabled him to answer truthfully that no such actions had been brought or claims made.

Using thought and investigation to limit the scope of interrogatories thus often provides a simpler yet equally effective alternative to filing objections. Defense counsel in the example above might have objected to the interrogatory as excessively broad in inquiring about products not involved in the action. He chose instead to narrow the question by his own construction.

A word or two of caution appears in order. An interpretation of interrogatories that works to one's own advantage must be an honest one and must be reasonable. An answer resting on a far-fetched construction of the question, or one that is palpably incomplete, exposes the answering party to a motion to compel further answers or to other sanctions.

A necessary safeguard in the kind of situation under discussion is the disclosure of one's interpretation. In the example above, defense counsel answered:

> No person has ever brought an action or made a claim against defendant arising out of the actual or alleged destruction of or damage to any crop as the result of using the product referred to in Paragraph 3 and elsewhere in the complaint.

This answer foreclosed any charge by plaintiff's counsel of perjury in defendant's answer to the interrogatory. Plaintiff's counsel might contend that the answer was incomplete or unresponsive, but defense counsel's candor in not concealing his construction would stand him in good stead in any resulting proceedings, as would the reasonableness of his interpretation of the question.

Looking into the background of your case will often enable you to make helpful constructions of your adversary's interrogatories. By studying the pleadings, for example, you may decide that it is reasonable to deem questions applicable to a particular period of time, geographical area or class of persons or trade. You may find that your adversary has himself construed terms, explicitly or implicitly, in a certain way. You are certainly entitled to make use of his definitions or interpretations to whatever extent they benefit your version of the case. Always remember, however, to let your answers show your construction or interpretation of a question.

Substantive law may help you construe interrogatories to your advantage. The statute under which you or your opponent is suing may contain definitions, or the courts may have defined some of its key terms. Perhaps your jurisdiction has enacted general definitions of some expression. Sources such as *Words and Phrases* may provide you with helpful definitions. So may an authoritative dictionary.

You will be asking for trouble if you impose upon an interrogatory a construction that contradicts the express words of the question. Suppose, for instance, the interrogatory hypothesized above, instead of referring ambiguously to "defendant's product," had said "any of defendant's fertilizers or other agricultural chemicals." Defense counsel could certainly never have made an honest construction limiting the question to the product in suit. He could narrow it only by way of an objection.

Similarly, your interpretation or construction of interrogatories must be consistent. If, as an example, one interrogatory asks for "gross sales" of a product and the next one asks for "returns and adjustments" of the same item, it would be foolish as well as improper to take the first question to apply to world-wide and the second to domestic transactions.

6. Doing Minimum Damage

Let us next consider the third objective in answering interrogatories. You will wish to make what admissions you must in the least harmful terms possible.

As we have pointed out before, "truth" in litigation is rarely an absolute. Two opposing lawyers, both men of integrity, can describe the same event, the same condition or the same relationship in drastically different terms without either version's involving a departure from the truth. As an easy example, take this paragraph from the introduction to defendant's trial brief in an automobile-accident case:

> On May 17, 1974, plaintiff's and defendant's vehicles collided at the intersection of Pine Avenue and 14th Street. Both parties sustained personal injuries, and both vehicles were damaged.

Plaintiff's attorney in the same action wrote:

> Defendant's vehicle struck plaintiff's vehicle on May 17, 1974, at the intersection of Pine and 14th. Plaintiff had the right of way. He sustained multiple fractures and a severe concussion. Defendant escaped with scratches and contusions. Plaintiff's vehicle was demolished.

This shows again why counsel, not the client or someone else, should draft answers to interrogatories. Lawyers have no monopoly on intelligence, and persons in many other walks of life are well endowed with resourcefulness and eloquence. The lawyer nevertheless, thanks to his education and experience if not to latent talent, has an all-but-unique combination of abilities. He has skill with language, comprehension of the effect of words, knowledge of the issues in a given action, and rigorous ethical standards. This combination enables him, better than anyone else, to set forth a version of sensitive facts that will damage his client's cause the least.

You may ask what good it does to struggle for wording that makes the answer to an interrogatory sound slightly more favorable to your client's side of the case. Your adversary, you may say, will not be convinced by your version of controverted issues. If he is worth his salt, he will hasten to point out to the judge any difficulty or unpleasantness in your case that you have glossed over by the adroit use of words. To what avail, then, is an answer that sets forth the facts as you prefer to have them rendered?

The answer is simple. Answers to interrogatories may usually be read into evidence as admissions.[51] If you have submitted an answer in terms that give aid and comfort to your adversary, the words, being your own, will carry many times what they would have, had they been composed by the side whose position they favor. If, on the other hand, your answers present matters in a light favorable to your client's cause, your adversary may prefer not to read them into evidence at all.

To disarm answers to interrogatories carrying unavoidable admissions, experienced lawyers sometimes apply a liberal rather than a restrictive policy of disclosure. To what they must disclose, they add a fact or two perhaps not called for under a narrow construction of their adversary's interrogatories. Within reasonable limits, this practice may deter the reading into evidence of what might otherwise stand out as a damaging admission. As an example:

> Plaintiff in an action for fraud in the sale of a tract of real property, asked this interrogatory about an allegedly deceptive sales brochure:
>
> 18. State whether defendant Manchester printed the brochure or pamphlet marked in this action as Plaintiff's Exhibit 1 for Identification and, if so, set forth the number of copies printed.

---

[51] See discussion at pages 232–233.

Counsel for the defendant in question could simply have answered the question thus:

> Defendant Manchester printed Plaintiff's Exhibit 1 in 5,000 copies.

Instead he chose to say:

> Defendant Manchester printed the brochure or pamphlet drafted by plaintiff's broker Arnoldson. Defendant caused 5,000 copies to be printed, all of which it turned over to Arnoldson for distribution.

Such an answer might well provoke remedial action by plaintiff's counsel, perhaps in the form of a motion to strike alleged surplusage. Defendant's attorney, however, could defend the answer as truthful and as containing no facts not relevant to the issues. His strategem, in any event, was certainly more astute than merely handing his adversary a damaging admission.

Sometimes your adversary will phrase an interrogatory in such a way that even a strictly responsive answer will risk a damaging admission. Take this example:

> Plaintiff sued an airline for slander, false imprisonment and assault. The action arose out of plaintiff's alleged arrest while a passenger on defendant's plane. Plaintiff posed, among others, this interrogatory:
> > Did you have a warrant of arrest with you when you arrested the plaintiff?
> Defendant objected. It alleged that any answer that it gave would imply that it had arrested plaintiff, which it denied. District Judge Fullam overruled the objection. He explained:
> > It is possible to phrase an answer so as to provide the details sought without inadvertently admitting anything.[52]

The lawyer who keeps that principle in mind will make few if any serious blunders in answering interrogatories. Answers that provide the essence of the information sought, even though they do not set it

---

[52] *Ballard* v. *Allegheny Airlines, Inc.*, footnote 50, 54 F.R.D. at pages 68–69.

forth as the interrogator would prefer, will not often be deemed unsatisfactory by a reasonable court.

7. A Tempting but Risky Shortcut

We have pointed out how the Federal Rules now simplify the job of answering interrogatories in one respect. If answers can be compiled from extensive business records, it suffices in some instances to give the interrogating party access to the records.[53]

Think twice before you take advantage of this time-saving opportunity. What you learn from going through the records yourself may be worth far more to your case than the time you save by avoiding the job. Also, opening the records to your adversary may give him more helpful evidence than his interrogatories request.

8. Keeping Your Answers Current

Your answers to interrogatories can only speak as of the time they are served and filed. Months or years may go by before the trial takes place. Do not forget in that interval that you may be required to amend your answers to insure their continued accuracy.

Some state practices impose an absolute obligation to keep answers to interrogatories current. As an example, Rule 90(c) of the Rules of Practice for the Circuit Courts of South Carolina says:

> The interrogatories shall be deemed to continue from the time of service until the time of the trial of the case, so that information sought, which comes to the knowledge of a party, his representative or attorney, after answers to interrogatories have been submitted, shall be promptly transmitted to the other party.

Federal practice and that of some states impose a limited obligation to keep answers to interrogatories up to date.[54] Some states make no such requirement unless the interrogatories themselves specify that they are continuing.[55]

---

[53] See pages 197–198.

[54] Federal Rule 26(e); *Clark* v. *Fog Contracting Co.*, 125 N.J.Super. 159, 309 A.2d 617 (1973).

[55] *Northwestern Mutual Ins. Co.* v. *Stromme*, 4 Wash. App. 85, 90, 479 P.2d 554, 557 (1971).

E. USING ANSWERS TO INTERROGATORIES

Interrogatories should always generate useful information. They may also produce admissible evidence.

No one should make the mistake of assuming that filing answers to interrogatories with the clerk puts them *ipso facto* before the trier of the facts. Like any other factual matter, they must be offered and received in evidence.[56]

As with deposition testimony, the rules of evidence control the use of answers to interrogatories at trial. Federal Rule 33(b), as an example, provides in part:

> Interrogatories may relate to any matters which can be inquired into under Rule 26(b), and the answers may be used to the extent permitted by the rules of evidence.

Answers to interrogatories, if they qualify as admissible evidence, will usually do so as admissions of a party against his interest, an exception to the hearsay rule.[57] They can provide potent, sometimes devastating proof.

A case from the District of Columbia provides an interesting example of the efficacy of answers to interrogatories skillfully used:

> A pallbearer was injured when the handle of a casket broke. He sued the funeral home and the wholesaler from whom it had bought the casket. To prove the casket defective, plaintiff offered the answer of defendant wholesaler to one of plaintiff's interrogatories. Defendants objected (1) that the wholesaler's answer was not based on his personal knowledge, (2) that it constituted inadmissible hearsay and (3) that even if admissible the answer should not have been received against the wholesaler's co-defendant, the funeral home. An appellate court held the objections to have been properly overruled. It unanimously affirmed a judgment for plaintiff against both defendants.[58]

Answers to interrogatories may be used at trial without being offered

---

[56] *Zamora* v. *New Braunfels Independent School District,* 362 F. Supp. 552, 554 (W.D. Tex 1973).

[57] See cases cited at footnote 5.

[58] *Johns* v. *Cottom,* 284 A.2d 50 (D.C. App. 1971).

in evidence. Counsel can use them, as he can deposition testimony, for impeachment purposes. The basic decision as to which of the two uses should be made of answers to interrogatories depends on the considerations discussed in our treatment of the use at trial of deposition testimony.

As the interrogatory procedure progresses from the drafting and revision of questions, through the presentation, resistance and resolution of any objections, to the framing and submission of answers, the attorneys for both the interrogating and the interrogated party should remember that they may be dealing with items which, as evidence, will play a decisive role in the eventual determination of the litigation.

Chapter VII

THE REQUEST TO ADMIT:
A SECRET WEAPON

A. WHEN TO USE IT

Many lawyers neglect the admissions procedure in their preparation for trial. Whatever the reason for this neglect, the request or notice to admit is a discovery tool that no astute practitioner can overlook.

In most jurisdictions, counsel for a party may serve on his adversary a notice demanding or requesting that certain stated items be deemed admitted. The notice may likewise usually be used to establish the authenticity of documents. The attorney who receives such a notice has a set time (30 days in federal practice) within which he must:

1. Deny the items set forth in the notice;
2. State why he can neither admit nor deny those items; or
3. Raise an objection to the request.[1]

If he fails to take any of these steps, the material in the notice will be deemed admitted for purposes of that action only without any further action on the part of the requesting party.[2] If, on the other

---

[1] See, e.g., Federal Rule 36(a); Calif. Code of Civil Procedure §2033; Pennsylvania Rules of Civil Procedure, Rule 4014.

[2] Sub-paragraphs (a) and (b) of Federal Rule 36; *Mangan* v. *Broderick & Bascom Rope Co.*, 351 F.2d 24, 28 (7 Cir. 1965), *cert. denied*, 383 U.S. 926, 86 S. Ct. 930, 15 L.Ed.2d 846 (1966). Some courts will, for cause, excuse a failure to make timely compliance with a notice to admit. *Moosman* v. *Joseph P. Blitz, Inc.*, 358 F.2d 686, 688 (2 Cir. 1966); *Heller* v. *Osburnsen*, — Mont. —, 510 P.2d 13 (1973).

hand, the party served with the notice denies or otherwise fails to admit an item in the notice, including the authenticity of a document, and if the party who served the notice proves the matter anyway, the court in some jurisdictions may assess the expense of such proof against the party whose failure to admit made the proof necessary.[3] In most instances this sanction applies only where the failure to admit has been found "unreasonable" or otherwise unjustified. A party, however, need not prevail in the action to be awarded the cost of proving what the court finds should have been admitted.[4]

Jurisdictions differ on whether the admissions procedure applies strictly to "facts." Federal Rule 36(a), as amended in 1970, permits a request for the admission of:

> the truth of any matters within the scope of Rule 26(b) set forth in the request that relate to statements or opinions of fact or of the application of law to fact. . . .

In some states, admissions still apply only to "matters of fact." [5]

The admissions procedure has advantages over other types of discovery. Like interrogatories, the request or demand for admissions involves relatively little time or expense. It has, however, a far more potent sanction than interrogatories. A party served with interrogatories may answer them evasively, equivocally or perhaps not at all. He knows that the interrogating party will have to move for an order compelling answers, whereupon he, the interrogated party, will probably have another chance to respond properly.

The notice to admit presents a more serious threat. The party served must do something, or his silence will be deemed an admission. If he denies a fact and the other side proves it over the denial, he may be out the cost of that proof. If he raises an objection, it may result in an outright determination by the judge that the request is proper, thereby leaving the served party no escape route whatever.

The admissions procedure has another advantage that commands attention. Whatever is admitted normally stands as proved. The admitting party will not be allowed on the trial or on appeal to contradict or qualify the admitted fact.[6] Federal Rule 36(c), for example, provides in part:

---

[3] See, e.g., Federal Rule 37(c); Calif. Code of Civil Procedure §2034(c).

[4] *Agranoff* v. *Jay*, 9 Wash. App. 429, 512 P.2d 1132, 1136–1137 (1973).

[5] See e.g., *Fredericks* v. *General Motors Corp.*, 48 Mich. App. 580, 587–588, 211 N.W.2d 44, 47–48 (1973).

[6] *Kuenne* v. *Loffler*, 266 Md. 468, 295 A.2d 219 (1972).

Any matter admitted under this rule is conclusively established unless the court on motion permits withdrawal or amendment of the admission.

In contrast, as a federal appellate court has said:

An answer to an interrogatory is comparable to answers, which may be mistaken, given in deposition testimony or during the course of the trial itself. . . . When there is conflict between answers supplied in response to interrogatories and answers obtained through other questioning, either in deposition or trial, the finder of fact must weigh all of the answers and resolve the conflict. . . . On the other hand, if a party makes a crucial admission in his formal pleading, or in response to a formal request for admissions, then the admitted fact is to be taken as established, absent a timely request for, and the granting of, relief therefrom.[7]

The admissions procedure thus may provide the basis for a motion for summary judgment.[8]

The request for admissions has its weaknesses. In some jurisdictions it may not be used to seek the admission of controverted facts going to the heart of the case. As one state court has expressed it:

It is not a proper use of [the admissions procedure] to request an adversary to admit, in effect, the truth of the assertion that he should lose the lawsuit.[9]

The usefulness of admissions may thus be curtailed by a limitation to matters as to which there is little or no dispute anyway. A 1970 amendment to Federal Rule 36(a) attempted to rule out this "loophole" by providing in part:

A party who considers that a matter of which an admission has

---

[7] *Victory Carriers, Inc.* v. *Stockton Stevedoring Co.*, 388 F.2d 955, 959 (9 Cir. 1968). See *Saum* v. *Venick*, 33 Ohio App.2d 11, 293 N.E.2d 313 (1972), where it was held error to receive testimony rebutting a defendant's answers to interrogatories. See also *Freed* v. *Erie Lackawanna Ry Co.*, 445 F.2d 619, 621 (6 Cir. 1971), *cert. den.*, 404 U.S. 1017, 92 S. Ct. 678, 30 L.Ed. 665 (1972); *Herring* v. *Texas Dept. of Corrections*, 500 S.W.2d 718, 720 (Tex. Civ. App. 1973); *Waldor Realty Corp.* v. *Planning Board of Westborough*, 354 Mass. 639, 241 N.E.2d 843 (1968).

[8] Federal Rule 56(c); *Shapiro, Bernstein & Co.* v. *Log Cabin Club Assoc.*, 365 F. Supp. 325 (N.D. W.Va. 1973). *Jackson* v. *Riley Stoker Corp.*, 57 F.R.D. 120 (E.D. Pa. 1972), and cases cited, notably *In re Mack*, 330 F. Supp. 737 (S.D. Tex. 1970); *Lawrence* v. *Southwest Gas Corp.*, 514 P.2d 868 (Nev. 1973).

[9] *Reid Sand & Gravel, Inc.* v. *Bellevue Properties*, 7 Wash. App. 701, 704, 502 P.2d 480, 482 (1972).

been requested presents a genuine issue for trial may not, on that ground alone, object to the request. . . .

As another weakness, the party served with a notice to admit in some jurisdictions need merely deny the facts asserted, often not even under oath.[10] The inability to obtain an explanation or justification of the denial may leave the serving party in more confusion than when he started out. Again, Federal Rule 36(a), as amended in 1970, seeks to remedy this flaw by providing in part:

> A denial shall fairly meet the substance of the requested admission, and when good faith requires that a party qualify his answer or deny only a part of the matter of which an admission is requested, he shall specify so much of it as is true and qualify or deny the remainder.

Counsel who served a request for admissions may, according to the same provision, test the sufficiency of his adversary's response by motion. "If the court determines that an answer does not comply with the requirement of his rule, it may order either that the matter is admitted or that an amended answer be served."

Finally, the court may sometimes relieve a party of the consequences of its failure to respond to a request for admissions.[11] It has discretion, too, to refuse such relief.[12]

As his case moves toward trial, the intelligent lawyer will be weighing these strengths and weaknesses to determine how the admissions procedure available to him can best serve his purpose. He will also consider alternative methods of proof. He will, for example, hesitate to use the request for admissions to establish a fact provable by a witness whom he intends to call anyway.

In his deliberations, counsel will also consider how much he is disclosing by his request. He does not wish to reveal more of his case than he must. Yet he knows that exposing proof damaging to his opponent may accelerate settlement.

Take this situation as an example:

Counsel is defending a personal-injury action arising out of

---

[10] The 1970 amendment to Federal Rule 36(a) eliminated the requirement of a sworn response to requests for admission.

[11] See *United States* v. *Cannon,* 363 F. Supp. 1045, 1049 (D. Del. 1973), and cases cited at footnote 2, this chapter.

[12] *Lawrence* v. *Southwest Gas Corp.,* footnote 8.

an automobile collision. He has found a statement that plaintiff made to her own collision carrier a week after the accident. Perhaps fearful of a cancellation of her policy, plaintiff said in the report, "No serious injuries to driver or any passengers." Defense counsel believes that plaintiff's attorney either does not know of this statement, or does not know that he, defense counsel, has it.

Let us consider the pros and cons of a notice to plaintiff calling for admission of the authenticity of the report. Viewing the negative first, we see at once that disclosing defense counsel's knowledge of the report forearms plaintiff. She will have time to prepare, with her lawyer's help, testimony reconciling the denial of injuries with her later allegations to the contrary. If defendant's lawyer keeps the report to himself until the trial, and if plaintiff is confronted with it on cross-examination, she may be too flabbergasted to manage any explanation at all. If we assume that the report is in plaintiff's own handwriting, we see that the value of pre-trial authentication is close to zero, and the loss from disclosure a major one.

Let us look at the positive side of using the admission procedure in this situation. Defendant's attorney knows that revealing this grave weakness in her case will encourage plaintiff to reduce her settlement demand. He knows that by forcing her to admit its authenticity, defense counsel is depriving her of any hope of keeping the paper out of evidence, even by the desperate tactic of failing to take the stand. Using the notice to admit may enable counsel to settle the case at once, and for next to nothing.

A common use of the admissions procedure involves the authentication of documentary and other evidence. By a page or two of requested admissions you may save yourself an hour or more of tedious deposition questioning about points not in dispute anyway. You may also save your client a substantial amount in court reporter's fees. Thus if a deposition is to concern nothing more than such routine matters as the authentication of documents, you might consider replacing it in its entirety by a request to admit.

The admissions procedure has another handy function. You can use it as a way to make a certainty of what you believe your other discovery has shown you. Consider this example:

> Plaintiffs' attorney in a stockholders' derivative suit contends that the corporation's board of directors acted out of improper motives in authorizing a construction contract with an affiliate.

He suspects defendants of trying to construct, after the fact, sound business reasons to justify the deal. By depositions of the several board members he believes that he has established what documentary and other material the directors had reviewed at the time they voted to authorize the transaction. He serves a notice on defense counsel asking the latter to admit that:

1. At the time of the meeting on January 10, 1974, of the board of directors of Montrose Foundries, Inc., no member of that board of directors had seen or read any written material concerning the pending contract with Candid Franchises, Inc., other than the items listed on Exhibit A to this notice.

2. At the time of the meeting on January 10, 1974, of the board of directors of Montrose Foundries, Inc., no member of that board of directors had discussed the pending contract with Candid Franchises, Inc., with any person other than Thomas Sayers and John C. Heenan.

If, as plaintiffs' attorney expects, he gains admission of these two items, he will know that his discovery program has achieved what he wished it to. If he does not, he will be disappointed, but at least he will have avoided the shock of learning the unexpected contentions at the trial, when it is too late to do anything about them.

The notice to admit, finally, has a special advantage in some jurisdictions. It may be served until almost the very day of trial.[13] This makes it possible for counsel who has allowed a discovery deadline to expire without establishing a certain crucial fact, to pursue the overlooked item anyway.

Lawyers tend to overlook the request for admissions as a discovery weapon. If properly understood and applied, it can confer substantial benefits.

B. FRAMING THE NOTICE

Once he has decided to present his adversary with a request or demand for admissions, counsel must decide how to make the notice most effective. Achieving that end is not quite so simple as may first appear to the practitioner inexperienced in the admissions procedure.

---

[13] Section 3123 of New York's Civil Practice Law and Rules, for example, permits service of a written request for admission "not later than twenty days before the trial."

We have seen that the party responding to the notice may issue a simple denial without explanation. If a "fact" sought to be admitted consists actually of a complex of facts, a denial may leave the serving attorney in total confusion.

Take an example from a stockholder's derivative suit. Plaintiff's attorney served a notice inviting defendants to admit, among other things that:

> 4. On May 7, 1974, the board of directors of Associated Enamelware Industries, Inc., consisting of each of the individual defendants plus Roger L. Turner and Grant S. Welbin, convened pursuant to notice as provided in the corporation's by laws, at Canton, Ohio, and elected as officers of the corporation:

> * * *

A flat denial of this statement, all that may be required of defendants, leaves plaintiff's counsel, who thought his statement one of undebatable fact, in a state of perplexity. He wonders where the flaw is that enabled his adversary to deny what he, plaintiff's attorney, thought undeniable. Is defendant's denial so frivolous or captious, he wonders, as to justify confidence in the court's application of the sanction of the cost of proving the denied matter? Or is further discovery necessary to reveal and mend a fundamental flaw in his own case?

This illustrates the first and most important rule of framing a request for admissions, namely, make your statements of fact as narrow and detailed as possible. Make them so precise and so simple that anything but an outright "yes" or "no" answer would be impossible.

For example, the request set forth above might be broken down to these statements:

> 1. On May 7, 1974, Roger L. Turner was a member of the board of directors of Associated Enamelware Industries, Inc.
> 2. On May 7, 1974, Grant S. Welbin was a member of the board of directors of Associated Enamelware Industries, Inc.

> * * *

> 7. The board of directors of Associated Enamelware Industries, Inc., met in Canton, Ohio, on May 7, 1974.
> 8. A notice of the meeting of the meeting referred to in Paragraph 7, above, was mailed to each director of Associated Enamelware Industries, Inc.

9. The notice referred to in Paragraph 8, above, complied, in both its contents and in its mailing, with the by-laws of Associated Enamelware Industries, Inc., and with all other applicable requirements.

— and so forth.

A denial of one or more of these broken-down statements will tell plaintiff far more than the refusal to admit the sweeping statement in the earlier example.

Here is a second rule to guide the draftsman of the notice to admit: Do not ask more than you must. Your objective, after all, is to encourage your adversary to admit the statements you are submitting. The more conservative and the less exaggerated you make them, the more likely your opponent is to concede them. Draft your requests or demands, therefore, in straightforward terms, omitting characterizations and unnecessary adjectives and adverbs.

For example, in the illustration above, you might wish to establish that the corporation's board of directors elected certain officers at the meeting in question. You might originally draft a proposed admission thus:

At the meeting referred to in Paragraph 7, above, the board of directors duly elected Jason W. White president of Associated Enamelware Industries, Inc.

You might then reconsider whether your chances of gaining an admission would be better without the adverb "duly." It probably adds nothing to what you are seeking to establish. It gives a resourceful opponent a handy means either to deny or to refuse to admit or deny your statement.

In the same way, if you are using the admissions procedure to establish medical expenses in a personal-injury case, you might include a statement that the injuries arose from "the serious personal injuries sustained by plaintiff" on the date of the accident. What good does "serious" do you? Your proof of your client's injuries will not depend on what your adversary admits in this remote context. You are merely providing him with a way to quibble over something that he might otherwise concede.

If properly used, the request or demand to admit provides the practicing lawyer with an effective discovery tool. It deserves not to be forgotten.

C. RESPONDING TO A REQUEST TO ADMIT

Because of the relative infrequency of the use of the admissions procedure, not all lawyers realize what can be at stake when another party to litigation resorts to it. Ignorance, oversight, or delay under such circumstances can prove disastrous.[14]

Upon receipt of a request for admissions or a corresponding paper, counsel should begin by finding out what options he has and what time he has in which to exercise them. Unless experience has familiarized him with the procedure, he must review the applicable statute or rules and the leading decisions interpreting those provisions.

Once aware of just where he stands, counsel must decide what to do. He can make this decision intelligently only if he first appraises the requested admissions in terms of their impact on his case. He will pose three principal questions:

1. Do the proposed admissions contain flaws sufficient to warrant objections or some other procedural challenge?
2. Will making the admissions effect substantive harm to the prosecution or defense of the action?
3. If total or partial denial appears desirable, will such a denial likely be deemed unjustified and thereby risk the imposition of the expense of the opposing party's proof of the denied fact or facts?

These are not counsel's only preliminary questions. He must ponder what other consequences can ensue from whatever course he selects. Denying a claimed fact, for example, may throw the area in question open to discovery by another party. Admitting it may foreclose such further inquiry. It may occur to the attorney of whom admissions have been requested that admitting a given fact may be of no consequence because of that fact's plain irrelevance or other disqualification as evidence. An objection to a requested admission may require the revelation of facts (or perhaps theories of the case) that counsel would prefer not to disclose.

The answers to such questions and to others will figure in the decision of what to do about requested admissions. Making that decision by no means ends the matter.

---

14 Admissions can provide the basis for summary judgment. See footnote 8.

If counsel decides to make the requested admission, he normally need do nothing. He may, however, take affirmative action to effect the admission, e.g., by a letter or notice to the requesting party. The latter procedure may prove wise when one wishes to prevent the requesting party from using the pendency or requests to admit as justification for delay. Where permissible, it may also enable counsel to qualify or amplify an admission.

Denying admissions that another party has requested calls for prolonged, meticulous thinking. One must determine the other party's purpose in seeking the admission. Finally, the attorney responding to the request must draft a denial that will accomplish its purpose without generating any harmful by-products.

If a requested admission consists of a single, relatively simple fact (e.g., the date of a meeting or the temperature at a given time and place), an outright denial may pose no problem. If, on the other hand, counsel for another party sets forth a statement of some length and complexity and demands that you admit or deny it, your task is more difficult. Such a request, to be sure, may justify an objection to the requested omission, but assume now that you have decided against such a course of action.

Generally speaking, your denial should be phrased as narrowly as possible. Consider, for example, a request that counsel admit that:

4. On July 30, 1973, R. T. Johnson, E. G. Marner and S. L. Berkely, all officers of the corporate defendant, attended a meeting at the Sutton Hotel and agreed to request plaintiff's resignation.

We have mentioned the general inadvisability of framing requested admissions in such broad terms. We are considering now the proper way to answer them.

Say that you consider the above proposed admission correct except for one thing. Marner was not on the date indicated a corporate officer. In a technical sense, you may be justified in simply denying the statement. In most instances, however, you would be better advised to limit your denial to the item that you consider incorrect. Depending on the standards applied in your jurisdiction, the court could deem the one misstated detail inconsequential and charge you with the cost of proving the statement as a whole.

As you draft the paper or papers embodying your denial, remember that the product of your efforts may end up as evidence. Do not overlook any legitimate opportunity to interject helpful material. In the example cited above, for example, you might respond thus to the requested admission:

> Defendants deny that on July 30, 1973, or at any other time before October 1, 1973, E. G. Marner was an officer of the corporate defendant. Defendants admit that the meeting referred to in said Paragraph 4 took place and that the participants reached a decision to request plaintiff's resignation for the reason set forth in defendants' Third Affirmative Defense, namely, plaintiff's repeated threats to commit a breach of his employment contract.

Painstaking analysis of the admissions requested of you, together with patient deliberation over the significance of the admissions to the various aspects of your case will enable you to prevent your adversary's use of the admissions procedure to inflict unnecessary damage.

Chapter VIII

MAXIMUM BENEFITS
FROM MEDICAL EXAMINATIONS

A. AVAILABILITY

As discovery has widened and as practitioners have grown more sophisticated in its use, new areas as well as new techniques have developed. The taking of a physical or mental examination of a party represents a significant expansion of discovery. Every lawyer shoud be aware of its availability, which is broader than many suppose.

Many practitioners tend to think of this type of relief as falling within one particular category. Typically, plaintiff in a negligence case claims injuries. Defendant, to verify those injuries and perhaps to disprove or minimize them, engages a doctor to examine plaintiff. That situation, to be sure, accounts for a large fraction of the physical examinations taken. However, it by no means accounts for all of the possible uses of a procedure that can materially strengthen a plaintiff's or a defendant's case.

The Federal Rules, for example, provide for the "physical or mental examination" of a party or "a person in the custody or under the legal control of a party" if such person's "mental or physical condition (including . . . blood group) . . . is in controversy." [1] The rule is not restricted to personal-injury actions, nor is it limited to parties.

---

[1] Federal Rule 35(a). New York CPLR, Section 3121(a), permits a physical, mental or blood examination in "an action in which the mental or physical condition or the blood relationship of a party, or of an agent, employee or person in the custody or under the legal control of a party, is in controversy. . . ." Calif. Code of Civil Procedure §2032(a) contains almost identical wording. See also Illinois Supreme Court Rule 215; Pennsylvania Rules of Civil Procedure, Rule 4010.

Some states have narrower provisions.[2] As an example, Section 269.57(2)(a) of Wisconsin Statutes Annotated provides in part:

> The court or a presiding judge thereof may, upon due notice and cause shown, in any action brought to recover for personal injuries, order the person claiming damages for such injuries:
> 1. To submit to a physical examination by such physician or physicians as such court or a presiding judge may order and upon such terms as may be just. . . .

Broader provisions of the federal type open the door to medical examinations in a variety of cases. In a negligence action, for example, a plaintiff might wish to show that a corporate defendant caused the accident in suit by negligently retaining in its employ a truck driver with defective vision or some other handicap. The driver, although not a party, is surely "under the legal control of a party," and proper drafting of the complaint will have insured that his physical condition is "in controversy."[3] The mental health of a party or its agent might be in controversy in a contract or other action.[4] We have referred[5] to a defamation case in which defendant, having pleaded truth as a defense to the allegation that he called plaintiff "psychotic," was held entitled to a psychological examination of plaintiff. The federal government has used blood tests to challenge the paternity claims of aliens in nationality cases.[6] Similar tests have been used elsewhere where paternity has been in controversy.[7]

One must remember, however, that the federal provision, like many state statutes and rules, applies to situations in which physical or mental condition is "in controversy."[8] This may be something

---

[2] Conn. Gen. Stats. Ann. §52–178a states that "In any action to recover damages for personal injuries the court or judge may order the plaintiff to submit to a physical examination. . . ." Conn. Gen. Stats. Ann. §52–184 governs blood tests in "any proceeding in which a question of paternity is an issue."

[3] Schlagenhauf v. Holder, 379 U.S. 104, 85 S. Ct. 234, 13 L.Ed.2d 152 (1964), involved such a situation, although the dispute over the driver's physical condition arose between co-defendants. The Supreme Court took a narrow view of the scope of Federal Rule 35.

[4] Bodnar v. Bodnar, 441 F.2d 1103 (5 Cir. 1971), cert. denied, 404 U.S. 913, 92 S. Ct. 232, 30 L.Ed. 186 (1971), involved the mental examination of plaintiff to determine whether he understood the nature and effect of the action. See also Donnelly v. Parker, 157 App. D.C. —, 486 F.2d 402 (1973); and Estabrook & Co. v. Masiello, 75 Misc.2d 784, 348 N.Y.S.2d 879 (1973).

[5] Pages 26–29, citing Gordon v. Davis, 267 So.2d 874 (Fla. App. 1972).

[6] See the cases collected at 4A MOORE'S FEDERAL PRACTICE ¶35.03[1].

[7] Wright v. Wright, 281 N.C. 159, 188 S.E.2d 317 (1972).

[8] See, e.g., N.Y. CPLR Section 3121; and Illinois Supreme Court Rule 215.

different from being "in issue." A plaintiff's physical condition is certainly "in issue" in a personal-injury action, but the mental stability of an attendant may be "in controversy" without being in issue in an action by a parent for injuries sustained by a child through allegedly negligent supervision at a playground.[9] On the other hand, a requirement that physical condition be "in controversy" may restrict the availability of physical examinations when compared, for example, to Federal Rule 26, which allows other forms of discovery to reach any material "relevant to the subject matter involved in the pending action." [10]

For a person's physical or mental condition to be "in controversy" for purposes of an examination, it need not have been placed there by the person himself. The institutors of an incompetency proceeding, for example, might win the right to have the alleged incompetent subjected to a psychiatric examination even though the latter had done nothing to place his or her mental condition in issue.[11] If the party sought to be examined did place his own condition in controversy, that may simplify the task of getting an examination.[12]

You are not necessarily limited to one examination of a party. Circumstances may entitle you to successive examinations, e.g., where you have reason to suspect a material improvement or other change since a previous examination.[13] A claim of diverse injuries or ailments may justify examinations by different specialists.[14]

Keep in mind a few more things about the availability of physical and mental examinations. First, this is almost the sole instance in federal practice where the party seeking discovery must take the initiative of obtaining an order. In most other phases of discovery, the opposing party must move against the discovering party's notice. The requirement that the applicant show "good cause" for a physical examination makes this distinction one of more than form.[15] Some

---

[9] For actual examples of the distinction, see *Constantine* v. *Diello*, 24 A.D.2d 821, 264 N.Y.S.2d 153 (1965); *Turner* v. *Town of Amherst*, 62 Misc.2d 257, 308 N.Y.S. 2d 547 (1970); and *Fisher* v. *Fossett*, 45 Misc.2d 757, 257 N.Y.S.2d 821 (1965). See also discussion in *Koump* v. *Smith*, 25 N.Y.2d 287, 295–299, 250 N.E.2d 857, 861–864 (1969).

[10] *Schlagenhauf* v. *Holder*, footnote 3, pointed out that distinction. 379 U.S. at page 117, 85 S. Ct. at page 242.

[11] *In re Stevenson's Estate*, 44 Ill.2d 525, 256 N.E.2d 766 (1970).

[12] *Schlagenhauf* v. *Holder*, footnote 3, 379 U.S. at pages 119–120, 85 S. Ct. at page 243, 13 L.Ed.2d at page 164.

[13] *Lewis* v. *Neighbors Construction Co.*, 49 F.R.D. 308 (W.D. Mo. 1969); *Vopelak* v. *Williams*, 42 F.R.D. 387 (N.D. Ohio 1967).

[14] *Marshall* v. *Peters*, 31 F.R.D. 238 (S.D. Ohio 1962).

[15] See the discussion and cases cited in 4A MOORE'S FEDERAL PRACTICE ¶35.03[5].

states, however, permit physical and mental examinations by notice, which requires the opposing party to take the initiative of moving against the proceeding but which may still leave with the party seeking the examination the burden of justifying it.[16]

That is not to say that the parties may not have a physical or mental examination by stipulation.[17] That procedure probably represents the rule rather than the exception.

Many jurisdictions have detailed local rules governing both the taking of physical examinations and the exchange of medical reports.[18] Study of any such rules and the cases decided under them must precede arrangements for an examination.

Such local rules may raise the question whether you wish to conduct an examination at all. Say you have provable information about the person whose physical or mental condition is in controversy. You must ask yourself whether resort to the examination procedure provided by your local rules will do your case more harm than good by forcing you to share that information with your adversary. Take an example:

> Plaintiff, a small corporation, sustained damages when the manager of a public market directed plaintiff's driver to unload a shipment of merchandise in an unsheltered area and then failed to move the shipment into a shelter. Plaintiff's attorney alleges negligence on the manager's part, having received evidence from an investigator that the manager had been suffering for some time from arteriosclerosis characterized by periods of forgetfulness. Plaintiff's attorney, if he moves for a physical examination of the manager, may be "tipping his hand" by enabling defendant to get a copy of the examining doctor's report. Defense counsel will then have the opportunity to collect evidence either that his client did not know of its employee's condition or that it took reasonable precautions in the light of that condition.

Plaintiff's attorney must look also at the advantages to be gained from a revelation such as this. Pointing out to defense counsel this weakness in his case may provide a catalyst to settlement negotiations.

Remember, finally, that by obtaining a physical or mental examina-

---

[16] See N.Y. CPLR Sec. 3121(a); *Koump* v. *Smith,* 25 N.Y.2d 287, 299, 250 N.E.2d 856, 864 (1969).

[17] *Liechty* v. *Terrill Trucking Co.,* 53 F.R.D. 590 (E.D. Tenn. 1971).

[18] See, e.g., the provisions cited in *Bowen* v. *Fiore,* 42 A.D.2d 960, 347 N.Y.S.2d 749 (1973); 12 Okl. Stats. Ann. §425.

tion, you may be exposing one more witness to potentially harmful cross-examination. If you, for whatever reason, fail to put your examining physician on the stand, you can be almost sure that your adversary will call him. To return to the example above:

> Plaintiff's attorney went ahead with the examination. His examining physician testified to the existence of arteriosclerosis. On cross-examination defense counsel elicited the admission that his examination did not and in fact could not show whether this patient suffered from intermittent forgetfulness. The physician witness admitted further that many arteriosclerosis patients do not suffer forgetfulness at all. Defense counsel then brought out that the manager's employer, even if it required periodic physical examinations, would have no reason to question the employee's day-to-day presence of mind.

If your case is a strong one, the fewer witnesses you have to expose to cross-examination the better. This factor will weigh against a physical or mental examination when the wisdom of such a procedure is in doubt. If your case is not so strong, you may have to take risks of this kind. In either event, your chances of making the right decision will improve if you have in mind the advantages and disadvantages of each alternative.

Do not let tradition or habit make so basic a decision for you. Your client or a fellow lawyer will probably tell you that "In this kind of case we always [or never] have an examination." That kind of advice is easy to accept. It spares one the pain of a decision that may win or lose the case. Such advice, however, is better done without. Independence of thinking and the courage to make crucial decisions stand as two of the foremost criteria of the professional.

B. CONDUCTING A PHYSICAL OR MENTAL EXAMINATION

1. Selecting the Doctor

a. The Choice: Yours Alone

You have decided to subject an opposing party to a physical or mental examination. Where do you begin? What are the precautions to take and the mistakes to avoid?

Your first step will be to pick a doctor. Your practice statute or rules may not give you this right unconditionally.[19] Even, however, if the examining physician is to be selected by the court, you may have the opportunity to nominate a doctor.

Your selection or nomination of a doctor will probably represent the most important decision of the proceeding. We cannot establish a formula for such a choice. We can agree upon a few rules to reduce the possibility of error.

You as attorney should select the examining physician. Do not let your client usurp this function. If you represent an insurance carrier or a frequent litigant such as a railroad, you may be told Dr. So-and-so "is our regular doctor for this kind of case." For the client's own sake, you must resist such pressure. If it proves irresistible, reconsider your decision whether to have an examination at all. Physicians employed or retained by insurance carriers and other corporations do not invariably represent the élite of their profession. Regardless of the competence of such a practitioner, the most cursory cross-examination will bring out his lack of objectivity.

b. What You Want in a Doctor

What standards will you apply in picking a doctor? You will remember that not only are you choosing an examining physician but also a key witness and the author of a crucial exhibit.
You are after, then, a plural talent. You want someone who can:

    1. Conduct an exhaustive, intelligent and honest examination;
    2. Draft a fair but convincing report in literate terms; and
    3. Present and defend his findings and conclusions on trial
or at a deposition.

Knowing what you want gives you a start. You must then proceed to find someone who comes as close as possible to satisfying your criteria.

c. How to Find Him

If your own experience does not provide a medical expert suitable to your needs, you will be best advised to consult other lawyers. No

---

[19] *Stuart* v. *Burford*, 42 F.R.D. 591 (N.D. Okl. 1967). Conn. Gen. Stats. Ann. §52–178a provides that "No party shall be compelled to undergo a physical examination by any physician to whom he objects in writing. . . ."

physicians' directory or medical-association roster can tell you who will and who will not meet the criteria above.

As a lawyer accumulates experience, particularly in personal-injury litigation, he builds up a roster of physicians whom he considers suitable for physical examinations and medical testimony. The neophyte can do more than question other lawyers whom he knows. He can look for reported cases in his jurisdiction involving medical problems such as the one confronting him. He can consult the lawyers listed as appearing in those cases. Such cases sometimes mention, favorably or otherwise, the name of the medical expert supporting the proof of one side or the other. If an attorney goes to some of the many medico-legal lectures and panel discussions given from time to time by bar associations and educational institutions, he will not offend the medical participants by asking them to discuss their participation in actual litigation. The lawyer confronted with a medical problem that is new to him can meet with and "size up" the authors of leading articles on the subject. A bit of inquiry and planning may enable him to observe medical witnesses on the stand.

In addition to the views of other lawyers, you will take into account any prospective medical witness's reputation, particularly if you are working in a smaller community. The doctor whom you are about to select may be disliked or mistrusted in his area, which is where your judge probably lives and where your jurors will be recruited from. If he has suffered a recent misfortune such as a malpractice suit or the untoward death of a patient, you can be sure that word of it will have reached at least one juror. Remember, however, that if you pick a doctor from some area other than your own, the question will arise, explicitly or implicitly, why a local man would not do.[20]

A given physician may be known as a "plaintiff's" or a "defendant's" man as the result of his courtroom experience. Even if he lacks the reputation of partisanship but falls in the "plaintiff's" or "defendant's" category as a matter of fact, cross-examination may damage his value to your case.

Herein lies one of the paradoxes of our problem. The physician most skilled in forensic examination, reporting, and testimony will be the one with experience in those fields. That experience, however, may be his undoing on cross-examination. Your adversary can create the impression, perhaps not totally unfounded, that your medical witness makes his living testifying rather than healing.

---

20 See *Stuart* v. *Burford*, footnote 19.

Ideally, counsel should engage a doctor with some litigation experience, but not too much, and not all on behalf of the same side. He wants someone who is articulate and persuasive on the stand, but not so smooth as to seem a professional witness.

d. Some Objective Standards

Because some of the elements going into your choice of an examining doctor are subjective, do not think that no objective criteria apply. You will prefer a practitioner with credentials that will favorably impress the trier of the facts. Membership in professional societies, hospital affiliations, teaching and lecturing experience and authorship all add weight to the value of your doctor's findings. They thereby increase the effectiveness of his testimony.

If your case is a substantial one, you should not settle for anyone other than a "boarded" specialist in the field with which you are concerned. If your adversary engages such a specialist and you do not, you can count on prolonged testimony from his doctor about the exacting standards of the specialty board in question, the difficulty in meeting those standards and the significance of such an achievement in the profession. Your doctor will be hard put not to agree with this testimony during his cross-examination. The slightest disparagement of "boarded" status, coming from one who has not attained it, will sound like "sour grapes."

We have seen that the choice of an examining physician presents a real challenge to counsel. Where someone's physical or mental condition will play a part in the determination of liability or in the computation of damages, the importance of medical testimony justifies your doing your utmost to meet that challenge.

2. Drafting the Papers

In order to conduct a physical, mental, or similar examination under applicable discovery rules, you will need a set of papers. They will probably consist either of a notice to your adversary or of an application for a court order.

Do not jeopardize or delay your examination by hasty or slovenly preparation of the necessary underlying documents. Go to the governing statute or rule and refresh your recollection as to just what it requires you to show. Take a look at how case law has construed the various provisions.

A good basic rule to follow in this as well as other discovery situations is to make your papers justify themselves. In federal practice, the physical or mental condition of the person to be examined must be "in controversy." In applying for an order permitting a physical examination, you might, therefore, include language like this:

> Defendant moves for a physical examination of Andrew Rhodes, an employee of third-party defendant, whose physical condition is placed in controversy by Paragraph 12 of defendant's answer.

You should then proceed to set forth the facts that place in controversy the physical or mental condition of the person whom you wish to examine. As always, you will adduce these facts first-hand, preferably by a witness having direct knowledge of them. Your own affidavit, unless you have first-hand information, will probably not count for much.

If your adversary opposes your effort to conduct an examination, he will have to challenge the papers you have prepared to obtain the examination. Careful preparation of those documents will improve your chances of prevailing. If your adversary consents, you need not consider wasted the time you have devoted to research and proper draftsmanship. The persuasiveness of your notice or motion may have been what deterred the other side from resisting an examination.

3. Preparing for the Examination

You have selected a physician to conduct your examination. You may not now simply make an appointment and hope for the best. You have a lot to do in getting ready for the event.

In preparing for a physical or mental examination, particularly in assembling medical records, you may encounter issues of physician-patient privilege. We shall not treat that topic in depth here. As a general proposition, a party, be he plaintiff or defendant, who puts his physical condition in issue in a personal-injury or other action thereby waives the privilege.[21] The waiver does not, however, necessarily extend to the litigant's entire medical history.[22]

---

[21] *Koump* v. *Smith,* 25 N.Y.2d 287, 294, 250 N.E.2d 857, 861 (1969).

[22] *Koump* v. *Smith,* footnote 21, 25 N.Y.2d at page 299, 250 N.E.2d at page 864; *Roberts* v. *Superior Court,* 9 Cal.3d 330, 107 Cal. Rptr. 309, 508 P.2d 309 (1973).

As a premise to our discussion of preparing for a physical examination, we must agree that a lawyer cannot competently handle personal-injury cases, or any other matters in which physical or mental condition figures, without steeping himself in medical knowledge. This means reading medical textbooks, attending medico-legal seminars and consulting appropriate medical experts as specific situations come up. You cannot do the job to which your clients are entitled if you settle for anything less.

In preparing for a specific case, the physician upon whom you rely for instruction and orientation need not be the one you engage to conduct an examination and testify about it. If the size of your matter justifies it, consider enlisting a physician solely as your consultant. He can help you in countless ways, such as by showing you how to make sure your examining physician is going to do a proper job, evaluating his report, suggesting points on which to cross-examine the other side's doctor, etc. A doctor with great learning and experience in his field but ineligible as a witness for one reason or another, might prove helpful in this way, especially if circumstances have forced you to select an examining physician of whom you are not perfectly confident.

Preparation for a physical or mental examination of an adverse party or his agent must nevertheless represent a joint effort by counsel and the examining doctor. Before the examination takes place, you should know, in detail:

    1. What tests your doctor plans to make, what other procedures his examination will consist of and what questions he proposes to ask of the person to be examined;

    2. The significance of each such item of his examination; and

    3. Why he plans to omit any other tests or procedures of which your study has made you aware.

All of this takes tact. You must not offend your doctor by appearing to tell him how to do something in which he justifiably considers himself exceptionally competent. You, on the other hand, know that questions about what he did not do in his examination pose a threat to the doctor on cross-examination. If you let him proceed on his own with a "routine" examination, as will probably be his inclination, you are subjecting him to acute embarrassment and your client's case to disaster.

This means that you must have at least one preparatory session with the examining physician. You should use that session, as we have seen, to acquaint yourself with every item of the contemplated examination and to communicate any suggestions or questions that you have. In addition, you should use it for one other major purpose.

Well before the time comes for the physical or mental examination, you should have collected every available scrap of information and opinion about the physical or mental condition in controversy. Whatever hospital records and doctors' reports you are entitled to should be in your hands. If you have conducted an undercover investigation, or if any of the depositions, interrogatories or other pre-trial work has touched on the condition, you should have the relevant material segregated and ready for delivery to and discussion with the doctor you have selected.

Your job does not end with turning this material over to your examining physician. You must see that he reads it, absorbs it and takes it into account in his examination and his findings. Here are two things you can do toward that end:

1. Rather than mailing the background material with a request to read it, actually go over it with the doctor, asking his opinion about the significance of various items and calling his attention to any gaps, contradictions or inconsistencies; and

2. Ask him to refer in his report to each item of the background material, relating his various findings to items in that material wherever possible.

Caution the doctor, however, in the latter regard that his report must stand on its own feet. A finding that depends even partially on background information may prove shaky. The background data may not get into evidence. It may be attacked as self-serving or otherwise unreliable. The examining physician's report should point out the extent to which his observations corroborate or contradict such items as the examined party's testimony, previous medical reports, etc., but he should not predicate his own conclusions on them. If he does, you should know about it, preferably in advance, and his report should show the reliance he has placed.

Adequate preparation for a physical or mental examination runs the risk of opposing counsel's asking your physician on cross-examination something such as:

Q. Now, doctor, didn't you discuss this report of yours with Mr. Sullivan, plaintiff's attorney, before you wrote it?
A. Yes, I did.

> **Q.** And in fact you discussed your report with him before you even conducted the examination, didn't you?
> **A.** Yes.

If you have foreseen this questioning, you should be able to elicit, as the truth, redirect testimony of this sort:

> **Q.** Doctor, Mr. Cannon asked you about the talk you had with me concerning your report. Do you happen to remember the first thing I told you in that conversation?
> **A.** Yes, I do. You said that you wanted a fair, honest report that I could stand behind and support under oath.
> **Q.** Did I ever qualify that request or tell you anything inconsistent with it?
> **A.** No, you did not.
> **Q.** And is that in fact the kind of report you turned in, as represented by Plaintiff's Exhibit 4?
> **A.** Yes, it is.

In preparing for the physical or mental examination, and in your later preparation of the doctor to take the stand, you will go over this and other potential subjects of cross-examination. The more skillful and comprehensive your preparation, the more potent will be the evidence you present.

4. The Examination

Once you have seen the necessary preparations made for a physical or mental examination, your part in the project will usually be substantially completed. You may in some situations still have a minor part to play.

When the person to be examined appears at the doctor's office, his lawyer may be with him.[23] You should be there too, if you are allowed to be. Your function should be to prevent your adversary from "coaching" his client during the interview that will usually precede the examination itself, and from interfering in any other way. You will take careful notes of all that happens. You should think very carefully before participating beyond that limited extent. Even if you are tempted to remind your doctor of a question or procedure he has omitted, remember that everything transpiring during the

---

[23] See footnote 27 for authorities on the right of the party examined to have counsel present at the examination.

examination may be the subject of cross-examination or other inquiry.

In the event your adversary does not accompany his client to the examination, you would probably be wisest to absent yourself as well. Remember, in any event, that you may not ethically communicate with a person represented by counsel except through his attorney.[24]

5. The Report

The doctor who conducts your physical or mental examination will probably render a report to you. In most instances that report will represent a crucial piece of evidence. Your adversary may be entitled to a copy of the report.[25] It almost surely will provide him with his principal tool for cross-examining the doctor.

Above all, make sure that the report is the doctor's alone, not yours. You may, with the precautions suggested above, consult with him beforehand about what his examination should consist of and about what his report should include. You may confer with the doctor afterwards and ask questions about his findings. The report itself, however, in words and in substance, should be solely the doctor's product. Do not let him submit a draft for your review or offer to make changes if the final product does not suit you.

In the event the report appears to you incomplete or deficient in some other way, you must proceed with circumspection. If the deficiency is minor, consider dropping it. If you think it serious, arrange for an amendment or correction. Do so openly, however, not surreptitiously.

The best way to remedy a defective report from your examining physician is the most candid way. It is a way that will never embarrass you or the physician you have retained. Write the doctor a letter such as this:

> Dear Dr. Jeffries:
>
> Thank you for your report of July 18. May I point out an apparent omission from an otherwise accurate and comprehensive piece of work?
>
> Your report makes no mention of Mr. Hornstein's claim of a diminution of strength in the grip of his left hand. You do

---

[24] American Bar Association Code of Professional Responsibility, Disciplinary Rule 7–104(A)(1).

[25] See footnote 18, and Calif. Code of Civil Procedure §2032(b)(1).

mention in your third paragraph that he is left-handed, and I understood that you intended to test the strength of his grip.

If I am correct in concluding that in writing your report you overlooked putting down the results of whatever strength test you conducted, please send those results in a separate letter. As I have said before, I am interested in having a complete, objective account of all of your findings.

If you did not make any such tests, we shall have to consider a further appointment to conduct them. The complaint is not a major item of plaintiff's alleged injuries, but I had hoped for findings from you on all phases of his condition.

Please let me hear from you soon. We are scheduled to go to trial in September.

Yours very truly,

Whatever you do in such a situation, do not send the report back, asking that it be destroyed and a new, corrected one issued. However you may try to justify such a maneuver, the preparation of two reports, one of which no longer exists, will look suspicious. Even worse is the practice, fortunately a rarity among doctors, of issuing two simultaneous reports, one written "for publication" to the other side, the other a "confidential" one for your use alone. Sooner or later a lawyer will regret having anything to do with such duplicity. He will probably also regret having anything to do with a doctor who will suggest or condone it.

The report that you want after a physical or mental examination is the report that says what the doctor found, no less and no more. Your client and you cannot afford any compromise with this goal.

C. WHEN YOUR CLIENT IS EXAMINED

1. The Application for Examination

When it is your client or your client's employee who faces a physical or mental examination, your attitude will naturally be different from that of the attorney wishing to have the examination conducted. Some of your problems will nevertheless be the same.

Before anything else, you must weigh your response to the proposal to have an examination. That proposal may take the form of a notice, an application for a court order or an informal written or oral request. In the vast majority of such situations, you will have no alternative to consenting. The question will usually arise in a personal-injury action or some other kind of case where the physical examination is available as a matter of right.

In less clear cases, you may think that your opponent seeks to harass or embarrass you or your client by a physical or mental examination. You may feel that yours is not a case in which any party's physical or mental condition is "in controversy," but rather one in which the other side is trying to create such controversy by its proposed examination.

Speaking generally, your recourse in such a borderline situation is two-fold. You must study your code or rules of practice and the decisions under them to determine if your adversary's proposed examination falls within the scope of what is permissible. Secondly, you should reread the pleadings, answers to interrogatories, briefs and other papers that the applicant has filed. This will help you determine whether the necessary "controversy," if that be the standard in your jurisdiction, is a genuine or simulated one.

Applicable rules may entitle you to challenge your opponent's choice of an examining physician. The Wisconsin statute quoted at page 246 states, for example:

> . . . but no court or judge shall order or compel any person
> to undergo a physical examination by a physician to whom that
> person objects in writing submitted to such court or judge.[26]

You may have a chance to disqualify the doctor selected or nominated by your adversary as interested, biased, of limited competence, etc. Think carefully before you exercise any such right. Your case may benefit more from the chance to cross-examine a vulnerable medical witness than from his replacement by an unobjectionable colleague. On the other hand, your exception to an initial selection may result in the appointment of an even less satisfactory examiner. The Wisconsin statute just cited continues:

> Only one such objection to a specified physician shall be allowed
> a person in any action.

In a jurisdiction which, like the federal courts, requires an order before a physical or mental examination may be had, your task of preventing an examination may be a somewhat easier one. If your

---

[26] See also the Connecticut statute quoted at footnote 19.

state permits examinations by notice, requiring the opponent of the examination to take the initiative of commencing court proceedings, you must consider carefully whether the prejudice or inconvenience likely to result from an examination makes opposition worth your while in view of your probably limited chances of success.

2. Preparation and the Examination

You are faced with a physical or mental examination of your client. A doctor engaged by and reporting to your adversary will conduct the examination. You know that opposing counsel initiated the examination for the purpose of collecting evidence to use against you. You have a lot to do.

Just as when you are getting ready to have an examination made for your own purposes, you will wish to know the subject-matter thoroughly. If you, as lawyer for the party to be examined, do not have a physician in your camp already, think of retaining one, if not to testify for your side then at least to help you prepare for the examination and to provide you with ideas for the deposition or cross-examination of the examining doctor.

Before you consult your doctor about the impending examination, study what technical literature you can find about the injuries or illness involved in the action. Review hospital records and whatever other background information your investigation and discovery have brought to light. Then when you confer with the doctor you have retained, you will have intelligent questions to ask. He will not have to waste his own time and yours with an elementary explanation.

Before the examination, you will confer with the person about to undergo the examination. To help him answer the examiner's questions truthfully, you should review with him his medical history. Tell him to give whatever information he is asked for, but no more. Impress on him that he will be doing his case no good by exaggerating his symptoms.

You should also tell your client to remain observant throughout the examination. Explain to him that you will interview him immediately afterwards. Let him know that you will wish to know all that happened, the substance of every question and answer and the nature of every test administered. If for some good reason it will not be possible to question the client, tell him to make careful notes at the earliest possible moment so that he can later make a comprehensive report to you.

By all means, attend the examination if you are permitted to.[27] Observe and make note of all that you discreetly can. Do not let your adversary interfere with the examination. If you are present when the doctor interviews your client, be particularly careful to make note of exactly what is said by both persons.

The astute plaintiff's personal-injury lawyer makes careful note of the exact time at which the examination of his client begins and ends. He hopes thereby to show on cross-examination that the physician's pressing schedule made a thorough examination impossible. As an added precaution, ask the client likewise to make note of the time taken to examine him. If the doctor then denies your questions indicating a hurried examination, your client may be able to take the stand on rebuttal and contradict the doctor on the basis of his own knowledge. Generally speaking, the examining physician will have kept no precise record of the time he took to conduct the examination.

3. After the Examination

As you have promised, you should interview the client after the examination and find out precisely and completely what happened. To be sure of getting everything, do not just rely on your client's memory. Have a list of testing procedures that you, as a result of your preparation, would expect to be followed at this kind of examination, along with a list of questions that you would expect a competent examiner to ask.

You may or may not, according to your practice, receive a copy of the doctor's report of his examination of your client.[28] If you do, your pre-examination preparation and the comprehensive report of the examination that you have built from your client's and your own observations and notes will enable you to analyze the examining physician's report. Your analysis may give you a wealth of material

27 *Whanger* v. *American Family Mutual Ins. Co.*, 58 Wisc.2d 461, 207 N.W.2d 74 (1973), discusses the right of an examined party to have counsel present and cites cases on the question from several other jurisdictions. 58 Wisc.2d at page 469, 207 N.W.2d at page 78, footnote 5. See also the discussion by Judge Latchum in *Warrick* v. *Brode*, 46 F.R.D. 427 (D. Del. 1969).

28 See footnotes 18 and 25.

with which to cross-examine the doctor or to refute whatever other medical evidence your opponent presents. If you do not receive a copy of the report, the other elements still give you ample material for helpful analysis.

Your local procedure may entitle you to take a physician's deposition after he has taken your client's deposition. Do not overlook this opportunity if it exists.[29]

You will be wise, in reviewing the doctor's report, to keep in mind that if you received a copy the author undoubtedly knew that you were to receive one and composed the document accordingly. You know that the significance of reports written for publication lies often as much in what they omit as in what they say.

With this premise in mind, take the three basic sources you have assembled, namely:

A. Your knowledge, from your pre-examination preparation, of what the examination should consist of;

B. Your knowledge, from observation, of what it did consist of; and

C. What the examiner in his report said it consisted of and what he found.

Note any element that appears in one category and not in another, and you have a worthwhile topic for cross-examination at trial or at least for further pre-trial discovery. Why, for example, did the doctor not conduct a Babinsky test on a person alleging damage to the central nervous system? Why did he take the party's blood pressure and pulse and not mention them in his report? Is the report's conclusion of no impairment of hearing scientifically supportable by no more than a simple tuning-fork test? Vast possibilities present themselves to the lawyer who has prepared himself.

True, if you have no copy of the doctor's report, you have not quite so rich a field to mine. However, you still have items A and B, above, to compare. That can be profitable. What is more, you can expect the examining doctor's trial testimony or deposition to supply you with item C. You must then be ready, on short notice, to make use of the three-part analysis recommended above.

The work you have done before, during and after the examination will serve you in another way. You should know, more or less precisely depending on your jurisdiction's discovery rules, what back-

---

[29] See, e.g., *Unit Rig & Equipment Co.* v. *East,* 514 P.2d 396 (Okl. 1973).

ground information the examiner has available to him. Both his conduct of the examination and his report should give you a good idea whether he took each item of that information into account in arriving at his conclusions. For example:

> A doctor has examined plaintiff in a personal-injury action. Plaintiff's attorney notes that the hospital report shows that upon admission an hour after the accident, the patient's pulse was slow and irregular. Accident reports and deposition testimony show that plaintiff received a severe blow to the chest in the accident. The examination report, made months later, does not mention etiher fact. This enables plaintiff's counsel to ask on cross-examination such questions as:
>
> 1. Whether the examining physician knew of this post-accident symptom;
>
> 2. Why, if he did know of it, he failed to mention it in his report; and
>
> 3. Whether he overlooked or ignored any other items of significance.

Thorough work in preparing for and analyzing opposing counsel's physical or mental examination of your client can benefit you in still another way. You will probably have a doctor of your choice examine the client. You will probably expect that doctor to testify on your client's behalf when the trial comes. If you defer this "friendly" examination until after your adversary's doctor has had and reported on his examination, you can remedy the first doctor's mistakes and omissions and thereby shift in your client's favor the weight of the evidence in what will probably be a difficult conflict of expert testimony.

We have seen in this chapter that in litigation, physical and mental examinations are too important a matter to be left in the sole charge of doctors. On whichever side he finds himself, the lawyer has a part to play.

Chapter IX

PUTTING TEETH IN DISCOVERY

A. ENFORCING YOUR RIGHTS

1. The High Price of Enforcement

We have reviewed the mechanics of each discovery device and discussed how best to make use of it. We shall now concern ourselves with making the various devices work when one element, the cooperation of the other side, is lacking.

Discovery today enjoys the status of a right, not a privilege. Thus to deprive a party of discovery may constitute the denial of his right to a fair trial.[1] Rights, however, if they are to mean anything, require means of enforcement. Here is where discovery shows some of its imperfections.

Our review has shown us that most discovery devices now require only a notice or its equivalent. No longer is it necessary, for example, in federal practice to make a motion under Rule 34 to obtain discovery and inspection. One simply serves a written request. The same applies, in many jurisdictions, to each of the discovery techniques we have mentioned.

This notice procedure works fine as a way to save the time of the court, the parties and the attorneys. It represents an advance over a procedure whereby the party seeking discovery bore the burden of initiating court action.

The notice procedure makes enforcement more difficult. Opposing counsel may ignore your notice or comply with it improperly or

---

[1] See, e.g., *Slatten* v. *City of Chicago*, 12 Ill. App.3d 808, 299 N.E.2d 442 (1973).

inadequately. You cannot rely upon the court to perceive the flaw and penalize it or even to disregard an unsuitable response.[2] You must launch some form of enforcement proceeding.

All discovery systems, therefore, provide for sanctions. They usually take two basic forms. The court may, on motion of the party who served the notice, issue an order directing compliance with the notice.[3] Where a deposition is involved, the order may direct that the witness answer questions to which he has, probably on advice of counsel, refused to respond.[4] As a more drastic alternative comes the order imposing actual punishment, perhaps in the form of striking the pleading of the offending party, taxing costs against him, etc, for failure to provide discovery.[5]

Most jurisdictions do not grant the latter type of order, i.e., they do not impose sanctions, for disobedience of a notice.[6] Their codes or rules of practice provide, or they are construed to provide that disobedience of a notice entitles the party seeking discovery to no more than an order compelling discovery.[7] The imposition of meaningful sanctions for disobedience of a notice, usually arises from aggravated circumstances.[8] If, therefore, you serve a notice of deposition, a request for discovery and inspection, or a set of interrogatories which your adversary ignores or answers inadequately, you must proceed in two steps, thus:

1. Move for an order compelling the disclosure that has been refused voluntarily,[9] and if the resulting order is disobeyed;
2. Move to dismiss the action or otherwise punish the recalcitrant party or witness for disobedience of the order.[10]

To make matters worse, some judges prolong the process by making

---

[2] *Moses* v. *Moses*, 505 P.2d 1302 (Colo. 1973).

[3] Federal Rule 37(a).

[4] *Heldmann* v. *Johnson*, 51 F.R.D. 3 (E.D. Wisc. 1970).

[5] Federal Rule 37(b).

[6] *Bower* v. *Chicago Transit Authority*, 4 Ill. App.3d 1021, 283 N.E.2d 250 (1972). See, however, *Anderson* v. *Froderman*, — Mass. —, 282 N.E.2d 893 (1972), where the complaint was held properly dismissed for plaintiff's defiance of a notice of deposition.

[7] *Anderson* v. *Home Style Stores, Inc.*, 58 F.R.D. 125, 129–130 (E.D. Pa. 1972); *Lathem* v. *Lathem*, 42 A.D.2d 909, 347 N.Y.S.2d 733 (2d Dept. 1973).

[8] See, e.g., *Marriott Homes, Inc.* v. *Hanson*, 50 F.R.D. 396 (W.D. Mo. 1970).

[9] *Chustak* v. *Northern Ind. Public Service Co.*, 288 N.E.2d 149, 153 (Ind. 1972).

[10] For an example of this two-step process, with some intervening complications, see *General Dynamics Corp.* v. *Selb Mfg. Co.*, 481 F.2d 1204, 1209 (8th Cir. 1973), *cert. denied*, — U.S. —, 94 S.Ct. 926, — L.Ed.2d — (1974). See also *Collins* v. *Wayland*, 139 F.2d 677 (9th Cir. 1944), *cert. denied* 322 U.S. 744, 64 S. Ct. 1151, 88 L.Ed. 1576 (1944).

the second order conditional upon the party's renewed refusal to grant
the discovery to which his adversary is entitled. In some jurisdictions,
on the other hand, courts shorten the procedure of enforcement to
some extent by ordering, upon disobedience of a notice, that the
party comply within a specified time or suffer default.[11] Sometimes,
although dismissal is not granted, the moving party is awarded costs.[12]
Instances of the direct imposition of sanctions for disregard or disobedience of a notice are rare.[13]

But an uncooperative party must, in some jurisdictions, disregard
three directions (the notice, the order compelling disclosure and the
order imposing sanctions for non-disclosure) before he suffers for
his conduct. The enforcing party must draft three sets of papers and
perhaps make three trips to the courthouse where one trip should
have sufficed. All of this costs heavily in the lawyer's most precious
commodity, his time.

Perhaps worst of all, the court will not necessarily grant sanctions
even where the violation of its order is proved conclusively. A default,
for example, granted for disobedience of a discovery order may be
vacated in the interests of determining the action on its merits.[14]
Disobedience must in some jurisdictions be "willful" or "deliberate"
before severe sanctions can be imposed.[15] An unexplained or unjustified failure to comply may provide the required willfulness,[16] but
the knowledge requisite to willfulness can not always be imputed
to a party through his attorney.[17]

Some courts, *e.g.*, in federal practice, have available the contempt
sanction in addition to those sanctions designed specifically for

---

[11] See the procedures outlined in *Matyas* v. *Albert Einstein Medical Center*, 225
Pa. Super. 230, 310 A.2d 301 (1973); and *Grahn* v. *Dade Home Services, Inc.*, 277
So.2d 544 (Fla. App. 1973). In *Synthetic Environmental Development Corp.* v.
Sussman, 275 So.2d 291 (Fla. App. 1973), however, the two-step enforcement pro-
cedure appears to have been followed.

[12] *Iessi* v. *Marino*, 42 A.D.2d 583, 344 N.Y.S.2d 520 (1973).

[13] *Sneider* v. *English*, 129 Ga. App. 632, 200 S.E.2d 469 (1973), and case cited at
footnote 8.

[14] *Dorbin* v. *Yellow Cab Co.*, 14 Ill. App.3d 586, 302 N.E.2d 633 (1973).

[15] *Société Internationale* v. *Rogers*, 357 U.S. 197, 78 S. Ct. 1087, 2 L.E.2d 1255
(1958); *Sapiro* v. *Hartford Fire Ins. Co.*, 452 F.2d 215 (7 Cir. 1971); *Dorsey* v.
Academy Moving & Storage, 423 F.2d 858 (5th Cir. 1970); *Lapp* v. *Titus*, 224 Pa.
Super 150, 302 A.2d 366, 370 (1973); *Morton* v. *Retail Credit Co.*, 128 Ga. App. 446,
196 S.E.2d 902 (1973); *Plonkey* v. *Superior Court*, 106 Ariz. 310, 312, 475
P.2d 492, 494 (1970); *Serpe* v. *Yellow Cab Co.*, 10 Ill. App.3d 1, 4, 293 N.E.2d
742, 744 (1973), and cases cited.

[16] *Norman* v. *Young*, 422 F.2d 470 (10 Cir. 1970).

[17] *Sisk* v. *McPartland*, 515 P.2d 179 (Or. 1973).

discovery.[18] Thus disobedience of a court order may lead to a fine for criminal contempt.[19]

Some states include built-in sanctions in their provisions for certain discovery devices. In Alabama, as one example, Equity Rule 39(a), dealing with a defendant's interrogatories to plaintiff, provides in part:

> . . . and upon his failure to answer within the time allowed, the bill must be dismissed as to such plaintiff, with costs, unless the time to answer the interrogatories is extended.[20]

Such provisions are, however, often far from airtight. Under the Alabama rule just quoted, for example, the court may extend a plaintiff's time to answer defendant's interrogatories even where application for the extension is made after the time has expired.[21]

A philosophy of leniency prevails. Courts show a reluctance to impose realistic sanctions lest they thwart substantive justice. As one state court has said, a discovery device:

> . . . cannot become a weapon for punishment or forfeiture in the hands of a party, or an instrument for avoidance of a trial on the merits.[22]

This high price of enforcement and the dubious benefits of enforcement proceedings tend to reward the lawyer whose professional conscience lets him treat discovery notices lightly. Steps can nevertheless be taken to eliminate or at least reduce the time and effort that enforcement of discovery rights consumes.

2. To Forearm Yourself

When you launch your discovery program, or when you decide to resort to a particular discovery device, you may have no idea of

---

[18] Federal Rule 37(b)(2)(D).

[19] *Southern Ry. Co.* v. *Lanham*, 403 F.2d 119 (5 Cir. 1968), *reh. denied*, 408 F.2d 348 (5 Cir. 1969).

[20] As another example, Section 269.57(2)(b) of Wisconsin Statutes Annotated provides that if compliance with an order directing discovery of X-Rays and hospital records is refused, "the court may exclude any of said [X-Ray] photographs, papers and writings so refused inspection from being produced upon the trial or from being used in evidence . . . on behalf of the party so refusing." A key word here, of course, is "may." See also 12 Okl. Stats. Ann. §425, relating to the delivery of a copy of the report of a physical or mental examination to the person examined or his attorney.

[21] *Phillips* v. *Phillips*, 49 Ala. App. 514, 519, 274 So.2d 71, 75 (1973), *cert. denied*, 290 Ala. 370, 274 So.2d 80 (1973).

[22] *Wolfe* v. *Northern Pacific Ry. Co.*, 147 Mont. 29, 40, 409 P.2d 528, 534 (1966).

the degree of cooperation to expect from your adversary. You may or may not, depending on the circumstances, find it wise to risk appearing hypertechnical by taking advance precautions.

If, as one example, you have any reason to anticipate difficulty in a party's or witness's compliance with your notice of deposition, why not serve him with a subpoena whether it is necessary or not? We have seen that one may usually take a party's deposition by notice alone, but this does not mean that use of a subpoena is forbidden. Since a subpoena is in most jurisdictions a court order, its use may eliminate the first of the steps to enforcement that we outlined above, namely, obtaining an order directing compliance with your notice.

Other discovery procedures, *e.g.,* interrogatories and discovery and inspection, do not have the equivalent of a subpoena. You can still take measures to save some of the time and trouble that their enforcement can involve. You can be sure, for one thing, that you always have something to enforce. This means serving and filing the proper paper even though you have made what you consider binding and adequate informal arrangements. After arranging for a deposition by a telephone conversation or for discovery and inspection by a casual exchange in the course of a deposition, you can confirm the understanding by a notice that conforms to the rules of practice. If the time then comes when you must seek the court's help, you will have the prerequisite to an enforcement order.

When you launch a given discovery proceeding, your adversary may oppose it, by motion for protective order or otherwise. If you are alert, this may give you the chance to remove one step from the enforcement procedure should the need arise. If the court denies the motion challenging your discovery, be sure that its order also directs your opponent to comply with your notice. Federal Rule 26(c) permits such a direction in these terms:

> If the motion for a protective order is denied in whole or in part, the court may, on such terms and conditions as are just, order that any party or person provide or permit discovery.

Note that this provision is permissive, not mandatory. If you do not think to ask the court to avail itself of this discretionary power, you may, for reasons shown, have to take two tedious steps instead of one to enforce your discovery rights.

When the time comes to resort to enforcement proceedings, you should act quickly and decisively. Say, for example, you serve interrogatories. The party served fails to respond or object within the required time. Neither does he ask for additional time. You must then give serious thought to moving immediately for an order compelling answers. If the delinquent party, having received your papers, calls or writes you and explains that he overlooked your interrogatories and needs additional time to comply, you can be as liberal as you think the circumstances call for. No harm will have been done by your having started the enforcement wheels moving, and you will have strengthened your position in the event of future delays. In such a situation, incidentally, you might tell your adversary that if he is going to answer your interrogatories anyway, he should have no objection to answering them under order, so long as the order contains the adjourned deadline he has requested. He should consent to your motion. This puts you in a still stronger position to cope with later non-compliance.

As yet another precaution, your consent order in such a situation might provide that in the event your adversary fails to serve timely and otherwise proper answers to your interrogatories, they shall be deemed answered in the terms (favorable to you, of course) set forth in the order. This technique enabled defense counsel in a New York federal case to dispose of an action by motion for summary judgment.[23]

3. Making the Right Kind of Motion

Whatever the stage at which you resort to court enforcement of your discovery proceeding, you should do so in the most effective way. Here are a few basic rules:

1. Make sure that you have complied with all conditions precedent to enforcement. Local court rules, for example, sometimes require proof by affidavit that counsel have conferred in an effort to resolve the issue before the court.[24]

2. Emphasize that the failure to make discovery has prejudiced your case. Point out how it has done so. Remember that even

---

[23] *Cabales* v. *United States,* 51 F.R.D. 498 (S.D. N.Y. 1970), *affd.,* 447 F2d 1358 (2 Cir. 1971).

[24] See, e.g., Rule 2(a)(6), United States District Court, Northern District of Ohio; Rule 12(d), United States District Court, Northern District of Illinois; *Beer Nuts, Inc.* v. *King Nut Co.,* 477 F.2d 326, 329–330 (6 Cir. 1973), *cert. denied,* 414 U.S. 858, 94 S.Ct. 66, — L.Ed.2d — (1973).

as to an out-and-out violation of the rules or of an order, the judge has discretion to grant or withhold sanctions.[25] He will probably not grant them for violations that will not affect the outcome of the action.[26]

3. Allege a "willful" failure to comply and set forth facts to back up your allegation.[27] List in detail your steps to obtain discovery by the notice procedure or other informal means you have pursued. Show exactly how your adversary has failed to comply. If he has failed to object to your request or demand or has objected only after the expiration of the appropriate time limit, point that out. Attach copies of relevant papers, including your notice and any stipulations of adjournment.

4. Point out any other facts of possible significance, *e.g.*, the urgency arising from an early scheduled trial date. Also, a recital of other instances of dilatory conduct by your adversary may persuade the court to impose a stiffer sanction.[28]

5. Finally, make sure that your motion demands relief of a type provided for by your practice act or rules. Cite in a conspicuous way all applicable provisions.

The last of these points merits amplification. In specifying the relief that you wish the court to grant, you must avoid overlooking any possibility and yet you must be realistic. The best policy, therefore, is to ask in the alternative for every type of relief available, including costs of the motion. Then in oral argument or in your brief you can indicate which remedy or remedies you consider appropriate and why.

Suppose you are plaintiff's attorney moving in a federal case as the result of defendant's failure to answer your interrogatories concerning one of its affirmative defenses. The prayer for relief in your motion might read:

WHEREFORE, plaintiff prays that an order be entered:
1. pursuant to Rule 37(b)(2)(C) of the Federal Rules of Civil Procedure, striking defendant's answer; or
2. pursuant to Rule 37(b)(2)(B), prohibiting defendant from

---

[25] See, e.g., *Marriott Homes, Inc.* v. *Hanson*, footnote 8; *Hollins* v. *Sneed*, 300 A.2d 447, 449, (D.C. App. 1973); *Hearst* v. *City of Chicago*, 9 Ill.App.3d 1085, 293 N.E.2d 738 (1973).

[26] *Hearst* v. *City of Chicago*, footnote 25.

[27] This technique won defendant a dismissal in *Morton* v. *Retail Credit Co.*, footnote 15.

[28] *Diapulse Corp. of America* v. *Curtis Publishing Co.*, 374 F.2d 442, 446–447 (2d Cir. 1967).

introducing any testimony or other evidence in support of the
"Third Affirmative Defense" in defendant's answer; [29]

3. pursuant to Rule 37(a)(2), directing defendant to serve
and file answers to plaintiff's interrogatories on or before April
10, 1974;

and plaintiff prays further that in addition to such of the
above remedies as the Court deems appropriate the Court award
plaintiff, pursuant to Rule 37(d), the expenses of this motion,
including a reasonable attorney's fee,[30] together with such additional or alternative relief as the Court may deem just.

Having to reply on something beyond your opponent's voluntary
compliance to secure your client's full rights to discovery can prove
an exasperating, expensive process. Knowing your remedies and
how best to apply them will make the procedure easier for you.
It will thereby diminish your reluctance to resort to enforcement.
That will make your discovery program more effective in each case
that you handle.

4. The "Surprise" Witness or Exhibit

One aspect of discovery enforcement calls for separate treatment.
If your opponent, although called upon to list in advance of trial his
witnesses, exhibits or both, nevertheless puts someone on the stand
or offers an exhibit that he failed to list, you have a special problem.
Anticipating it may help solve it.

In this situation, you cannot resort to conventional enforcement
techniques. The other side has enumerated its witnesses and exhibits, say in answer to your interrogatories. You could not have
moved at the time to compel further answers or to impose sanctions
for incomplete answers, for you had every reason to believe that
your adversary had given you a complete list. Only in the midst
of trial, when it is too late to resort to regular sanctions, do you
discover the omission.

In such a situation, you have but one real remedy, exclusion of

---

[29] *Iaconelli* v. *Anchor Lines, Ltd.,* 51 F.R.D. 144 (E.D. Pa. 1970); *Ward* v. *Hester,*
32 Ohio App.2d 121, 288 N.E.2d 840 (1972), *affd.,* 36 Ohio St:2d 38, 303 N.E.2d
861 (1973); *Philadelphia Housing Authority* v. *American Radiator & Standard Sanitary Corp.,* footnote 44, Chapter VI.

[30] Federal Rule 37(a)(4) allows such relief in the case of a motion to compel
discovery. It was granted, for example, in *Bar Harbour Theatre Corp.* v. *Paramount
Film Distributing Corp.,* 5 F.R. Serv.2d 37d.2 (E.D. N.Y. 1961).

the testimony or other evidence that the other side has kept from you.[31] On its face, such relief seems only fair. You may find, however, that it does not come automatically. Unless you can show both surprise and the threat of prejudice to your case, the court may let the challenged testimony or exhibit into evidence, particularly if the failure to make disclosure is found not to have been deliberate.[32]

As one step in trial preparation, therefore, you wish to avoid any surprise witness or exhibits and to exclude them from evidence in the event they are presented. What can you do to anticipate and solve the problem?

To begin, make sure that you have your opponent firmly committed as to his witnesses and exhibits. You might, if it is permissible, serve supplemental interrogatories just before trial and thereby see if counsel has changed his list of witnesses or exhibits but neglected to inform you. This can be done, of course, even if applicable rules require a party to bring his answers to interrogatories up to date anyway.[33]

Secondly, your practice may permit a clause in the pre-trial order or elsewhere prohibiting the calling of a witness or the offering of an exhibit not listed in advance.[34] Even if such is not the rule or custom, a suggestion that the court add such a clause to the pre-trial order in your case may receive a favorable reception. You know, at least, if your adversary objects to such a clause, that you have cause for concern and reason to take other precautions.

Thirdly, make your discovery as exhaustive as possible, and direct it against all parties and other persons likely to have relevant knowledge. This will foreclose an argument that any surprise resulting from the calling of an unnamed witness or the offering of an unlisted exhibit is your own fault.[35]

It may sound paradoxical, but you should do what you can to build in advance an argument to convince the court that the evidence you are challenging has surprised you. By definition, you will not know until the moment of crisis what evidence you are trying to exclude, so your preparatory work must be general in character,

---

[31] *Von Brimer* v. *Whirlpool Corp.*, 362 F. Supp. 1182, 1186 (N.D. Calif. 1973); *Clark* v. *Fog Contracting Co.*, 125 N.J.Super. 159, 309 A.2d 617 (1973).

[32] *Neider* v. *Chrysler Corp.*, 361 F. Supp. 320 (E.D. Pa. 1973), affd., 491 F.2d 750 (3 Cir. 1974). See *Hollins* v. *Sneed*, 300 A.2d 447, 449 (D.C. App. 1973); *Plonkey* v. *Superior Court*, footnote 15; *Wolfe* v. *Northern Pacific Ry. Co.*, 147 Mont. 29, 40, 409 P.2d 528, 534 (1966); *Ocasio-Morales* v. *Fulton Machine Co.*, 10 Ill. App.3d 719, 295 N.E.2d 329 (1973); *Jones* v. *Atkins*, 120 Ga. App. 487, 171 S.E.2d 367 (1969).

[33] See, e.g., Federal Rule 26(e)(1).

[34] As an example, see *South Carolina State Highway Dept.* v. *Booker*, 260 S.C. 245, 260, 195 S.E.2d 615, 623 (1973).

[35] See *Wolfe* v. *Northern Pacific Ry Co.*, footnote 32.

but a thorough knowledge of your own and your adversary's case will enable you to make the best use of what resources you have.

In the case of a witness, you may claim that counsel's failure to identify him deprived you of the opportunity to take his deposition. His appearance, unannounced, at the trial limits your ability to verify the testimony that he gives and perhaps to prepare and present contradictory testimony. You have lost the opportunity to look into his background for material that might bear on his credibility. The lack of advance notice will surely handicap your cross-examination.

All of these arguments will apply in almost every case. The facts of a given action should supply still more ammunition for the fight to keep the surprise witness off the stand.

When it comes to exhibits, your job will be harder. Particularly if you have had possession of or access to a document or other item for some time before the trial, you will have difficulty arguing surprise or, what is more important, prejudice to your case. The exhibit that you have never seen before the trial will, of course, present you with ample arguments for its exclusion if it is a potent enough item to be worth objecting to.

It will do no harm in a situation of this kind to point to your own conscientious adherence to the rules. Remind the judge that opposing counsel has obtained the benefit of your complete and timely listing of witnesses and exhibits. This should help him see the unfairness in your adversary's failure to reciprocate.

Some day you may find the shoe on the other foot. You will wish to call a witness or offer an exhibit which for some reason you did not list in your answers to interrogatories or their equivalent. How can you get this important material in evidence over your adversary's claim of surprise?

In general, you would probably be best advised not to wait until the evidence is objected to. Apply to the court, as far in advance as you can, for permission to amend your answers to interrogatories or the pre-trial order and to introduce the evidence not previously listed. A brief memorandum of law might accompany your application, but you will almost surely wish to have an affidavit. It should show, to the extent possible under the circumstances:

    1. That you have legitimate reasons for not having previously listed the witness or exhibit;

    2. That you made the application as promptly as possible upon discovering the need for the unlisted evidence;

    3. That you likewise notified the other side at the earliest

possible opportunity and, in the case of a witness, offered to
consent to the taking of a deposition or, in the case of an exhibit,
furnished a copy;

    4. That any claim of surprise will not be legitimate in view
of your opponent's knowledge of the evidence or at least his
reasonable opportunity, given due diligence on his part, to learn
of it; and

    5. That reciept of the evidence in question will not prejudice
the rights of any party but will further the interests of justice
by bringing material and weighty evidence before the trier of
the facts.

You will, of course, make these points in factual terms, not as bald
conclusions. If the affidavit that you submit is your own, you should
consider supplementing it with the affidavit of your client, the witness
whom you wish to call or some other knowledgeable layman.

B. PROTECTING YOUR RIGHTS

1. Follow the Book

Let us consider the problem of enforcement of discovery from the
opposite side. Let us discuss it from the standpoint of the attorney
for the party against whom enforcement is sought.

If you pay attention to your practice code and rules, observe all
deadlines and obtain timely extensions where necessary, and if you
meet all other requirements imposed by applicable discovery provisions, you will have little if any occasion to deal with enforcement by
your adversaries.[36] The suggestions below, therefore, will be mainly
of a preventive character.

Just as you should do as an initiator and potential enforcer of
discovery, you should make sure to protect the record in advance.
Be able to prove, by documentary evidence, that you have complied
with every requirement imposed on you by your adversary's notice.
If that is not the fact, be able to show good reasons for the impossibility
of full compliance. If your practice requires you to make objections
to a notice or other paper by a certain date, either do so within the
allotted time or get the time extended. When, incidentally, you need
an extension of time of any kind, you should ask your opponent
for it in advance. This means far enough in advance that if he turns

---

[36] See *Sapiro* v. *Hartford Fire Ins. Co.*, footnote 15, 452 F.2d at page 217.

down your request you have time to apply to the court. You put yourself in a poor light by appearing to have ignored a deadline, particularly one imposed by court order, until your opponent institutes proceedings for sanctions.

The pressure of time and other cases can induce shortcuts and oversights that we later regret. It may work to your advantage sometimes to overlook or forgive the omissions and oversights of opposing counsel, but you will spare yourself substantial embarrassment, and perhaps avoid prejudice to the rights of your client, if you hold yourself to strict, literal compliance with every detail of discovery practice.

2. Keep Exhaustive Records

You will also improve your chances of successfully defending an enforcement motion if you can document in detail the amount of work that went into your own and your client's response to the other side's notice. Diligent and exhaustive research will not excuse your ignoring a notice. It may nevertheless help when you are charged with something such as submitting incomplete answers to interrogatories or failing to produce all of the records called for.

In the type of case that involves large numbers of documents, you should ask that someone in your client's employ be appointed to help you with the file searching and other factual research necessary for discovery and other trial-preparation purposes. Suggest that this person or these persons keep a detailed diary or log. It should show both the general nature of each item of work done and the amount of time spent on it. Such a record, if kept faithfully and accurately, will come in handy in several ways.

3. The Motion Itself: To Defend or Not

When preventive measures, whatever they have been, have failed, and you find yourself face-to-face with a motion challenging your client's or your own compliance with discovery requirements, you have several decisions to make. The first of these is crucial but not often difficult.

Should you defend an enforcement motion at all? If the motion asks only for an order compelling disclosure, or if you feel confident that such is the only relief the court will grant, you might well consider consenting. This suggestion assumes that you either have no objection to any part of the discovery that your adversary initiated or that if you have, you have made timely objection.

Under some circumstances, you may wish to put up resistance to an enforcement motion even though you have no real objection to the order compelling discovery. The motion filed by opposing counsel may have painted so black a picture of your client's alleged noncompliance that you wish to clarify the record. You do not wish the judge, particularly if he will be trying the case, forming an early impression of your side as difficult or obstreperous.

4. A Short-Cut Solution

If you have decided to resist your opponent's motion, you can probably defeat it by making it moot. Do this by complying at once with the notice or other paper he is trying to enforce. If you can achieve this by the time the motion comes up for argument, you should find the judge reluctant to waste his time on an omission that has already been remedied. Indeed, upon your compliance your opponent will often withdraw his motion as having lost its purpose.

5. The Counteroffensive: The Best Defense?

When confronted with a motion to compel discovery, counsel must assemble every legitimate resource. One effective weapon for this purpose may be your opponent's conduct of his discovery and other pre-trial proceedings. If he has been dilatory or evasive, you may be able to make effective use of a *tu quoque* argument. This will be particularly true where his delays have been unauthorized ones, *e.g.,* where instead of obtaining adjournments when necessary he has simply helped himself to whatever extra time he needed. Even more useful is the ability to point out how opposing counsel's delay has hindered your efforts to comply with his notice or demand. Such a situation might arise, for example, where you have asked interrogatories about the other side's contentions and cannot select the information or documents that they have demanded until you know what those contentions are.

In discussing the strategy of enforcing discovery, we dwelt on the importance of building a proper procedural record. If your adversary has failed to follow this advice and is demanding some kind of enforcement, you should be alert to his oversight. You might, for example, point out that your client has not disobeyed an actual notice but has merely failed to live up to an informal telephone stipulation. You would then add a reference to the appropriate section or rule to show that the relief being sought has as its predicate the failure to observe a written notice.

In making this kind of argument, you must avoid the appearance of resorting to a technicality to justify a failure to honor a promise to a fellow lawyer. You might use language such as this for that purpose:

> 8. Although, as shown in Paragraphs 6 and 7, above, the Federal Rules do not entitle plaintiff to the drastic relief he seeks, I nevertheless wish to explain to the Court my client's inability to abide by the commitment that I made to Mr. Heath by telephone on March 12. I submit that the facts stated below and in the accompanying affidavit of defendant's secretary-treasurer more than justify that failure.

6. Hardship and Emergency as Defenses

The task of opposing a motion to compel discovery or a motion for sanctions for disobedience of a discovery order becomes more difficult when a lawyer must try to justify his client's failure to appear for a deposition. If counsel can present a valid excuse, he must do so. He must include every scrap of corroborative detail and documentation available. For example, if reasons of health have prevented an appearance, counsel should do more than state on information and belief that his client "has been indisposed." He should show, preferably by affidavit of the client, his doctor or both, just what the illness has been, how long it has lasted and why it has made an appearance impossible.

Whether your excuse be illness or some other crisis, proving the emergency may not be enough. You should also show what you did to obtain an extension of your time to comply with the notice or order you are charged with having disregarded.[37]

The sophisticated lawyer hestitates in this kind of situation to argue

---

[37] *Hodges* v. *Youmans*, 122 Ga. App. 487, 177 S.E.2d 577, 578 (1970).

or try to prove that his client has been kept from a deposition by "pressing business commitments" or something of the like. As we have noted before, telling a judge that a party has given private business priority over a matter in that judge's court may create greater danger than offering no excuse at all. The attitude may strike the layman as realistic or not, but it is a fundamental one and an important one, that to any court the law comes first, commerce and industry somewhere thereafter.

Where a true business emergency has arisen and must be relied on, the attorney and his client must therefore proceed with caution. They should not only explain the facts in exhaustive and well-documented detail, but also make it plain that they recognize and acknowledge the precedence that the legal system takes over a litigant's daily affairs, however pressing. Here, for example, is how a client's affidavit might introduce an explanation of his failure to appear at a deposition:

ARTHUR J. SAWYERS, being duly sworn, deposes and says that:

1. I am defendant in the above action. I make this affidavit to explain to the Court my failure to appear for a deposition on March 6, 1974. I am asking the Court to deny the motion by plaintiff's attorney to strike my answer and enter judgment for plaintiff.

2. As shown by the facts below, a business crisis of the acutest character kept me from attending the deposition. I recognize that, as my attorney has repeatedly advised me, my obligations to this Court as a litigant take precedence over the demands of my business. In the situation outlined below, however, an unforeseen emergency required my presence in the vicinity of Tuscaloosa, Alabama, to prevent the shut-down of a factory. Such shut-down would have deprived over 215 persons of several days' work and jeopardized my company's relations with its largest customer.

3. The suddenness with which the crisis emerged, together with the limited access by air transportation to the area of our factory, gave me only the shortest time to decide whether to attend to the crisis above or to appear for my deposition. I had no time to consult my attorney. Inasmuch as my opponent, Mr. Mendoza, had asked for and obtained four postponements of his deposition, and since I knew that a deposition would not involve an actual court appearance, I made the snap judgment to go to Alabama.

I apologize to the Court and to all concerned for any inconvenience that my decision caused.

[Full details of the emergency should follow.]

An Illinois decision [38] shows how counsel's resourcefulness can rescue a party from the most extreme of sanctions for apparently outright defiance of a court order for discovery. It involved a corporate defendant's failure to produce an employee for a deposition notwithstanding an explicit order entered after a notice had failed to secure the employee's attendance. The trial court struck defendant's answer and entered judgment for plaintiff. The appellate court reversed, pointing to the corporate defendant's proof that it had ordered the employee to attend, that he had refused to do so and that under a collective-bargaining contract the employer lacked the power to punish the employee by discharge or otherwise.

As an officer of the court, you have a duty to obey statutes, rules and orders applicable to your case. It should not take enforcement or the threat of enforcement to make you comply with proper discovery proceedings instituted by other counsel. You must, on the other hand, protect your client's and your own rights against the substantive damage that procedural errors or omissions can sometimes effect.

7. The Client's Responsibility

Sometimes a lawyer faces the situation in which he has done his best to comply with a discovery notice, or even an order, but he simply cannot enlist the indispensable cooperation of his client. Take the case of counsel who has prepared comprehensive, accurate answers to interrogatories. For no known reason, his client fails to sign them. Perhaps more common is the situation of the lawyer whose client fails to show up for a deposition, sometimes even under the stimulus of a court order. Far from unknown is the client who simply moves away, neglecting to tell his lawyer (or sometimes anyone else) where to reach him.

The lawyer in any of these situations must decide the basic question whether the attorney-client relationship can continue without the client's active participation. At the moment, however, we face the immediate question what to do when, without the semblance of an

---

[38] *Serpe* v. *Yellow Cab Co.*, footnote 15.

excuse, one is confronted with a motion to impose sanctions for failure to obey one or another kind of discovery notice. Fortunately, one potent argument can always be advanced no matter how flagrant the client's negligence or inaction may appear. It is an argument you should make in any situation where you are threatened with a substantive penalty for a procedural infringement. In the painful situation of the kind under discussion, it may be all you can say.

8. An Indispensable, Potent Argument

In defending your client's disregard or disobedience of a discovery notice, always stress the merits of his case. Do this whether you have a valid excuse or not. You should first state the facts that show him to have a good cause of action or defense. Then point out that granting the extreme relief your opponent is requesting would defeat the ends of substantive justice. Most judges today hesitate to deprive a litigant of his day in court because he infringed a procedural requirement. This attitude may have the regrettable effect of encouraging defiance of procedural rules, but if your client is on the verge of a dismissal of his case, you will not be concerned with the long-term consequences of your rescuing him.

You may be confronted with the ultimate sanction for disobedience of a court order, namely, dismissal of your pleading or, if you represent defendant, the entry of a default judgment. If your situation strikes you as hopeless, consider this example:

> Defendant in a treble-damage antitrust suit declined to produce its sole stockholder, a celebrated recluse, for a deposition pursuant to court order. Judge Metzner of the U. S. District Court in New York City entered default judgment aggregating after trebling and the addition of attorneys' fees and interest, over $145,000,000.[39] With a minor modification, the Court of Appeals affirmed.[40] The Supreme Court of the United States reversed. It held defendant, by virtue of the rulings of a federal administrative agency, immune to antitrust sanctions.[41]

Severe sanctions have, however, held up in other cases.[42]

---

[39] *Trans World Airlines, Inc.* v. *Hughes Tool Co.,* 32 F.R.D. 604 (S.D. N.Y. 1963); *Trans World Airlines* v. *Hughes,* 308 F. Supp. 679 (S.D. N.Y. 1969), further proceedings, 312 F. Supp. 478 (S.D. N.Y. 1970).

[40] *Trans World Airlines* v. *Hughes,* 449 F.2d 51 (2d Cir. 1971).

[41] *Hughes Tool Co.* v. *Trans-World Airlines, Inc.,* — U.S. —, 93 S. Ct. 647, — L.E.2d — (1973). Other proceedings in this litigation are reported at all federal levels. For a narrative account, see Tinnin, JUST ABOUT EVERYBODY VS HOWARD HUGHES (Doubleday & Co., Garden City, N.Y., 1973).

[42] See, e.g., *General Dynamics Corp.* v. *Selb Mfg. Co.,* footnote 10, Chapter VI.

The party whose attorney complies scrupulously with all of his opponent's legitimate discovery demands and interposes timely objections to all that are not legitimate has spared himself and his client time and trouble and has escaped embarrassment and possible substantive prejudice. Avoiding conflicts over one's compliance with discovery requirements is far better than winning them.

This review of enforcement procedures concludes our study of discovery techniques. That should not exaggerate the importance of those procedures. We all know that discovery works largely through the voluntary compliance of attorneys and that the system would break down if resort to compulsion became necessary in every instance. We also know, however, that to give our own discovery proper scope and to impose proper bounds on the efforts of our adversaries, we must be aware of what we and they can and cannot do if voluntary means fail.

CHECK-LIST FOR PREPARATION OF PARTY OR WITNESS ABOUT TO TESTIFY AT DEPOSITION

I. THE PROCEEDINGS THEMSELVES

A. Place of Deposition

B. Persons Present

1. Absence of Judge or Other Presiding Officer
2. Witness
3. Counsel for Each Party
4. Court Reporter
5. Notary (usually same person as reporter)
6. Parties or Their Officers

C. Sequence of Events

1. Administration of Oath
2. "Direct" Examination by Opposing Counsel
3. Objections
   a. with instructions not to answer
   b. without such instructions
   c. point of objections
4. "Cross-examination"

5. "Redirect," etc.
6. Termination

D. Post-Deposition Events

1. Interval for Transcribing Testimony
2. Reading, Correcting, Signing & Filing Transcript
3. Later Use of Transcript

II. RULES OF TESTIFYING

A. Telling the Truth

1. Witness's Version, Not Adapted to Satisfying Examining Counsel
2. Testimony Unaffected by Examiner's Apparent Incredulity
3. Phrasing Answer in Most Helpful Terms Consistent with Accuracy
4. Propriety of Lack of Knowledge or Recollection
5. Admitting Preliminary Talk with Counsel

B. The Art of Answering the Question

1. Listening to the Question
2. Studying the Question
3. Giving No More and No Less than Asked
4. Refraining from Volunteering:
   a. unsolicited explanations or "background"
   b. alternative sources of information unless asked for:
      1. other possible witnesses
      2. records, etc.
5. Insisting on Finishing
6. Stopping When Answer Completed

C. Testifying About Documents

1. Reading Entire Paper if Feasible
2. Noting Author, Addressee & Recipients of Copies
3. Distinguishing Between Actual Knowledge and Recited Facts
   a. signature, mailing, etc.
   b. substantive content of writing

D. Technique of Answering on "Cross-examination"

E. Common Mistakes to Avoid

  1. Garrulousness
    a. as product of questioner's interest and apparent friendliness
    b. as product of relaxation of initial nervousness
  2. Anger
  3. Humorous, Facetious or Sarcastic Answers
  4. Argument Instead of Facts
  5. Speculation or Conjecture
  6. Interrupting Questions
  7. Answering by Nods, Gesticulation, Etc.

III. MISCELLANEOUS POINTS

A. Consulting Own Counsel Before Answering

B. Requests to Produce Papers or Look Up Further Facts, etc.

C. Talks "Off the Record"

D. Conduct Before and After Session

INDEX